REAL LOVE
IN MARRIAGE

REAL LOVE
IN MARRIAGE

The Truth About Finding Genuine Happiness

Now and Forever

GREG BAER, M.D.

GOTHAM BOOKS

GOTHAM BOOKS
Published by Penguin Group (USA) Inc.
375 Hudson Street, New York, New York 10014, U.S.A.
Penguin Group (Canada), 90 Eglinton Avenue East, Suite 700, Toronto, Ontario
M4P 2Y3, Canada (a division of Pearson Penguin Canada Inc.); Penguin Books Ltd, 80
Strand, London WC2R 0RL, England; Penguin Ireland, 25 St Stephen's Green, Dublin
2, Ireland (a division of Penguin Books Ltd); Penguin Group (Australia), 250 Camber-
well Road, Camberwell, Victoria 3124, Australia (a division of Pearson Australia Group
Pty Ltd); Penguin Books India Pvt Ltd, 11 Community Centre, Panchsheel Park,
New Delhi–110 017, India; Penguin Group (NZ), cnr Airborne and Rosedale Roads,
Albany, Auckland 1310, New Zealand (a division of Pearson New Zealand Ltd); Penguin
Books (South Africa) (Pty) Ltd, 24 Sturdee Avenue, Rosebank, Johannesburg 2196,
South Africa

Penguin Books Ltd, Registered Offices: 80 Strand, London WC2R 0RL, England

Published by Gotham Books, a member of Penguin Group (USA) Inc.

First printing, September 2006

1   3   5   7   9   10   8   6   4   2

Copyright © 2006 by Greg Baer
All rights reserved

Gotham Books and the skyscraper logo are trademarks of Penguin Group (USA) Inc.

LIBRARY OF CONGRESS CATALOGING-IN-PUBLICATION DATA

Baer, Greg.
Real love in marriage : the truth about finding genuine
happiness now and forever / by Greg Baer.
p. cm.
Includes index.
ISBN 1-592-40250-X (hardcover)
1. Marriage. 2. Love. 3. Man-woman relationships. I. Title.
HQ503.B34 2006
646.7'8—dc22
2006015092

Printed in the United States of America
Set in Adobe Garamond with Diotima Display
Designed by Elke Sigal

Contents

Introduction

In *Real Love: The Truth About Finding Unconditional Love and Fulfilling Relationships,* I talked about the importance of Real Love—unconditional love—in our lives. With Real Love, we uniformly experience a profound and lasting happiness that enables us to have richly fulfilling relationships with the people around us.

I did not suppose, however, that I would address all relationship issues in one book. Because marriage is a special relationship, we need to discuss more of the questions that pertain to it. It's obvious that we need a greater understanding of marriage: 56 percent of the people in this country are married, but more than half of those marriages will end in divorce. In light of this widespread failure in marriage, we must ask these questions:

- Why do so many marriages fail?
- How is marriage different from other relationships? Why is it important to understand the differences?
- Why do many couples fall in love, get married, and then fall out of love?
- What exactly should we do when our spouses are angry, demanding, or withdrawn?

- Why do we keep having the same destructive arguments with our spouses, over and over?
- How do we make a fair division of the many jobs that must be done in the family?
- What can we do to settle our differences with our spouses about sex, the children, and other issues?
- Is it really possible to eliminate conflict in marriage and find the consistent love and happiness we've always wanted, regardless of the injuries we've already experienced?

In *Real Love in Marriage*, we'll answer these critical questions. The principles we'll discuss have proven to be consistently successful in improving the success of marriages across the country. If you've read *Real Love*, you'll find *Real Love in Marriage* easier to understand. If you haven't, don't worry: I'll summarize most of the first book in the first two chapters of this one.

A word about gender: To avoid the tiresome repetition of the phrases "him or her," "his or hers," and "he or she," I will often use the pronoun of one sex or the other. I might say, for example, "When someone feels sufficiently threatened, *she* will react with behaviors she learned in the past, even when those behaviors are harmful to herself and others." It should be understood that any such description applies to both men and women.

REAL LOVE
IN MARRIAGE

1

❧

The Great Secret

The Real Reason for Marriage Problems

What's the secret to a great marriage? What can you do to make yours better? Because any relationship is a natural result of two people making independent decisions, we can't meaningfully talk about the relationship between two people until we understand the nature and causes of individual human behavior. In these first two chapters we'll discuss why we behave as we do and what we can do about it. Then we'll talk about the specific things we can do to create a richly rewarding marriage. Let's begin by observing an interaction between Mark and Susan, a married couple.

Mark comes home one evening after an unusually long day at work and finds ketchup splattered on a wall near the front door. Stomping into the kitchen, where Susan is busy working at the sink, he says in a harsh tone, "What's that mess on the wall?"

Looking up from her task, Susan angrily replies, "You wanna be useful, for once? Why don't *you* clean it up?"

Offended, Mark snaps back, "Hey, I was only asking a question," and then he stalks out of the room, muttering something about her moods. For the rest of the evening, they silently avoid each other.

The next day, Mark learns what happened the day before. After work, Susan picked up the children from school and arrived home moments before he did. One of the children stumbled while running with a plate of food, spilling fries and ketchup everywhere. Susan had cleaned up the floor and was preparing to wash the wall at the very moment Mark had demanded an explanation of the mess. She'd already had a tough day, and Mark's accusatory question was more than she could stand.

Our Spouses Are Not the Cause of How We Feel and Behave

We've all had experiences like that. When our spouses are late, or fail to do something we've requested, or don't give us the attention we want, we tend to become irritated, or withdraw, or act like we've been treated unfairly. And we naturally hold our spouses responsible for our reactions, as Mark and Susan both did. Susan blamed Mark for her irritation, reasoning that she wouldn't have become angry if he hadn't first attacked her about the ketchup on the wall. Mark, in turn, blamed Susan for his anger, since he wouldn't have reacted as he did if she hadn't snapped at him.

Although blaming our spouses for how we feel and behave often seems reasonable—how else *can* we feel and respond, we ask ourselves, when they say and do those thoughtless and unkind things?—our blaming is never justified. Until we see that, we'll continue to point fingers at each other and repeat the unproductive feelings and behaviors that cause so much harm to our relationships and to our own happiness.

Imagine that you're fifty years old. You're sixty pounds overweight, and you haven't seriously exercised in many years. Although your cholesterol and blood lipids are sky-high, you eat a half pound of bacon every morning. You have high blood pressure, but you don't take the medication that was prescribed for it.

Even though your doctor has told you it will kill you, you smoke two packs of cigarettes every day. And, finally, both your parents died of heart attacks before they were forty.

One day you and I go shopping at the grocery store, and when we get home I insist that you help me carry the heavy bags of food into the house. You protest, but I pick up a bag and put it in your arms, and as you start walking up the steps to the front door, you keel over with a heart attack.

Did I cause your heart attack? That might seem like a reasonable claim. After all, if I hadn't insisted you carry the bag of groceries, you might not have had the attack. But it's still ridiculous to say that I caused it. Your heart attack was caused by your weight, diet, smoking, genetics, cholesterol, and lack of exercise, all of which had nothing whatever to do with me. You were a heart attack waiting to happen—essentially, you'd *chosen* to have one—and I just gave you an opportunity to have it.

In a similar way, although our spouses do affect the way we feel in any given moment, their contribution is minor. When we get angry or feel hurt in response to something our spouses have done, there are always many other factors that powerfully affect our feelings and behavior, none of which are determined by our spouses. In any given moment, we're reacting to a lifetime of events and feelings, not only to something our spouses have done or not done. In fact, if we're sufficiently unhealthy emotionally and spiritually, our spouses don't have to do *anything* wrong to provoke a negative reaction from us.

Other people are never responsible for how we feel. If we understood that, our marriages would change dramatically. How could we keep being angry at anyone after realizing that he or she is not to blame for our feelings?

So what *does* cause our feelings? Just as age, weight, lack of exercise, genetics, and other factors are the causes of heart attacks, what are the underlying factors that really determine how we feel and how we interact with our spouses?

Real Love—The Essential Ingredient for Happiness and Success in Every Marriage

The most important requirement for our emotional health and happiness is Real Love. *Real Love is caring about the happiness of another person without any thought for what we might get for ourselves.* It's also Real Love when other people care about *our* happiness unconditionally. With Real Love, they're not disappointed or angry when we make our foolish mistakes, when we don't do what they want, or even when we inconvenience them personally.

When I use the word *happiness,* I do not mean the brief and superficial pleasure that comes from money, sex, power, and the conditional approval we earn from others when we behave as they want. Nor do I mean the temporary feeling of satisfaction we experience in the absence of immediate conflict or disaster. Real happiness is not the feeling we get from being entertained or making people do what we want. It's a profound and lasting sense of peace and fulfillment that deeply satisfies and enlarges the soul. It doesn't go away when circumstances are difficult. It survives and even grows during hardship and struggle. True happiness is our entire reason to live, and it can only be obtained as we find Real Love and share it with others. *With Real Love, nothing else matters; without it, nothing else is enough.*

Sadly, few of us have sufficiently received or given that kind of love—not just during our marriages but in our entire lives. From the time we were small children, we observed that when we didn't fight with our sisters, didn't make too much noise in the car, got good grades, and were otherwise obedient and cooperative, our parents and others smiled at us, patted our heads, and spoke kindly. With their words and behavior, they told us what good boys and girls we were.

But what happened when we did fight with our sisters, made too much noise, got bad grades, and dragged mud across the clean living room carpet? Did people smile at us or speak gentle, loving words? No—they frowned, sighed with disappointment, and often spoke in harsh tones. Just as the positive behaviors of other people communicated to us that we were loved, the withdrawal of those behaviors could only mean that we were *not* being loved. Although it was unintentional, our parents and others taught us this terrible message: "When you're good, I love you, but when you're not, I don't—or I certainly love you a great deal less."

This conditional love can give us brief moments of satisfaction, but we're still left with a huge hole in our souls, because only Real Love can make us genuinely happy. When someone is genuinely concerned about our happiness, we feel connected to that person. We feel included in his or her life, and in that instant we are *no longer alone.* Each moment of unconditional acceptance creates a living thread to the person who accepts us, and these threads weave a powerful bond that fills us with a genuine and lasting happiness. Nothing but Real Love can do that. In addition, when we know that even one person loves us unconditionally, we feel a connection to everyone else. We feel included in the family of all mankind, of which that one person is a part.

Without sufficient Real Love, we can only feel empty and alone, which is our greatest fear. In any given negative interaction with your spouse, it is the long-standing lack of Real Love in *your* life that determines how you feel, not the behavior of your spouse in that moment—just as a heart attack is really caused by many long-standing factors, not just by a single moment of stress. In any given moment, you react to the amount of love you feel from everyone, past and present, not just from the person you're interacting with.

The Effect of Real Love

Before we can really understand the effect of Real Love in our lives, we need to actually *feel* it. Without that experience, the intellectual understanding is shallow—like trying to *understand* a strawberry without *tasting* it. Take your time as you read the following paragraphs. If possible, read them in a place where you won't be distracted, so you can visualize and feel the experience as you read.

Imagine that you're having a difficult day. Several people have confronted you about mistakes you've made or assignments you've not completed, and you're feeling both inadequate and irritated. The computer isn't working—again—and your car is in the shop for the third time in the past two months. You want to pound your fists on the wall and scream.

In the midst of your frustration, a man and a woman walk into the room and address you by name. Even though you've never seen them before, you feel as though they've known you all your life. Somehow you sense from their peaceful and inviting expressions that you can trust them completely. They ask you to go with them, and without hesitation you get up and follow them.

Side by side, you walk between this couple for some time, finally turning into the driveway of a beautiful home. Walking through the front entryway, you enter a spacious, well-lighted room, where many people are talking to one another. After seeing you, several of them come over to greet you. Although you've never met them before, you feel no anxiety, because you see in their faces and gestures nothing but a sincere and unreserved welcome.

In a way you can't describe, you sense that everyone in this room feels loved and happy, and you know that no matter what mistakes you've ever made or what flaws you have, these people accept you completely. As you sit and talk with them, you realize you don't need to do anything to impress them, nor do you have a need to hide anything from them.

Utterly relaxed, you begin to tell them the story of your life. You talk about your mistakes, your foolishness, your weaknesses, your fears, and your successes. They understand everything you're saying, and they accept you and care about you. You know there is nothing you could do that would disappoint or irritate them, nor would it be possible to feel embarrassed or ashamed around them. For hours you talk and laugh with these new friends.

Allow yourself to enjoy this feeling. Let it sink in and fill your entire being. Allow yourself to float in a calm, sweet ocean of the peace you feel. You'd like to stay in this place forever, but the day draws to a close, and eventually you must go home. As you leave, your friends invite you to return anytime you wish, and you know they mean what they say.

Now come back to the real world and consider this question: While you were with those people, did you feel any inclination at all to be angry at them—or to lie to them or withdraw from them? The idea is ridiculous—how could you feel angry or otherwise react negatively toward people who unconditionally accept and love you? Moreover, while you were with those people, did you feel any inclination to be angry at *anyone else*—at any of the people you know in real life? Were you irritated about the dysfunctional computer or the car in the shop? While you were with those loving people, you didn't have any of those negative feelings, because when we feel unconditionally loved, we have the one thing that matters most in all the world, and then we lose our need to be angry, to feel hurt, to lie to people, and to withdraw from relationships.

Have you ever experienced an interaction with your spouse like the one Mark and Susan had? Have you ever said something you thought was innocent, only to have your partner react much more negatively than you ever would have predicted? And then did you react by getting angry in return, or by acting hurt or running away?

We take offense—understandably, I might add—when our partners lash out at us or otherwise behave in ways we don't like. But when we react to someone with anger or withdrawal, or by acting hurt, we never feel genuinely closer to that person. Instead we feel more alone and miserable. So why do we keep doing those unproductive things? Why do we consistently react to our partners in ways that can only make us more unhappy and undermine the health of our marriages? Why don't we just stop these behaviors that cause so much pain?

The answer is simple. When you do feel unconditionally loved—as you did with the people in that house—you lose your tendency to feel hurt and alone, and to react with anger, deceit, and withdrawal. You have these negative feelings and respond in these negative ways, therefore, only because you *don't* feel loved. Human behavior is usually that simple.

There is much to be learned from the fact that when you were with those loving people, you didn't feel anger at the *other* people in your life. Real Love *from any source* makes us happy, and we only feel empty, alone, angry, and so on when we don't have enough Real Love from *anyone*. When you get angry at your wife, therefore, it's not only because you don't feel loved by *her*. Your anger is a reaction to a lifetime of insufficient Real Love from everyone.

Conditional Versus Real Love

Conditional love is distinguished from Real Love by the presence of *disappointment* and *anger*. You can point out the mistakes of your spouse, for example, while you're unconditionally caring about her happiness. You can describe her mistakes so she can avoid the behaviors that affect her in a negative way. The instant you become disappointed or angry, however, your primary concern is no longer *her* happiness. You're thinking about *yourself* and how she has failed to do what *you* want.

We often try to justify our disappointment and anger by explaining that we're disappointed or angry at our spouses' *behavior* but not at *them*. That is rarely the entire truth. Let's suppose, for example, that your wife fails to give you an important phone message. You might claim that you're irritated only at the inconvenience, but be honest here: After her mistake, do you feel any differently toward her? Before you deny it, ask yourself whether you tend to avoid her—physically or verbally—or speak to her in a different tone. When she makes mistakes like this, you probably give off a hundred signals that something is different in the way you feel about her, and she *feels* that. Almost all of us feel some disappointment and irritation when our spouses inconvenience us, and those feelings always indicate that we didn't get something *we* wanted. In those instances, we can't be unconditionally concerned about *their* happiness.

If you continue to have doubts about whether you often love your spouse conditionally, ask *her* if you treat her differently when she does something you don't like. When we're disappointed or angry, our spouses know that our primary concern is for *ourselves*. That's not Real Love, and the effect is uniformly damaging.

What We Use Without Enough Real Love—Imitation Love

Without sufficient Real Love in our lives, the pain and emptiness are intolerable, and in order to eliminate or reduce those feelings, we're willing to do almost anything. Everything we use as a substitute for Real Love—to temporarily make us feel better in the absence of what we really need—becomes a form of Imitation Love, and all those substitutes are one or more variations of four things: *praise, power, pleasure,* and *safety*.

Praise

When people give us their approval, we feel praised and worthwhile, and if we can't get the Real Love we need, we'll do a lot to win that approval. Regrettably, we almost always have to *earn* it. In order for people to smile at us, compliment us, and want to spend time with us—all signs that they accept or "love" us—we have to be talented, beautiful, wealthy, witty, cooperative, grateful, successful, or otherwise worthy of acceptance. That kind of acceptance is conditional, because all the signs of it—the smiles and kind words, for example—disappear when we make mistakes, inconvenience people, and fail to live up to the expectations of others.

Because the absence of Real Love is painful, we're willing to do a lot to earn the approval that temporarily makes us feel good, even if it's conditional. For example, we make ourselves look good physically with exercise, clothing, makeup, dieting—even starvation—and plastic surgery, all in the hope that someone will say, "You're looking good." We work hard to succeed at school and our jobs in order to be complimented for our intelligence, creativity, and diligence.

But consider how you feel—after working hard for hours, days, even years—when you finally get that precious morsel of praise from a spouse or anyone else. How long does it last? In just a moment or two, the feeling is gone, and then you have to work to earn it all over again. Buying praise with our behavior or appearance is a lot of work, and because it's usually not given unconditionally, we're left with an empty feeling even when we get it.

Another reason praise is often unfulfilling is that when most people praise us, they're rarely saying something about *us*. They're saying that when we're cooperative and perform according to their expectations, they like how we make *them* feel—but we're quite willing to keep on doing whatever it takes to earn the sensation of praise, gratitude, and acceptance, because it's still much better than the emptiness that accompanies a lack of Real Love.

Power

Although it's mostly unintentional, anytime we successfully manipulate or control someone, we enjoy a sensation of power over that person. We use money, authority, sex, flattery, and personal persuasion to influence, control, and even hurt people. When you control someone, you actually feel more connected to him or her in a brief, shallow way. It's not Real Love, but when you control the people around you, you feel less powerless; you feel less of the emptiness and helplessness that are always associated with a lack of Real Love.

We tend to deny our efforts to control our spouses—it's not a flattering behavior to admit—but whenever we try to *get* people to do anything, we're controlling them and using power as a form of Imitation Love. If you doubt that you control your spouse, consider how you feel when he *doesn't* do what you want. Your disappointment or anger indicate that you want to control his behavior—however unconscious your efforts may be.

Pleasure

When we don't feel unconditionally loved, we often use pleasure—food, sex, drugs, and many forms of entertainment and excitement—to feel better temporarily. Certainly there's nothing inherently wrong with pleasure, but when we compulsively seek it, we're using it to fill a deep emptiness.

Safety

Without sufficient Real Love, we're already experiencing an insufferable pain, and we'll go to great lengths to keep ourselves safe from anything that might prolong or worsen our pain. To minimize painful disapproval, we stay away from unfamiliar situations, tasks, and relationships, and then we confuse that feeling of relative safety with real happiness. I've known many couples who believed they had a "good marriage" until they discovered that their "happiness" was only an avoidance of conflict, not a sharing of Real Love.

By no means are praise, power, pleasure, and safety always unhealthy. In the presence of Real Love, money, authority, sex, and praise, for example, can all add to our genuine happiness. These things are dangerous only when they're used as substitutes for unconditional love.

Falling in Love—The Nature and Effect of Imitation Love

People who consistently use addictive drugs soon discover that the effect becomes increasingly brief, and more of the drug is required in order to achieve the same outcome. All the forms of Imitation Love are like an addictive drug. Despite all the effort required to earn Imitation Love, the beneficial effects of praise, power, money, and sex become increasingly brief, we have to work harder to get more and more, and eventually we become exhausted and frustrated. And no matter how successful we are in obtaining Imitation Love, we never get the feeling of connection with other people that comes with Real Love, so we're still painfully alone.

Regrettably, Imitation Love *does feel good,* and it's easy to confuse that temporary satisfaction with genuine happiness. That self-deception distracts us from pursuing the life-giving steps that lead to Real Love.

When we see the role and effect of Imitation Love, we can more easily understand interactions like the one I described earlier between Mark and Susan. When they first met, they fell madly in love and were certain it would last forever. So what happened? How did these two go from violins playing and birds singing to the place where they bit each other's heads off over something as meaningless as ketchup on a wall?

In the absence of sufficient Real Love, we're strongly attracted to anyone who gives us Imitation Love. When Mark met Susan, he found her physically attractive—which gave him immediate pleasure and suggested the possibility of more physical pleasure in the future—and he sensed that she accepted him and was willing to behave in certain ways to win his approval, which gave him feelings of praise and power. She was attracted to him because he was good-looking, funny, smart, and kind to her, and because he had a good job—all of which gave her a sense of praise, pleasure, and safety. Unwittingly, they were both *trading* Imitation Love with each other.

Susan and Mark married because they found in their partner the qualities that would entertain them, make them feel worthwhile, and give them safety, not because they unconditionally loved each other. Most of us pick our partners for the same reasons—we look for someone who has qualities that will temporarily make *us* feel good, and in return we're quite willing to do the same for that person.

In order to get the Imitation Love that temporarily makes us feel better in the absence of Real Love, we *buy* it with whatever forms of Imitation Love we have to offer. Let's arbitrarily measure Imitation Love in dollars, and we'll suppose that when you give a dollar of Imitation Love to someone, that person gives you twenty cents in return. To a second person you give a dollar and receive fifty cents. Without being aware of the reason, you naturally prefer the company of the person who gives you a 50 percent return on your investment—that's why we "like" some people more than others. Then you give a dollar of Imitation Love to someone who gives you a full dollar in return. Excited about this dramatic improvement in your investment return, you give him or her two dollars, then three, then more, and to your delight, you are rewarded equally each time. You are now "in love."

Mark had said complimentary things to other people all his life, but when he gave them a dollar of praise, he rarely got a dollar of praise, power, pleasure, and safety in return. Then he met Susan. When he gave her a dollar of praise—verbal and nonverbal—she immediately responded by accepting him (praise), doing some of the things he wanted (power), and physically touching him (pleasure)—at least a dollar all together. So he gave her even more Imitation Love—the best he had to offer—and when she responded generously, he was so thrilled with the exchange that he called the feeling "falling in love." Falling in love usually means that two people have found someone with whom they experience an abundant and relatively fair exchange of Imitation Love. That's not very romantic, but that's how it is when Real Love is lacking.

As I've said, however, the effect of Imitation Love always fades, and Mark and Susan felt that. They really enjoyed the initial exchange of Imitation Love, but it wasn't long before that level of praise, power, and pleasure wasn't as rewarding as it once had been. When people say the "excitement has worn off " in a relationship, they're just describing the fleeting effect of Imitation Love. As we experience less "happiness" with Imitation Love, we naturally turn to our spouses to supply what we're missing, and our partners understandably feel resentful of our increased demands. They married us based on an unspoken understanding of how much Imitation Love they'd have to give us to make us happy, and then we changed the rules. Our spouses don't like that.

As couples discover the transient effect of Imitation Love, they also invariably find that the exchange of Imitation Love becomes unfair. We can roughly quantify the trading—and fading—of Imitation Love over the course of Mark and Susan's marriage. In the beginning, they exchanged Imitation Love as summarized below:

Type of Imitation Love	Imitation Love (in Dollars) Received in the Relationship by	
	Mark	Susan
Praise	5	5
Power	5	5
Pleasure	6	2
Safety	1	5
Total Imitation Love	17	17

In the beginning of their marriage, they both received five dollars of praise as each of them complimented the other for a variety of qualities, including sexual desirability. They were equally successful in getting the other to do the things they wanted (five dollars of power each). Mark got more physical pleasure from the relationship (mostly from sex) than Susan (six dollars versus two), but Susan got a greater sense of security (safety) from the relationship than Mark did (five dollars versus one). Because they experienced more Imitation Love from each other—and with a better rate of return on their investment—than with anyone else they had known, they were in love and happy with their marriage. After several years, however, the trading had changed:

Type of Imitation Love	Dollars Received in the Relationship by	
	Mark	Susan
Praise	1	1
Power	3	1
Pleasure	4	1
Safety	0	1
Total Imitation Love	8	4

They both discovered that the effect of flattery had quickly worn off, and that constantly earning it was exhausting, so neither of them was willing to continue their initial efforts to praise each other. After years of marriage, Susan discovered she could hardly get Mark to do anything she wanted (one dollar of power versus the five dollars she got in the beginning of their relationship), so she tended to reward him with nagging instead of praise. Without sufficient praise and appreciation, Mark had even less motivation to keep doing what Susan wanted. Susan, however, still did most of the housework and child care, so Mark got three dollars of power from getting her to do what he wanted (compared with the five dollars he once got). He still got four dollars of pleasure from the relationship (mostly from sex), while she got only one dollar (virtually nothing from sex but some from other forms of entertainment they enjoyed together). Susan's sense of safety had been reduced to a single dollar, because he often criticized her and because she wasn't sure of his fidelity when he looked at other women. Mark felt no safety at all as Susan nagged at him about everything.

What a miserable state of affairs. When they got married, what Mark and Susan both needed was Real Love, but neither of them had ever felt much unconditional love, so there was *no way* they could have loved each other as they needed. We simply can't give what we don't have, but they did offer each other what they had— Imitation Love in its various forms—and they gave as much as they could. Imitation Love does feel good, and because they were both giving it with all their hearts, they were satisfied in the beginning of their marriage. But when the effect wore off and they each gave the other less of the various forms of Imitation Love, they felt like the rules of exchange had been violated. They were both faced with the horror that they were not going to get the happiness they'd wanted all their lives.

Susan experienced more disappointment later in their marriage than Mark did. Not only was she disillusioned with the decline in her overall happiness (four dollars of Imitation Love versus seventeen in the beginning), but she sensed that their relationship was unfair (four dollars for her versus eight for Mark). It's common for one partner to believe the relationship is worse than the other partner does, because although both partners are far from genuinely happy, one of them—in this case, Mark—is getting more Imitation Love than the other. In addition, although Mark wasn't ecstatic about his marriage, he was relatively satisfied, because even though his total was down from seventeen dollars to eight, it was still better than he'd ever gotten before he was married.

We can learn a lot from Mark and Susan. Although the details of our marriages vary, all unhappy couples experience the failures and injustices of Imitation Love. In 2003, a study was released that described the self-assessed level of happiness of 24,000 people over a period of ten years. Although marriage gave people an initial emotional boost, on average that effect completely wore off after a period of a few years, leaving married people no happier than they were before marriage.* This is quite consistent with what I've said about the effects of Imitation Love.

Many unhappy couples experience brief improvements in their marriages as they attempt to increase the Imitation Love in their relationship. Often with the guidance of therapists or self-help books, they try to improve the sex in their marriage, for example, or their communication—which increases the amount of praise, power, pleasure, and safety they enjoy—without attending to the Real Love they need. Such efforts rarely produce lasting results.

What We Do Without Enough Love (Real or Imitation)—Getting and Protecting Behaviors

Insufficient Real Love creates an emptiness we cannot ignore, especially when we also don't have enough Imitation Love to make us feel better temporarily. Our subsequent behavior is then often

*"Reexamining adaptation and the set point model of happiness: Reactions to changes in marital status." Lucas, Richard E.; Clark, Andrew E.; Georgellis, Yannis; Diener, Ed. *Journal of Personality and Social Psychology*. March 2003, Vol. 84(3), 527–539.

determined by our *need* to be loved and our *fear* of not being loved. Without Real Love, we do whatever it takes—Getting Behaviors—to fill our sense of emptiness with Imitation Love. To eliminate our fear, we use Protecting Behaviors. The Getting Behaviors include lying, attacking, acting like a victim, and running. The Protecting Behaviors include lying, attacking, acting like a victim, and clinging.

Lying

We use lying as a Protecting Behavior when we make excuses, shade the truth, or do anything else to avoid the disapproval of others. We don't lie because we're bad; we lie because we've learned from countless experiences that it *works*. People really do disapprove of us less when we hide the truth about our flaws, and we'll do almost anything to keep from feeling that withdrawal of acceptance.

We use lying as a Getting Behavior when we do anything to get other people to like us—when we tell people about our accomplishments but not our flaws, communicate positive feelings that are not true, change our physical appearance to attract people to us, or tell people what they want to hear so they'll like us. We don't think of these behaviors as lying, but they are, because we don't tell other people we're manipulating them. We lie so often that we don't even realize we're doing it most of the time. If you watch two people in conversation, for example, you'll usually see that each of them is carefully and unconsciously studying the other for any hint of disapproval—a forehead wrinkling into a frown, an eyebrow lifting into an expression of doubt, a change in tone of voice—and when that happens, the speaker immediately modifies what he or she is saying until those signs of disapproval disappear. Again, although we do this unconsciously, it's still lying, because we don't tell people we're trying to get them to like us.

From the time we were young, we were told by our parents and others, "Put your best foot forward." That sounds like good advice, but the results are usually undesirable, as illustrated by Mark and Susan's dating experiences, long before they married. When they went out on their first date, they were both nervous about being accepted, so they put their best foot forward. Susan prepared for hours—makeup, hair, clothing—to look good so Mark would like her. Mark, too, made himself as physically attractive as possible. In addition, they were each careful to talk in a way they thought would be pleasing to the other.

As they each put their best foot forward, they succeeded in winning each other's acceptance, but now they'd started on a path that often has disastrous consequences. When I show you only my best foot and you indicate that you like me, I clearly hear that you like me *because* of my best foot—and that's almost invariably exactly what you mean. When people tell us *why* they like us, they're also telling us that if we *didn't* have those characteristics, they almost certainly would *not* like us as they do. When someone tells you that he or she likes your best foot, there's a strong implication that you must hide the rest of you from that person so you won't lose his or her affection and attention. But we still love to hear people say, "I like you because . . ." We're just dying to hear what comes next: ". . . because you're witty, intelligent, handsome, beautiful, strong, responsible, whatever."

It's understandable that Susan was delighted to see Mark's good-natured, sensitive, and loving side. We want our partners to have the positive qualities that would make a relationship enjoyable. Susan was also trying to buy *his* approval with *her* best foot. That approach really does seem to work in the beginning—Mark and Susan were both thrilled to find someone who "made them happy," but then they discovered what we all do: that our partners have more than just a best foot. There's that other foot, and a lot more besides. He doesn't smell nearly as sweet after a long day at work as he did on the first date, nor is he as entertaining or accommodating. Her hair and smile don't have quite the same glow after a rough night's sleep. Neither partner is quite as eager to please the other as he or she was in the beginning.

We don't *intend* to deceive each other early in a relationship, but we're willing to do it because we're so anxious to be accepted. A serious problem then arises if our lies succeed in gaining the acceptance we want, because our partner *will* eventually discover the rest of us. After Mark and Susan were married, they began to see the qualities they hadn't noticed while they were dating, and they were disappointed. We often complain that after we get married, our partners change. You may think, *He is just not the person I dated.* Yes, actually, he is, but you didn't see him clearly in the beginning. After you got married, however, you saw more of him, not just the parts he wanted to show you—which are also the parts you wanted to see. Our partners do change in some ways. They become less willing, for example, to work hard to earn the Imitation Love we gave them initially, because the exchange becomes less rewarding than it once was.

When we lie to a spouse, or potential spouse—however unconscious it may be—we establish a foundation that cannot support a healthy and happy relationship. In the following chapters, we'll discuss how we can change that.

Attacking

Attacking is any behavior that motivates another person through *fear* to behave in a way we want. We attack people when we criticize them, physically intimidate them, withdraw our approval, make them feel guilty, and use our positions of authority at work, at home, and elsewhere, all to get Imitation Love—usually in the form of power—and to protect ourselves from fear. With anger, for example—the most common form of attacking—you may be able to make your wife sufficiently uncomfortable (afraid) that she'll do whatever you want in order to stop you from making her feel bad. With your anger, you can get her to give you attention, respect, power, flattery, approval, even sex. But of course if she's giving you these things not because she's genuinely concerned for your happiness but simply to avoid your anger, all you're receiving is Imitation Love.

Earlier in the chapter, Mark didn't just *ask* Susan about the ketchup on the wall—he attacked her. Attacking involves disappointment, anger, and shaming, all for the purpose—however unconscious—of motivating others with fear. Let's explore why Mark chose to attack Susan rather than simply ask her a question. Early in their relationship, Susan usually gave Mark what he wanted quickly and willingly, in great part because he gave her what *she* wanted. It was a fair trade. But when the effect of Imitation Love began to wear off, Susan responded less quickly and willingly to Mark's desires. If he increased his positive attentions toward her, she was more responsive, but the ever-increasing level of attention that Susan unknowingly required of him became inconvenient, even exhausting, for Mark. He began to experiment with ways he could get what he wanted more reliably and with less effort.

From past experience, Mark had learned the motivational benefits of anger. As a child, he hurried to avoid his parents' displeasure when they were angry, so he eventually learned to apply this motivating force to others. In the schoolyard, he noticed that he could persuade his peers to do what he wanted when he raised his voice and physically intimidated them, and in business, he discovered that when he became irritated, fellow employees would often hurry to do what he wanted in order to make him happy and thereby stop his anger.

Having learned the power of anger, Mark increasingly used it to motivate Susan, and that's what he was doing when he said to her, "What's that mess on the wall?" Although he was not consciously aware of his intentions, he nonetheless hoped that if he spoke in anger, she would more likely and more quickly respond by giving him what he wanted (attention, respect, a clean wall, and so on).

Earlier in their relationship, Susan had become afraid whenever Mark attacked her, and she did whatever it took to make him happy. But eventually she realized that pleasing him was exhausting and ultimately futile, so she began to protect herself from his anger with the Protecting Behavior *she* had also learned as a child: her own anger. All her life she'd felt the painful emptiness and fear that result from a lack of Real Love. In that condition, Mark's attack was more than she could bear, so when he attacked her about the ketchup, she attacked him in return, saying, "You wanna be useful, for once? Why don't *you* clean it up?" To protect himself, Mark then responded with another attack. Had he stayed in the room, they would have continued to attack each other, adding yet more wounds to their relationship.

Although anger can be an effective way to protect yourself and to manipulate others to do what you want, you need to consider these questions: Have you ever been angry at your spouse and at the same time felt more loving toward him or her? Or more loved? Or enjoyed your relationship more deeply? Of course not, and yet we continue to get angry at our partners. Shortly we'll talk more about why we do that, and in subsequent chapters we'll discuss how to eliminate anger from our lives and our marriages.

Acting Like a Victim

If we can convince people that we've been injured and treated unfairly, they'll often stop hurting us and may even give us their sympathy, attention, and support. That's why we act like victims. Victims communicate—verbally and with their behavior—with variations on the following three themes: (1) Look what you did *to* me; (2) Look what you should have done *for* me (and didn't); and (3) It's not my fault. Victims have excuses for everything and blame everyone but themselves for their own mistakes and unhappiness. We all act like victims at times. Whenever we're confronted with a mistake we've made and say, "I couldn't help it," we're acting like victims. When we complain that we've been treated unfairly by our spouses, we're acting like victims.

When Mark spoke harshly to Susan, she responded with anger, but she was also acting like a victim. She thought, *How could you talk to me like this? Look how you're hurting* me!—a question and an accusation typical of victims—and then she felt entirely justified in attacking Mark with her own anger. We can't act like victims until we've first identified a perpetrator who's doing something *to* us—or is wickedly refusing to do something *for* us—and then we feel justified in responding however we want. When you believe someone is hurting you, defending yourself—even harshly—can seem like the only effective response.

Again, however, acting like a victim has the same detrimental effect as the other Getting and Protecting Behaviors. Have you ever acted like a victim and felt unconditionally loved by anyone? Does that behavior lead to a more richly rewarding relationship? Never. Acting like a victim is an attempt at manipulation, and what we get as a result cannot feel like Real Love.

Running

If we simply move away from a source of pain, we're less likely to be hurt. Withdrawing from conversations (verbally and physically), avoiding people, and leaving relationships in a state of fear or anger are all forms of running. When people say they're shy, what they're really saying is, "I've felt empty and afraid all my life, and I've learned that when I allow people to see who I really am, they criticize me or laugh at me, making me feel even more unloved and miserable. So to minimize that pain, I simply stay away from people or avoid speaking." Drugs and alcohol are other ways to run.

After Susan attacked Mark, he briefly attacked her in return, but he knew he'd only experience more pain if he stayed in the room with her and battled it out. So he walked out—he ran.

Not all withdrawing is running. Sometimes withdrawing is actually the healthy course to take, but only under certain circumstances, as I'll explain in Chapter Four.

Clinging

Clinging is obvious when a child grips tightly to his mother's skirt, but as adults we also cling emotionally to the people who give us attention, hoping we can sometimes squeeze even more out of them. We may do this by flattering the people who do things for us, or by being excessively grateful. Sometimes we're clinging to people when we tell them how much we love them and need them—we hope our words will encourage them to stay with us and return our expressions of love. Effectively, we're begging for more Imitation Love.

On the occasions Mark went out with his friends, Susan often said, "Do you really have to go? You never stay home with me anymore." She was clinging, begging Mark to love her. At one point in their marriage, Susan threatened to divorce Mark, and when he saw that she meant it, he said—several times—"Please don't leave. I couldn't make it without you." Mark was clinging.

The Destructive Effect of Getting and Protecting

When you lie to your spouse, get angry at him, act like he's hurting you, withdraw from him, or cling to him, you are not primarily concerned about *his* happiness—the definition of Real Love. You use those behaviors—mostly unconsciously—because you want to protect *yourself,* or get something for yourself, or both. When we use Getting and Protecting Behaviors, our primary concern is for *ourselves*. On these occasions, the people around us can't possibly feel like we unconditionally care about *them,* and they're quite right—we *don't*. That has a terrible effect—on us and on others.

The Effect of Getting and Protecting on Others
When Mark attacked Susan, she already felt unloved, empty, and afraid—as a result of a lifetime of not feeling unconditionally loved by her parents, other family members, teachers, friends, and Mark. When he spoke to her in anger, she saw his behavior as yet another confirmation that no one really cared about her, and in order to protect herself from that intolerable feeling, she lashed out at Mark. His angry words didn't cause her outburst. They were only the straw that broke the camel's back. She was reacting

to a *lifetime* of the emptiness and pain that always result from insufficient Real Love.

Mark had never felt unconditionally loved, either, a condition that existed long before he met Susan. When she spoke to him in anger, he, too, felt like Susan didn't really care about him and his needs—which she didn't. She couldn't feel a concern about his happiness while she was feeling the effects of a lifetime of emptiness and fear. Her attack was more than he could bear, so he reacted with more Protecting Behaviors, and the destructive cycle worsened. When we feel unloved, we tend to react to our partners in the very ways that make it *more* likely he or she will respond to us with additional Getting and Protecting Behaviors.

Keep in mind that although Mark's anger certainly wasn't kind or loving, he did *not* cause his wife's reaction to him. We'll talk more about that in the next chapter.

The Effect of Getting and Protecting on Ourselves

Even if our spouses don't respond badly to our Getting and Protecting Behaviors, *we* still experience an awful effect when we use them. Let's suppose you're out of work, penniless, and hungry. Every day you see me on the street carrying an armload of bread, and every day you walk up to me and say something to persuade me to give you one of the loaves:

- "You probably didn't know that my mother is sick." (lying) "Could you give me some bread to take to her?"
- "I haven't eaten in days." (lying, since you ate yesterday) "If you don't give me some bread, I don't know what I'll do." (acting like a victim)
- "I need something to eat. Do you remember last year when I helped you fix your car?" (attacking with guilt)
- "Could I borrow one of those loaves from you? I'll pay you back tomorrow." (lying)
- "Give me some of that bread right now!" (attacking)

• "Say, you really look nice today." (lying, because you're trying to exchange your compliment for my bread, and you're not being honest about your intention)

Each time you speak, I give you some bread, but what you don't know is that each morning I've baked a loaf specifically to give you. I'm trying to offer you a gift, but you can't *feel* it as a gift, because each morning you manipulate me in some way before I can say anything. Because of your manipulation, my gift can feel only like a result of something you have said or done. I'm offering you a small piece of Real Love, but with your behavior you turn it into Imitation Love—quite unconsciously. How sad that you're missing out on the effect of my gift.

Each time we use Getting and Protecting Behaviors with other people, we cannot feel the moments of acceptance they may offer us from time to time. We can only feel Imitation Love—the acceptance, power, pleasure, and safety we're given after we *earn* them. With our Getting and Protecting Behaviors, we effectively turn gold into lead.

On many occasions, Mark *did* choose to spend time with Susan and do the things she enjoyed, but she didn't feel loved on those occasions. Instead she felt like he was giving her what she wanted only because she'd nagged him about it so many times, or because he felt obligated as a result of something nice she'd done for him. She felt like she'd *paid* for his attention with her behavior—which was true.

Getting and Protecting Behaviors Are Always Wrong

Our primary goal in life—our very reason to exist—is to be genuinely happy, and we achieve that condition only as we feel unconditionally loved and share that love with other people. Whatever contributes, therefore, to feeling loved, loving, and happy is right, while anything that interferes with feeling loved, loving, and happy is wrong.

When you're angry at your spouse—to use just one example of getting and protecting—do you ever feel closer to him or her? Do you ever feel loved, loving, and happy? All the Getting and Protecting Behaviors are selfish and destructive. From extensive personal experience we've all learned that when we're lying, angry, acting like victims, and withdrawing from relationships, we're never happier, nor do we contribute to the health of our marriages. Because the Getting and Protecting Behaviors detract from feeling loved, loving, and happy, they are always wrong. Instinctively, we even know they're wrong, because when we're confronted about them, we usually deny them.

Anger, for example, is always wrong. I am not saying you *shouldn't* be angry, nor am I suggesting that you can't talk about your anger. I'm only stating in the strongest possible terms that anger—along with all the other Getting and Protecting Behaviors—is destroying our happiness and our marriages. With Real Love, we can learn to eliminate those behaviors and replace them with joy.

So Why Do We Use Getting and Protecting Behaviors?

If Getting and Protecting Behaviors have such a consistently destructive effect, why do we use them? Because they *work*—at least temporarily. In the absence of Real Love, these behaviors often produce an immediate and predictable relief from our pain and emptiness. When, for example, you drop hints here and there about your husband doing something for you, you may wait years without getting the desired result. When you get angry and make a fuss, however, you can sometimes get him off the couch in seconds or minutes. We're seduced by the immediate rewards of anger, and we've experienced that since childhood. Our parents effectively used anger to motivate us, so we tend to do the same with our spouses.

Even though Mark and Susan were miserable every time they lied, got angry, and withdrew from each other, they kept doing those things, because for a moment they felt stronger or safer. Susan knew that when she got angry at Mark, she wouldn't feel loved or loving, but with her anger she often succeeded in getting him to stop doing whatever was threatening her—being critical and angry, for example—and he might even do some of the things she wanted.

ༀ

We also use Getting and Protecting Behaviors because we simply don't know anything better. When I first began to play tennis, I played only with people who were as inexperienced as I was. No matter how hard I tried, I played badly. I didn't *want* to keep playing badly—I just didn't know a better way to hit the ball. After some skilled players showed me a better way to do the basic strokes, I was soon able to increase my level of play significantly.

Similarly, we all want to be unconditionally loving and happy, but who ever showed us how to find these qualities? When we were young and failed to please our parents, teachers, and friends, they became impatient and angry. We saw people lie to us when they became afraid. They acted like victims when we did things they perceived as unfair or hurtful. When we didn't satisfy their expectations, they often withdrew from us. Everywhere we looked, we saw Getting and Protecting Behaviors. We also saw that they *worked*—the people who used them were successful in protecting themselves and in controlling the behavior of others, including us. We've seen these same patterns as adults.

We've learned to use the behaviors we were taught. How could we not? We really do have an innate desire to be truthful and loving, but we also have a powerful tendency to do what we've *learned*, and to do what temporarily makes us feel better in the absence of sufficient Real Love. That's why we continue to use these behaviors that leave us feeling empty and cause so much harm to our relationships.

The Origin of Getting and Protecting Behaviors

I've stated that in the absence of sufficient Real Love, emptiness and pain always result, and then Getting and Protecting Behaviors are natural responses to those conditions. Does that mean that whenever we use these behaviors, we can blame them on our parents and others who failed to love us? Yes and no.

Let's take Susan as an example. Clearly, she and Mark would have been happier if she had responded to him in a loving way when he asked her about the ketchup on the wall. But she was already carrying the emptiness and fear that resulted from a *lifetime* of not feeling unconditionally loved by her parents and others, so in the moment when Mark confronted her with anger, she reacted not only to him but also to her considerable past experience. She was not a prisoner to her past—we can always work at making better conscious decisions instead of just automatically responding to past conditioning—but she *was* significantly affected by it. Real Love is absolutely essential to the health of our souls, just as vitamins and minerals are essential to the health of our bodies. A person with malnutrition—of the body or soul—simply cannot be as strong as someone who has been adequately fed. In subsequent chapters, we'll discuss in detail what we all can do to eliminate our Getting and Protecting Behaviors—with increased understanding, self-control, and Real Love.

Exercises

Exercise One

Identify the forms of Imitation Love you use. If you devote considerable time and effort to your appearance and success so people will notice and accept you, you have a *need* to be praised—a need to fill your emptiness. If you're disappointed or irritated when your spouse doesn't do what you want, you have a need for power. If you think about sex in an obsessive way and feel deep disappointment and impatience when you don't get it as often as you'd like, you have a need for pleasure to fill your emptiness. If the happiest moments in your life are associated with pursuing some kind of physical excitement—skydiving, skiing, and so on—that is another indication that you use pleasure as a form of Imitation Love.

Write down some of the forms of Imitation Love you use. We

don't like to see how attached we are to praise, power, pleasure, and safety, but if you can see this in yourself, you can begin to realize that you're trying to fill an emptiness created by a lack of Real Love. Knowing that, you can begin to recognize how you use your spouse to fill your emptiness, and you can begin to take the steps to get what you really need for your own happiness and for the enrichment of your marriage.

🍂

Exercise Two

Write down the Getting and Protecting Behaviors you use: hiding, exaggerating, making excuses, anger, acting like a victim, clinging to other people, and running from relationships. Regardless of what your spouse does, admit how much harm each of *your* Getting and Protecting Behaviors causes to your marriage and to your own happiness.

2

The First Steps to Success in Marriage

When the Head Understands, the Heart Can Follow

When we lie, attack, cling, run, or act like victims, we hurt our partners and ourselves, but because we don't understand why we do those things, we keep repeating them and causing more injury. Although most of us have been stuck in this destructive pattern all our lives, there is a way out. With an understanding of Getting and Protecting Behaviors, we can

- eliminate the mystery and frustration of human behavior.
- change the way we feel about the behavior of others—including our spouses—which dramatically changes the way we react to them.
- eliminate our own unproductive feelings of guilt.
- overcome the frustration of trying to change other people.
- identify what we need to change about ourselves.

Eliminating the Mystery of Human Behavior

In the last chapter, you met Susan and Mark, who had an unpleasant interaction characterized by Getting and Protecting Behaviors. Shortly after their angry conversation, Susan called a friend and said, "I just don't understand Mark. An hour ago, one of the kids made a mess, and while I was working to clean it up, he came in and snapped at me. He didn't ask what he could to do help. Then he got mad and stomped out of the room."

Although Mark's actual attack certainly contributed to Susan's feelings of emptiness and fear, she also experienced a large portion of frustration that came from not *understanding* his behavior. Here she was doing the best she could, and Mark attacked her for no obvious reason. *Why,* she thought, *does he keep doing this to me?* And Mark couldn't understand why Susan bit his head off when he was "only asking a question." Many of us are mystified by the behavior of our spouses, and in our ignorance we're guaranteed to repeat the same unproductive reactions. How frustrating.

When we understand our need for Real Love and how we're affected by its absence, we can see that all the lying, anger, withdrawal, whining, and other manipulations used by ourselves and others are just Getting and Protecting Behaviors that result from feeling empty and afraid. Never again wonder *why* your spouse is behaving badly. Don't make it complicated. Just remember that he or she is empty and afraid. Once you see that, the mystery of these behaviors vanishes, and then you can change forever the way you feel about your partner, as well as how you behave toward him or her.

Changing Our Feelings About Other People with a Knowledge of Getting and Protecting Behaviors

Imagine that you and I are in the Bahamas, enjoying a pleasant lunch, a warm tropical breeze, and the soothing music of a live band as we sit together by the side of a pool. We're having a perfect day, but then someone in the pool starts splashing you—first on your shoes, then higher up on your pants. You can't see who it is because there's a deck chair between you and the person in the pool. At first you ignore it, but eventually you begin to get wet and irritated, and finally you get up from your chair to say something to this idiot who's being so thoughtless. As you stand up, however, to look over the chair that's in your way, you see that the man splashing you is *drowning*. He's only splashing you because he's thrashing and kicking in the water to keep his head from going under.

How do you feel now? Are you still angry at this man? Of course not—who in their right mind could be angry at someone who's drowning? In fact, as soon as you see why he's splashing you, you not only lose your irritation, but you try to help him out of the water. Let's ask some important questions about this event:

- How long did it take for your feelings of anger to be replaced by a feeling of complete acceptance? It happened in an instant. As soon as you understood that the man was drowning, your anger vanished.
- After seeing the truth of the situation, how much effort did you exert to control your anger? None. When you saw that the man was splashing you only in an effort to save himself, your anger simply disappeared. You didn't have to *control* yourself or *work* to make your anger go away.
- What did the drowning man have to do to persuade you to help him? Did he have to pay you? Apologize to you? Beg you? Of course not. You offered him your assistance without any conditions. With a simple flash of understanding, your feelings of anger were replaced not only by acceptance but by an unconditional concern for his welfare (Real Love).

With an understanding of Real Love and Getting and Protecting Behaviors, the way you feel toward other people in real life—notably your spouse—can change just as quickly and dramatically as your feelings changed toward the man in the pool. You now realize that without sufficient Real Love—without the single most important ingredient required for happiness—people feel like they're drowning all the time, and then they'll use the Getting and Protecting Behaviors that allow them to temporarily keep their heads above water. Regrettably, as they're splashing about in the water with these behaviors, they often affect us in negative ways. When you understand that, the effect is powerful:

- Your feelings change immediately. When you understand that every time your spouse uses Getting and Protecting Behaviors, he or she is simply drowning—not trying primarily to annoy *you*—you can't stay angry at him or her for one minute longer.
- You don't have to work at controlling your anger. It will usually go away on its own.
- Your negative feelings are actually replaced by a desire to help your drowning spouse.

When your head understands, your heart can follow.

Mark came to see me shortly after the ketchup incident, and as I explained Getting and Protecting Behaviors to him, a look of understanding crossed his face as he said, "So when Susan snapped at me, she was just drowning and protecting herself?"

"Yes," I replied. "She was empty and afraid as a result of a *lifetime* of not feeling loved unconditionally, and your critical, unloving words just pushed her head a little farther under the water. It was more than she could take, so she lashed out at you in an attempt to get you to stop pushing her under."

"So she was already drowning and I just made it worse."

"Right, and now that you know that, are you still mad at her about what she did?"

"Well, not as much, no."

"Remember how this feels," I suggested, "to have your feelings change toward Susan when you understand her better. The next time she gets mad, if you make a conscious effort to remember that she's just drowning, you'll be much less angry at her, if at all. In fact, instead of being angry at her, which only makes things worse for both of you, what *could* you do?"

"I don't know."

"You could help her out of the water."

"How?" he asked.

"When she's drowning, what does she need?"

"To feel loved, I guess."

"There's no guessing about that. Every time Susan is angry at you, she's drowning—she's telling you she doesn't feel enough Real Love, not just from you but from anyone. If you can remember that, and not be angry, you'll be able to see how to give her the love she needs."

"Like how? What could I do?"

"You could smile at her and ask, 'What can I do to help?' Give her a gentle hug. And if you're already angry, you could say, 'Wait a minute. I'm getting irritated, and that's not helping. What do *you* need?' When you do that, you're helping her out of the water, and that's what she really needs when she's drowning, not your criticism or anger. Can you imagine how different things would be if you did that instead of getting mad?"

Mark was quiet for a moment before he said, "She'd fall over dead from shock if I did any of those things. This really changes the way I see her. I've gotta say, though, that when she gets mad, I don't know if I could hug her."

"Think," I suggested, "about how it goes every single time you get angry or run away when she's irritated at you. Does it *ever* make you happier or make your relationship better?"

Mark smiled and shook his head.

"So, do you want to keep doing what never works—using the behaviors that make both of you unhappy—or do you want to try something different? If you'll make a conscious decision to remember what we've talked about today, and do whatever it takes to help her out of the pool, you'll change the way both of you feel. It's well worth the effort."

A week later, Mark called me to say that earlier that day Susan had been angry at him, and he'd begun to get angry in return, but then he remembered our conversation. He saw that she was drowning, so instead of saying another word, he walked over to her and gave her a hug. She dissolved into tears in his arms. "I would not have believed she could change that fast," he said, "and it felt pretty good to me, too."

When your head understands, your heart can follow.

A few days later, Susan came to see me. "What did you do to my husband?" she asked. I told her what I'd said to him about Real Love and Getting and Protecting Behaviors. She wept as she said, "I've been drowning all my life, but I didn't know it."

"Few of us do," I said.

"I understand better now why I got angry at Mark, but why did he get mad about the ketchup on the wall in the first place?"

"When you're drowning, almost *everything* becomes more inconvenient or stressful than you can stand. Imagine that you're out on the water in a sturdy boat. How much would small waves bother you? Or how much would it bother you to hold small weights in your hands?"

"It wouldn't, I suppose," said Susan.

"But what if you're drowning and barely keeping your nose above water? Now how would you feel about small waves washing over your face? Or holding small weights in your hands? Now those 'little' things would drown you, wouldn't they? That's what happened with Mark. He already felt unloved—as a result of a lifetime without enough Real Love, not because of any particular thing you'd done or not done—and in that condition, the ketchup on the wall became one more inconvenience or stress than he could stand. He felt helpless and alone, and by lashing out at you, he experienced a moment of power that made him feel better. He didn't even realize he was using you, and he didn't think about how it would affect you. He was only trying to make his own pain bearable."

"I never understood any of this," she said.

"Of course not. All our lives we've seen people lash out at each other, or withdraw, or act hurt, without understanding what was going on. No one has ever told us *why* we do all these things."

Days later, Susan called me and said, "It's working."

"What's working?" I asked.

"Today Mark was angry because the tape measure was missing from his toolbox. He came in from the garage and asked me where his (expletive) tape measure was. I was about to tell him where he could put his stupid tape measure, when I remembered that he was just drowning and thrashing around in the water. Suddenly, I wasn't afraid or angry. I said that it must be frustrating to not know where his tools are. I said I'd be happy to look around the kitchen for it, and I suggested he might look in the kids' rooms or in our bedroom, where he'd been doing some remodeling. I couldn't believe what happened then. He stopped fuming—immediately. It was a miracle. In the past, we'd have argued and probably wouldn't have spoken to each other again for days."

"Feels nice when you understand what's going on, doesn't it?"

"I wouldn't have believed it if I hadn't seen it work."

Every time your spouse lies, attacks, acts like a victim, clings, or withdraws from you, he or she is saying that he doesn't have enough of the Real Love that makes life worth living. He's drowning and using the behaviors he's used all his life to protect himself and to get the Imitation Love that temporarily distracts him from the pain that always results from a lack of Real Love. When you don't understand that picture, you naturally want him or her to stop those behaviors, which are inconvenient and even painful to you. Unfortunately, that's like telling a drowning man that he should stop struggling, stop bothering you, and just drown. How foolish is that? Even worse, you often jump into the water with him and demand that he save *you* from drowning. So now there are two of you drowning, and you're both choking the other as you demand help. It's an impossible situation. When you understand Getting and Protecting Behaviors, you can stop jumping in the water with your spouse. You can stop yelling at him or her from the sidelines and actually help him out of the water instead.

❧

As I tell people that their Getting and Protecting Behaviors are a result of a lifetime of not feeling loved, not just a response to something their spouse did in a given moment, many people still object, and they explain—in great detail—how their partner's behavior really did cause their subsequent feelings. They commonly say—in a variety of ways—"He (or she) makes me so angry." Every time we get angry *at* someone, we're implying that *she* is the cause. After all, we reason, we wouldn't be angry if she hadn't done what she did, so it must be her fault. Because we're all flawed and frequently do inconsiderate things with one another, other people will always give us plentiful opportunities to blame them for our anger. We absolutely must understand, however, that other people do not make us angry, and to prove that point, let's examine a scenario from my book *Real Love*.

Imagine that you have only two dollars left in the world, and you're starving. Putting the money on a table, you get ready to go out and buy some bread. Suddenly, I dash into the room, snatch the two dollars off the table, and run away before you can stop me. You'd almost certainly be angry at me and would claim that I *made* you angry.

Now imagine that the next day I do exactly the same thing—steal two dollars off the table as you're getting ready to go out and buy some bread—but this time you have *twenty million* dollars in the bank. How would you feel now? Compared with twenty million, two dollars is nothing, and losing it would be insignificant.

We just proved that I didn't *make* you angry when I took your money the first time. If *my* behavior caused your reaction the first time, then doing the exact same thing the second time would have made you angry then, too. But it didn't. Your anger was a reaction to *your* lack of twenty million dollars, and I wasn't responsible for that.

Every time your spouse, or anyone else, does something inconsiderate—she's late, he gets angry, she withdraws her affection—he or she is taking two emotional dollars from you. If that's your last two dollars—which is how you feel when you don't have enough Real Love—the loss is a big deal. When you have enough Real Love, however, you feel like you have twenty million dollars, and then the loss of two dollars seems relatively meaningless. With enough Real Love—with twenty million in the bank—other people can't "make" you angry anymore when they take two dollars. Their behaviors become minor inconveniences, not major catastrophes. At this point you may think this sounds like a fairy tale, but it's not. When we understand Getting and Protecting Behaviors, and when we have enough Real Love, our feelings and behavior really do change. If you can put aside your skepticism—understandably born of a lifetime of experience—and take the steps described in this and subsequent chapters, you'll learn for yourself the effect of feeling Real Love and having an accurate understanding of human behavior.

❦

Let me suggest another way to prove that other people don't make us angry. Imagine someone who loves you completely and unconditionally, like the people you met in the house you visited on pages 5–7. Imagine that she says, "Because I care so much about you being happy, I'd like to share an observation with you. I think you're doing something that's interfering with your happiness."

You ask what it is, and she calmly continues: "When people have an opinion different from yours, you often try to bring them around to your point of view. You browbeat them with facts and intimidate them with the force of your presentation. When you do that, you do succeed in getting many people to agree with you, but they don't feel closer to you emotionally, nor do you feel closer to them. You win the argument, but you still lose—bigtime. I know you'd be a lot happier if you just let people have their opinions, whatever they are."

Remember that you *know* she loves you. Are you angry as she expresses her loving concern about something that's hurting you? Of course not. Now picture in your mind someone who has often been critical of you and angry at you—perhaps so consistently that you regard him as an enemy. How would you take it if that person told you that you boss people around and try to control them? You'd feel quite differently now, even though he's saying the same thing your loving friend did. Your anger, therefore, is determined not by what someone—like your spouse—does in the moment, but mostly by your past experience and how you perceive that person.

Eliminating Our Own Unproductive Feelings of Guilt

After Susan realized what her husband needed from her, she began to feel guilty. "All these years, what Mark really needed from me was unconditional acceptance, but instead I've been angry at him and criticized him when he didn't do what I wanted. I've done that with the kids, too—and a lot of other people, come to think of it. I feel bad about all that."

"Why does Mark get angry at you?" I asked.

"Because he's drowning. He's trying to protect himself or get something from me."

"If that's why Mark gets angry at *you*, why do you think *you* get angry at *him*?"

When you treat your spouse badly, you're drowning and trying to protect yourself or get something from him or her. That doesn't *justify* your behavior, but it does explain it. Some guilt can be good—it can motivate us to change—but excessive guilt only makes us feel bad. In fact, if you feel guilty enough, you'll likely hide the behavior that makes you feel bad, and then you'll never change it. You don't need to beat yourself when you make mistakes in your marriage, but you do need to *recognize* your mistakes and take the steps necessary to avoid making them in the future.

It can be especially difficult to avoid feeling guilty when your wife is telling you—with her words and behavior—that you *are* responsible for her anger, sadness, pain, and so on. Certainly you need to be compassionate and not dismiss her pain—you need to do whatever you can to accept and love her—but in the same way that she is not responsible for *your* feelings, you are not responsible for *hers*. If your spouse is drowning, almost everything you do will become threatening, and she'll react badly to you. Although you can certainly make things worse for her when you're thoughtless and uncaring, you are not responsible for her drowning, which is a result of a lifetime of insufficient Real Love.

Overcoming the Frustration of Trying to Change Other People

Almost every day I speak with married people whose complaints boil down to this: How can I *get* my partner to stop being critical, angry, neglectful, and so on—in other words, how can I get my partner to stop using Getting and Protecting Behaviors?

Imagine again that you're standing by the side of a pool and watching a man who's drowning. You wouldn't say, "Stop it. You're getting me wet. Why don't you just put your hands at your sides and slip quietly under the water?" But that's just what we're doing when we insist that our partners change their behavior. They're using the Getting and Protecting Behaviors they believe will keep their heads above water, and we respond by insisting that they stop it and simply drown. No wonder our demands for change are ineffective and cause so much frustration for ourselves and our spouses.

When Susan realized why Mark got angry at her and withdrew from her, she began to let go of her insistence that he stop those behaviors. Instead she gave him the unconditional acceptance and love he needed. As a result, she was a great deal happier, and with her love, he no longer had a *need* to use Getting and Protecting Behaviors with her. Of course, these changes didn't happen overnight.

The Law of Choice
Drowning people are not primarily trying to hurt us, just doing whatever it takes to save themselves—and they have the right to do that, even if their efforts inconvenience *us*. That doesn't make their behavior right, but they must be allowed to make their own choices about what they do. *Everyone has the right to choose what he or she says and does.* That is the Law of Choice, and it's the most important

principle in any relationship, including marriage. On many occasions—each of which can seem so very justifiable—you may want to control the choices of your spouse, but the results would be awful. Where would it end? If you have the right to control what *he* does, it's only fair that he gets to control what *you* do. Without the Law of Choice, everyone would become a puppet dangling from strings controlled by others—an intolerable thought.

If you control me in any way, I'm no longer myself. I've become an extension of you, like your shoes or gloves. But when you're with your shoes or gloves—or anything else you control— you're still alone, the worst condition of all. You might think you want to control what your spouse does, but if you succeed in that effort—if you make all the decisions and do all the thinking— you'll only guarantee your own loneliness. You won't have a partner but a prisoner. Is that what you really want? To be in control but alone? Or do you want to have a relationship with a real person as you allow your spouse to make his own choices?

What you truly want is a real relationship with your spouse, and *a relationship is the natural result of people making independent choices.* In the process of making independent choices, we all make mistakes, and as we do, it is simply unavoidable that the people around us will be inconvenienced, even hurt. If *you* expect to make mistakes, how could you expect that your *spouse* would not make mistakes, including those that inconvenience you? We have that expectation because when we're suffering from the intolerable condition of being empty and afraid ourselves, we naturally expect that everyone around us—especially our spouses— will avoid hurting us and even give us something to fill our emptiness. When they don't fill those expectations, we're disappointed and angry.

Honoring the Law of Choice for the Benefit of Others, and Making Our Own Choices

A woman named Anne came to visit me one day and said, "For days I've been telling Parker [her husband] that whenever I pull out of the driveway, there's a small puddle of green liquid where my car was parked. He said he'd do something about it, but he never did. Yesterday when I got home, there was steam coming out from under the hood, and when I told him about it, he waved his hand at me—like he was brushing away a fly—and said he'd fix it. But this morning, I found a river of green stuff running down the driveway, and now I'm afraid to drive the car anywhere. I have some important errands to run, but he's gone somewhere in his car, so I can't go anywhere. I'm stuck."

"You sound pretty angry about it," I said.

"Sure I am. Who wouldn't be? He didn't listen to me—again—and I'm tired of it."

"That's his choice to make."

"What do you mean?"

"Remember how we talked about the Law of Choice?"

"Yes."

"Parker has chosen not to listen to you, and you don't get to control that."

"But he—"

"There is no *but* here," I reminded her. "You don't get to control his choices, even when they're selfish and inconvenient to *you*."

"Then what am I supposed to do if he keeps ignoring me like this?"

"Oh, you have lots of options."

"Like what?"

"In every interaction or relationship, we have three choices. We can live with it and like it, live with it and hate it, or leave it. You don't get a fourth choice—the one many of us want—which is to control another person. Living with Parker and hating it wouldn't make much sense—you'd just be guaranteeing your own unhappiness. So let's deal with the other two choices. Do you want to divorce Parker over this?"

Anne smiled. "Not really."

"Then you're left with one choice: Live with it and like it."

"How am I supposed to like it when he doesn't do what he says he'll do? Am I supposed to like it when I don't have a car to drive?"

"When I say 'live with it and like it,' I don't mean you should like Parker ignoring you, or enjoy not having a car to drive. But no matter what Parker does or doesn't do, you can learn to enjoy your life and your relationship with him. Although it's certainly inconvenient that you don't have a car right now, that's not what's bothering you most. What you want most is to feel unconditionally loved. You want Parker to love you, and when he ignored you about the car, he was clearly telling you that he didn't care about you—and that's what really hurts."

"I've never seen it that way," said Anne, "but that's right."

I described to her the visualization from Chapter One about being with a group of unconditionally loving people, and then I asked, "If you felt completely loved by a group of people like that, or by Parker, how much would it bother you if he didn't fix the car when he promised?"

"Probably not much."

"It would just be an inconvenience, not the big deal it is to you now. So it's clear that you *don't* feel loved, and that's what you need to address rather than trying to control your husband's individual behaviors. If you can find the love you really need, you can live with any situation and like it."

After I described to Anne what she could do to find the Real Love she needed—which we'll talk about in the next chapter—she had one more question: "I still don't have a car for the errands I have to do today. What can I do about that?"

"Living with a situation or a relationship and liking it does not mean you can't do something about it. There are lots of things you can do, actually. You're not helpless. You could get the car fixed, for example. You could call a repair shop and have someone come out to look at it, or if they won't come to you, you could have the car towed to them. Then, while the car is being repaired, you could get a taxi to do your errands, or call a friend to take you, or borrow her car, or rent a car. Or you could wait on repairing the car, leave it in the driveway until Parker finally gets around to it, and in the meantime you could rent a car to get where you want. There are lots of options."

"Do you know what would happen if I had the car towed and called a taxi? It would be expensive, and he'd blow up."

"It always costs money to fix cars and get where you need to go. That's just the way it is. But notice that I'm not telling you what to do here. I said you had *many* options. One of them is to leave the car there and rent a car. I'm just suggesting that since Parker has chosen not to participate in the process of making the decisions about this situation, you might have to make your own decision today. When he comes home, tell him—calmly, without criticizing him—what you did about the car and the errands today, and then discuss what you plan to do in the days to come."

"He'll probably get mad."

"That will be *his* choice. As I've said before, we don't *make* other people angry. If Parker gets mad, that will be his choice, not something you caused. All you're responsible for is your own behavior. You need to be certain that if you get your own ride or have the car fixed, you're just doing what needs to be done, not trying to get back at Parker."

In every situation or relationship, you have three choices:

- Live with it and hate it. This is never a smart choice, since it guarantees only that *you* will be miserable.
- Live with it and like it. This doesn't mean you can't do anything about the way things are. You can make requests, negotiate agreements, take action on your own, and make decisions that change the way you feel and behave. We'll be talking about these options in this and subsequent chapters.
- Leave it. Sometimes it's not possible for us to be happy—to feel loved and loving—in certain situations or relationships. It may then be best to walk away from an individual interaction

or even a relationship. We'll talk more about that in a later chapter.

We try to control other people—including our spouses—only because we are empty and afraid, and we believe that as we control others we will feel safer and less helpless. The truth is, we already have great power. We can *always* make decisions that will enable us to see the world differently and will bring into our lives more of the Real Love that will make us truly happy. *That* is real power—the ability to change our own feelings and behavior—not the ability to control the behavior of others.

Identifying What We Need to Change About Ourselves

Anne called me a few days later to talk about some other inconsiderate thing Parker had done, and again I said, "You sound pretty mad about it."

"Of course."

"It seems like you get angry almost every time he does something you don't like."

"What else *can* I do? He doesn't ever think about me, just himself."

"I have a suggestion. Let's go down to the hardware store and get a large brass ring. We'll put it through your nose, fasten a chain to it, and hand the chain to Parker."

It was clear—as she raised her voice and said, "What?!"—that my suggestion was not the answer she was looking for.

"You wouldn't *like* having a ring in your nose?"

"*No*, I *wouldn't.*"

"But you already have one. Whenever Parker does something you don't like, you get angry. He *controls* your behavior—just as though he were leading you around with a ring in your nose."

There was a long pause before Anne replied, "I see what you mean."

"Do you want to stay a slave to whatever he does, or would you rather be free?"

"Free."

"Then you have to determine your own behavior, which can only happen when you understand it. When you get angry, what are you doing?"

She wasn't sure, so we talked about Getting and Protecting Behaviors again. She saw that she got angry because it made her feel stronger and more in control—she got Imitation Love in the form of power. Sometimes with her anger she even got Parker to do what she wanted: He was willing to comply with her demands in order to avoid her disapproval. Her anger also protected her from the feelings of helplessness and loneliness that came from not feeling loved.

"Each time you get angry," I suggested, "you might try to remember that you're using a Getting and Protecting Behavior that helps you deal with the emptiness and fear you experience because of a lifetime of not feeling loved. That has little to do with Parker, and it's something you can change." Again we talked about how to find the Real Love she needed.

When we see our Getting and Protecting Behaviors as signs of our own emptiness and fear, we don't focus any longer on the mistakes and flaws of other people. We can then begin to change the way we feel and behave. Until we understand the cause of our Getting and Protecting Behaviors, however, we're doomed to repeat them.

The Law of Expectations

Imagine that you're starving in the middle of the desert. In that condition, you'll do just about anything to get food and to protect yourself from losing what little you have. When a man walks by with a backpack full of food, you naturally expect him to help you. After all, if he has what you desperately need, how could he possibly refuse to help?

Being without Real Love is like being without food. Without

sufficient Real Love, we have enormous expectations of other people—for Real Love if they have it, and for Imitation Love if they don't. It's from your spouse that you usually have the greatest expectations of all, and for two reasons: First, it's very likely that he or she actually did fill your expectations for "happiness" in the beginning of your relationship—but filled them with Imitation Love. *That* is why you fell in love with your partner: because he or she gave you enough Imitation Love that you temporarily felt pretty darned good.

But then the effect of Imitation Love wore off, and you wondered why you weren't happy anymore. *When I fell in love with my partner,* you thought, *he made me happy.* We like to think that someone else can *make* us happy—for one thing, it relieves us of the responsibility we have for our own happiness. And we like it when people tell us that we make *them* happy, because then we feel worthwhile and important. But giving this responsibility to our spouses has awful consequences—we then have huge expectations that they will *continue* to make us happy, and if we do become unhappy, we can only conclude that our partners are responsible for that condition.

The second reason we have huge expectations of our spouses is that they actually *promised* to make us happy. Regardless of the words actually spoken at the wedding ceremony, what we *hear* our spouses say is this: "I promise to make you happy—always. I will heal your past wounds and satisfy your present needs and expectations—even when you don't express them. I will lift you up when you're discouraged. I will accept and love you no matter what mistakes you make. I give to you all that I have or ever will have. And I will never leave you."

Neither partner is consciously aware of making this bushel of promises, but each partner still hears them and insists that they be fulfilled. When both partners lack sufficient Real Love, however, they can't possibly make each other happy, and then their efforts to do that yield only disappointment and anger, no matter how hard they try.

Expectations can only kill the potential happiness in a marriage, as illustrated by Rachel, a woman who complained to me that her husband, Kevin, never gave her flowers anymore, didn't look at her with affection as he once did, and didn't talk to her when he came home from work. She was in the process of listing more of his failings when I said, "It sounds like you expect Kevin to do a lot of things."

She looked at me like I was stupid. "Why *wouldn't* I? He's my husband."

"What if I *expected* you to give me a dozen roses on my birthday," I said, "and you only gave me nine? I'd only have one thing on my mind, wouldn't I?"

"The three roses you *didn't* get," she said.

"In fact, even if you did give me a dozen roses, I wouldn't be thrilled by them—I'd only be *satisfied* that you filled my demand. It can't feel like a gift when I'm essentially *making* you give me something with my expectations. But if I expect *nothing* from you, even a single rose from you will feel like a delightful gift, real evidence that you care about me. I'll love it.

"With your expectations," I continue, "you make it impossible for anything you get from Kevin to feel like a gift. Everything he does seems like nothing to you. He can never do enough to please you. In addition, he *knows* he can never do enough, and eventually he gets to the point where he doesn't *want* to do anything with you or for you."

"I'd never thought of that."

The Law of Expectations states that we never have the right to expect anyone to do anything for us. That makes sense when we understand the Law of Choice. If we understand that other people really do get to make their own choices—and mistakes—how can we possibly expect them to change their choices to please us? Rachel doesn't have the right to expect Kevin to give her what she wants.

After I explained the Law of Expectations, Rachel said, "But if

I don't have any expectations, Kevin won't do anything. How do I get what I want?"

"You can always *ask* Kevin for what you want—nothing wrong with that—but you haven't been making *requests* of Kevin. You've been making *demands*."

"How do you know that?" she asked.

"When Kevin doesn't give you what you 'ask' for, do you feel either disappointed or irritated?"

Throughout our discussion, Rachel had made it clear that she was experiencing both of those feelings, so she could hardly deny it. "I guess I do," she said, "but isn't that natural?"

"Sure, it's natural, but it also shows that you're making demands and having expectations, and it's killing your happiness and your marriage. Kevin is empty himself, so he feels your expectations as a huge burden to carry and as an accusation that he's not acceptable. He responds with Getting and Protecting Behaviors, and those never make the two of you feel closer."

Each time we're angry, we demonstrate that we have expectations that are not being filled. When we understand the Law of Expectations, it's much more difficult to remain angry at anyone.

There is an exception to the Law of Expectations. If your spouse makes a promise to do or not do something, you have a right to have expectations about his or her behavior. We'll talk about promises, requests, and agreements in Chapter Six.

Realizing the selfishness of expectations is often quite a blow to married people. The very reason most of us get married is to have someone we *can* expect to love us and make us happy, and when we hear that those expectations are unreasonable, we wonder, *Why should we bother to get married at all?* Indeed, if our goal is primarily to get what we want from our spouses, marriage often will be unfulfilling and even unfair. When we understand, however, that marriage is really an opportunity to learn how to love our spouses, our perspective on marriage changes considerably. We'll talk more about a new perspective on marriage in Chapter Five.

Exercise

Write down some of the things your partner does that irritate you, or disappoint you, or hurt you. Here are some examples:

- "When he comes home, he goes in the other room and just reads the newspaper. He doesn't look at me, talk to me, or touch me. I feel like he doesn't care about me."
- "Instead of seeing all the things I try to do for her, she just nags me and tells me what's wrong with me."
- "He never spends time with the kids anymore, and he expects me to do everything for them: feed them, help them with their homework, take them places—everything."

You can change how you feel about all these behaviors you've listed—and how you react to them—as you use the principles you've learned in this chapter. Following are some examples of applying these principles, which you can use in a similar way with each of the irritating behaviors you've written down:

- Why we use Getting and Protecting Behaviors. When you get up in the morning, do you ever say to yourself, "I *could* be loving toward my spouse today and make a huge contribution toward the happiness of our marriage, but no, instead I'll withhold my love and express my anger, or be deceitful, or withdraw, or act like a victim, which will hurt both of us." You wouldn't ever do that intentionally, and *neither would your spouse*. Carefully examine each of your spouse's behaviors and ask yourself:

  1. Which Getting and Protecting Behaviors is he or she using here?
  2. Why do people use Getting and Protecting Behaviors? (Because they feel unloved, empty, and afraid—because they're drowning and trying to save themselves.)

3. Would I be angry at someone who was drowning? Does it make any more sense to be angry at my husband when he's drowning emotionally?

- The Law of Choice. Read the following to yourself:

  1. Do I have the right to make my own decisions about how I feel and what I say and do? The alternative would be unthinkable. My partner has the same right, even when he or she doesn't do what I want.
  2. I do not have the right to control my partner, even when I really want something from him or her.
  3. When I try to control my partner, I'm selfishly trying to protect myself or get something for myself. I do not have the right to do that, and my selfishness cannot lead to a genuinely loving marriage.

- In understanding the Law of Choice, we also understand that we do not have the right to expect our spouses to make us happy. Read the following to yourself every day until you firmly believe it: When I have expectations of my spouse, I'm demanding that he/she give me what I want. Those expectations cause disappointment and anger in me, and create a sense of distasteful obligation in my partner. I cannot be happy, and we cannot have a loving relationship, while I'm having these expectations.

3

Taking Action

Finding and Sharing Real Love

In Chapter Two, after you learned he was drowning, you experienced a dramatic change in your feelings toward the man who was splashing you. Now imagine that you see another man drowning, but this time you jump into the pool with him, where he grabs you by the neck and pushes you under the water. Although you understand that he's doing this only to save his own life, that *understanding* alone won't keep you from drowning.

Similarly, when your husband or wife is attacking, lying, acting like a victim, or running, it may not be enough just to *understand* that he's only drowning, because when you don't have enough Real Love yourself, you're drowning, too, and in that condition everything he does can seem quite threatening. If you then respond with your own Getting and Protecting Behaviors, effectively you're grabbing him by the neck and demanding that he save *you* from drowning, and that will only make things worse for both of you. At that point, you may need more than just an intellectual understanding of Getting and Protecting Behaviors. You'll need to actually *feel loved*, which will pull you out of the water, where you'll feel safe and will be able to make more rational and loving decisions.

We use Getting and Protecting Behaviors only to protect

ourselves and to fill the emptiness we feel in the absence of sufficient Real Love. When we get enough Real Love, our emptiness and fear will go away, and we'll have no *reason* to use the Getting and Protecting Behaviors that have such an adverse effect on our happiness and relationships.

How do we find this Real Love that most of us have been lacking all our lives? Let me begin by sharing a story from *Real Love.*

The Tale of the Wart King and the Wise Man

Once there was a rich and beautiful kingdom that stretched beyond the horizon in all directions. But the prince of that kingdom was very unhappy. He had warts all over his face, and everywhere he went, people teased him and laughed at him. So he mostly stayed in his room, alone and miserable.

Upon the death of his father, the prince became king and issued a decree that no one—on pain of death—would ever laugh at his warts again. But still he stayed in his room, ashamed and alone. On the rare occasions that he did go out, he put a cloth bag over his head, which covered his warts but also made it difficult for him to see.

Finally, after many years, the king heard about a Wise Man living on top of a nearby mountain. Hoping the Wise Man could help him, the king climbed the mountain and found the old man sitting under a tree. Taking the bag off his head, the king said, "I've come for your help."

The Wise Man looked intently at the king for several long moments and finally said, "You have warts on your face."

The king was enraged. That was not what he'd climbed all that way to hear. "No, I don't!" he screamed. Ashamed and angry, he put the bag back over his head.

"Yes, you do," the Wise Man insisted gently.

"I'll have you killed!" shouted the king.

"Then call your guards," the Wise Man said.

"My guards aren't here!" the king shrieked helplessly. "I climbed all the way up this mountain to ask for your help, and all you can say is that I have warts on my face?! How cruel you are!"

Angry and frustrated, the king ran from the Wise Man, falling repeatedly because he couldn't see very well with the bag on his head. Finally, the king fell down a steep slope and into a lake, where he began to drown. The Wise Man jumped in, pulled the king to shore, and took the bag from his head so he could breathe.

The king was horrified when he saw the Wise Man staring at him. "You're laughing at me," the king said.

"Not at all," the Wise Man replied, smiling.

With his eyes fixed on the ground, the king said, "The boys in the village laughed at me, and my father was ashamed of me."

"I'm not one of the boys in the village," the Wise Man immediately responded, "and I'm not your father. That must have been hard for you."

"Yes, it was," the king admitted, with tears in his eyes.

"But as you can see, I'm not laughing at you, and I'm not ashamed of you," the Wise Man repeated.

Somehow being with the Wise Man did feel different to the king. He looked into the lake and saw his reflection. "I really do have a lot of warts."

"I know," the Wise Man agreed.

"And you don't find them disgusting?"

"No, and I don't find my own warts disgusting anymore, either."

The king noticed for the first time that the Wise Man also had warts. "Why do *you* not wear a bag over your head?"

"I used to," the old man replied, "but with the bag over my head, I couldn't see. And I was lonely. So I took it off."

"Didn't people laugh at you?" asked the king.

"Oh, sure, some did. And I hated that, just as you do. But gradually I found a few people who didn't laugh, and that made me very happy."

The king was thrilled. No one had ever looked at his warts without laughing at him or showing their disgust. "I think I won't wear the bag when you're around."

The Wise Man smiled. "When you go home, you might even leave the bag here."

"Will I find other people like you, who won't think I'm disgusting?" the king wondered aloud.

The Wise Man nodded. "Of course you will. And with the love of those people, you won't care when other people laugh."

The king dropped the bag on the ground and went back to his kingdom, which was far more beautiful without the bag over his head. And he did find people who didn't mind his warts at all. For the first time in his life, he was very happy.

How to Recognize and Find Real Love: Truth → Seen → Accepted → Loved

We all have warts—if you have any doubt about that, ask your wife and she'll be more than happy to point them out—but it's not our warts that make us unhappy. Our misery comes from the chilling fear that other people will *see* our warts—our mistakes, flaws, and fears—and will then laugh at us, ridicule us, or otherwise fail to accept us. To prevent that from happening, we hide who we really are, as the Wart King did. With that approach, we can temporarily avoid the disapproval of others, but when people can't see us as we are, we also can't feel loved, only terribly alone.

We can summarize the path to feeling loved in this way:

Truth → Seen → Accepted → Loved

What you want most is Real Love, but before you can believe that people actively care about your happiness—the definition of Real Love—you need to know that they *accept* you. You can't know that people accept you as you really are unless you know that they *see* who you really are, and how can they see the truth about you unless you *tell* them? If you tell the truth about yourself—as the Wart King did—you will create opportunities for people to see, accept, and love you.

When people are empty and afraid themselves, they can't see who you really are. They can see only what you might do *for* them (to help eliminate their emptiness) or *to* them (to worsen their pain and fear). Without the ability to see you clearly, these people can't accept or love you. When someone does feel sufficiently loved, however, that person is not empty and afraid, and he or she can see, accept, and love you. That person becomes a wise man or wise woman for you in much the same way as the Wise Man was for the Wart King. On the many occasions in this book when I use the term *wise man*—to include, of course, wise women—I am not talking about a mystical sage sitting on top of a mountain, or a therapist, or someone formally designated as a counselor. A wise man is anyone who feels loved enough that he or she can clearly see you, accept you, and love you when you tell the truth about yourself. As you share yourself, you'll discover that many of the people around you are capable of being wise men: your friends, coworkers, family members, and, it is hoped, your spouse. Sometimes they will be accepting and loving only for moments at a time, but those moments are life-changing.

Telling the Truth About Yourself to Your Spouse

Although we're usually not aware of it, most of us lie to our spouses every day. We lie to protect ourselves from criticism, anger, and other forms of disapproval, and we've done it for such a long time that we've become accustomed to it—we don't even recognize our lies anymore. To illustrate how we lie, and to demonstrate what we can do to change our behavior, let's consider my experience with Kirk, who'd been married to Jill for more than ten years.

Kirk was obviously irritated as he said, "I don't know what to do with Jill. I'm not a bad husband. I have a good job, spend time with the kids, go to church, but Jill never stops complaining. From morning till night, she's nagging me about something."

"Like what?" I asked.

"Everything."

"Give me an example."

"Yesterday she whined about the lawn not being mowed. She said if I wouldn't do it, we ought to hire somebody in the neighborhood. And then she—"

"Is it your job to mow the lawn?"

"Well, yeah, I suppose, but—"

"Does the lawn need mowing?"

"It *is* getting kinda high, I guess, but I haven't had time to cut it. She doesn't understand all the stuff I have to do."

When he said "kinda high," I pictured a giraffe peeking over the top of the grass in Kirk's lawn. "Did you watch the football game two days ago?" I asked.

Kirk looked relieved at the apparent change of topic. "Sure did. Great game, wasn't it?"

"Could you have mowed the lawn during the first half of the game?"

He stopped smiling. "Look, I work hard during the week. I have to relax sometime."

With more questions, I learned that Kirk had watched television most of the day Saturday—but not all day, because he'd also gone fishing for four hours. There were many other jobs around the house he hadn't finished—or started—and he had excuses for all of them.

"I've done that many times," I said. "I've put off doing stuff that needs to be done because it's hard work, or boring, and there are other things I'd rather do."

"Exactly." Kirk was pleased that I understood.

"There's a word for that—when you put off doing what needs to be done, and you play instead. If an employee did that where you work, what word would you use to describe him?"

Kirk looked uncomfortable as he thought for a moment. "Irresponsible?"

"Sure, and we're all irresponsible at times. What really hurts us, though, is *denying* that we're irresponsible. When Jill nags you about something, have you ever said, 'Jill, I'm sorry about that.

That was irresponsible of me. I'll go and take care of that job right now.' "

Kirk laughed and said, "No."

I told him the story of the Wart King and said, "You're just like him."

"You're saying I have a bag over my head?" he asked.

"When it comes to jobs around the house, are you responsible or not?" He started to make excuses, and I reminded him, "If someone filled their assignments at work like you do at home, would you call them responsible?"

"No, I guess not."

"Then this isn't complicated, right? Are you responsible—are you reliable—about doing your jobs at home?"

"Not really."

"No, you're not. This is not an accusation of you, just a truthful description of how things are. And do you admit that to Jill?"

"You're kidding. If I admitted that, it would be awful. She'd just criticize me even more."

"That's what the Wart King thought, too," I said, "but he discovered that when he told the truth about himself, the results were quite different from what he thought they'd be. He felt loved only when he told the truth about himself, even though he was afraid. You won't feel loved until you do the same thing."

"I don't understand."

"You can feel loved by Jill only when you let her see who you really are, but you don't let her. When you're irresponsible, you don't tell the truth about that. That's understandable, and mostly unconscious, but it's still lying."

"I never thought of it like that."

"Until you tell Jill the truth about your being irresponsible, you're protecting yourself from her, just like the Wart King did with the people around him, and you'll always feel like you have a bag over your head."

"I just can't imagine telling her I'm irresponsible."

"You told *me*. Did I think less of you?"

"That's different. *She'll* rub my nose in it."

"Have you ever admitted to *anybody* that you're irresponsible?" I asked.

"Other than you? Probably not."

"How did you know how *I'd* react when you told me?"

"I didn't."

"No, you didn't, and you found out that I accept you as you really are only because you told me the truth. The only way for you to find out whether Jill will accept you is to tell *her* the truth, too. Until you take the bag off your head, you'll be protecting yourself, you won't feel like Jill cares about you, and you'll feel alone."

After we talked more about how to begin telling the truth, Kirk went home. I saw him several days later, and he said, "You won't believe this. Yesterday Jill started in on me about something I hadn't done. I started to get mad and tell her to leave me alone, but I remembered what you and I had talked about, so I decided to take the bag off my head. I was pretty nervous about it at first, but I did it anyway."

"What did you say?"

"I said, 'That's really irresponsible of me. I should have done that a long time ago, but I just didn't feel like it. Do you want me to do it now, or would tomorrow be soon enough?' She went into shock. I hugged her and told her I was sorry for all the times I'd made things difficult for her when I was irresponsible and resistant."

"Was she mad?"

Kirk laughed. "No. In fact, she hugged me back and apologized for nagging me so often. She said she hadn't been very loving. It was a pretty great experience, actually."

Kirk was not aware that for years he'd been hiding the truth about himself to avoid Jill's disapproval. Each time he lied—justifying himself and making her wrong—he felt a sense of safety and power, but he also felt alone under the bag on his head. When Kirk told the truth about himself, he made it possible for Jill to accept him *while* he was being irresponsible—with his warts—and that's Real Love. He could feel the difference immediately.

Jill also had been lying for years. Instead of admitting that she was angry and unloving, she'd blamed Kirk for how she felt and behaved, saying, "I only nag him because I have to." When she told the truth about herself, she took the bag off her head and felt Kirk accept her as she really was.

Not with **My** Partner

As you tell the truth about yourself, you create opportunities for your spouse to accept you unconditionally. The effect can be powerful, as demonstrated by Jill and Kirk. You might be inclined, however, to think—as many people have—*This would never work in* my *marriage. My wife wouldn't be as accepting as Jill. She'd say, "It's about time you admitted that. I've been telling you that for a long time. Now we'll see if you do anything about it."*

Let me address that concern in three ways. First, you can't know what's going to happen until you actually tell the truth about yourself. Until he was honest, Kirk had no idea what Jill would do.

Second, what have you got to lose? If you continue avoiding the truth, you're guaranteed to be stuck in a relationship that's not based on the truth and Real Love. Is that really what you want? If you tell the truth, however, you'll at least create an *opportunity* to feel loved and have a loving relationship.

Third, you might be right about your spouse. He or she might be critical and unloving when you tell the truth about yourself. If so, you still benefit in two ways:

- You'll experience the wonderful sense of freedom that comes from being truthful, regardless of the response of others. Although we've become accustomed to lying through the years, our lies are still a great weight on our shoulders, and it feels great to throw off that burden.
- It's good practice. Most of us have lied so many times and for so long that telling the truth is now an unfamiliar behavior. We have to *learn* how to do it, and we learn it like we learn anything else—with practice. Even if your spouse

doesn't accept you, your truth-telling will nonetheless prepare you for positive experiences with people who *can* love you. We'll talk more about that shortly.

What Can You Actually Say?

Every day we have many opportunities to be more truthful with our spouses. Following are just a few examples:

- When your wife asks you why you're late getting home, don't just grumble, or get angry, or offer some excuse, even though you might feel justified. Instead say, "I stayed late to finish an important job, but I should have called you and explained that. I wasn't thinking about you, and I'm sorry. I'll try to remember that next time."
- When your husband asks if you called the repair shop to check on the lawn trimmer that's being fixed, don't say, "I didn't have time," even if you can provide detailed evidence of how busy you are. Tell the truth: "I chose to do some other things instead of what you wanted. I should have made the call or at least told you why I couldn't. I'll call them now."
- When your wife comments about your clothes being all over the bathroom floor—again—you *could* make excuses (lying), or you could tell her you're sick of her nagging (attacking, acting like a victim), but it works so much better when you answer, "I was just too lazy to put them where they belong. No excuse. I'll go pick them up."
- When your husband asks why you're being grouchy, you could attack him with a list of the hundred things he's done in the past week to inconvenience Your Royal Highness, or you could tell the truth: "I'm just feeling selfish and not very loving. I want everything to go my way, and when it doesn't, I get irritated. Actually, it has very little to do with you."

To find many other examples of telling the truth, see the Additional Resources on page 325.

When we use Getting and Protecting Behaviors, they inconvenience and/or frighten our spouses, who tend to respond with similar behaviors of their own, and then—before you can blink an eye—the conversation goes straight downhill. And we keep repeating that foolish pattern because we can't see a way out. When you tell the truth about yourself, however, you're not adding to your partner's emptiness and fear, which removes his or her reasons to protect himself with arguing, anger, or withdrawal. And then you can create those golden opportunities where your partner can see, accept, and love you.

❦

Every time we talk to our spouses, we're choosing between telling the truth or using Getting and Protecting Behaviors. Carol learned that as she talked about her husband, James, to her wise friend Grace.

"James is always—" Carol began, before her friend, who had heard it all before, interrupted.

"I know it feels pretty good," Grace said, "to point out the things James does wrong—I've done that with my husband many times—but have you ever felt happier or closer to him when you do that?"

Carol was surprised and confused. "Are you taking his side?"

Grace smiled. "Not at all. He probably does all the terrible things you say, but be honest: Has it ever made you or James genuinely happier when you complain about him?"

"But he—"

"You can talk about him all you want, but wouldn't you rather be happier and have a better relationship with your husband? You can't have that while you talk about *him*."

"So what can I talk about?"

"Yourself."

"Okay," said Carol. "*I* feel angry when James doesn't listen to me or care about me."

Grace laughed. "You're talking about *him* again."

"No, I'm talking about how *I* feel. *I* feel angry. That's about me."

"Sure, but you're still criticizing *his* behavior. Try speaking without saying anything about James being wrong."

Carol couldn't speak. Most of us cannot talk about being unhappy without blaming someone else. We've heard other people do that all our lives—when they use the expression "He makes me so mad," for example.

"When James doesn't do what you want," Grace asked, "how do you feel?"

"Hurt. Disappointed. Sometimes he's pretty annoying."

"And when you feel disappointed and irritated, in that moment are you concerned about *his* happiness or *yours?*"

"But if I don't say something to him, I'll never get what I want."

"You might be right, and in a minute we'll talk about how you can ask for what you want, but for now, stay with this question: When you're irritated, are you concerned about *his* happiness or *yours?*"

"Mine, I guess."

"Yours, for sure. If you're mad at him, it's because he didn't do what *you* wanted, and when you're more concerned about yourself than about him, there's a word for that."

"Selfish?"

"Right. When you're angry, you're being selfish and unloving. When you don't feel loved, being angry is quite understandable, but it's still selfish and unloving. When you blame James for how you feel, you're attacking him, which creates even more distance between you and makes both of you feel more alone."

Carol then realized that despite anything James had done, *she* had been selfish, and she wanted to change that. Certainly, James had made many mistakes—we're not minimizing those—but if Carol had kept talking to Grace about them, she would have walked away from the conversation feeling even more angry, victimized, and alienated from her husband. After admitting her self-ishness to Grace, however, she felt accepted and was able to summon the courage to share the same thoughts with her husband.

Days later, Carol became irritated at something James had done, but instead of telling him that *he'd* done something wrong, she said, "James, whenever you do something I don't like, I get irritated and try to control you. I'm just beginning to see how selfish that is, and I apologize. I've done that a lot, but I want you to know that I'm learning how to be less demanding and more loving with you."

You can imagine how surprised and delighted James was to hear that. From that point, their relationship gradually became what they'd always wanted.

It's our emptiness, fear, mistakes, and Getting and Protecting Behaviors that we most often hide from our spouses, and that hiding keeps us alone. We need to talk about the times we're wrong, lonely, afraid, selfish, angry, acting like victims, running, and so on. Most of us have rarely—if ever—been truthful in this way, so we need help getting started. Let me suggest a few more examples here:

- "Earlier today, you asked me to pick up the kids from school tomorrow, and without thinking about it I frowned and told you with my tone of voice that I didn't really want to do it. I knew you were busy and couldn't pick them up yourself, but I couldn't resist telling you with my facial expression that you were inconveniencing me. I was being selfish, and I'm sorry about that. I'll be happy to pick up the kids tomorrow."
- "A few minutes ago, you asked me if I'd done the taxes yet, and I said, 'Almost.' Well, that's not quite right. I've barely started, but I didn't want to admit that I've been lazy."
- "I'm feeling irritated, as you can probably tell, and when I get like that, I tend to start finding fault with you. Normally, I keep doing it, but then I just feel more and more separated from you, and I hate that. Maybe I can stop blaming you in my mind if I just tell you I'm feeling selfish and demanding. How I'm feeling is not your fault."
- (After you've just answered a question with an edge in your voice) "Whoa, hang on. I just snapped at you a little—maybe more than a little—and I apologize."

• "Yesterday you were trying to tell me something about the kids, and I didn't really listen to you. I felt responsible for what the kids had done wrong, so I was trying to avoid hearing you talk about it. Finally, I left the room to do something else, remember? My mistake. Do you want to talk about that some more now?"

Telling the truth in these ways can seem difficult at first—most of us have no experience with this at all—but the rewards are plentiful.

The Humor of Telling the Truth About Yourself

As a Boy Scout leader, for years I supervised young men on many campouts and hikes, where we explored trails, mountains, caves, and rivers. On one occasion we were crossing a stream, and one of the boys slipped from the rock he was stepping on and fell into the rushing water. He immediately panicked and began to thrash wildly in the water as he screamed for help. Being familiar with that part of the river, I simply told him to stand up. When he did, he discovered that the water was only four feet deep, and he was easily able to walk to the shore. Moments later, he laughed as he pictured how silly he looked as he thrashed for his life when all he had to do was stand up.

Similarly, in our relationships, we often thrash and kick in the water—using our Getting and Protecting Behaviors—when all we need is to stand up on the firm foundation that Real Love provides. Once we have enough Real Love and no longer feel like we're drowning, our previous gyrations do look pretty unproductive, even ridiculous, and when we can laugh at them, it's much easier to learn from them and take significant steps toward feeling accepted and loved.

Telling the Truth About Yourself to People Other Than Your Spouse

Sometimes your spouse simply won't be able to give you all the Real Love you need. Living without Real Love is intolerable, so you'll have to get it from people who have it, which will in turn enable you to bring that essential element back to your marriage. To illustrate how this can work, we'll listen to Marilyn talk to her wise friend Angela. Remember that a wise man is anyone who feels loved and loving enough in a given moment that he or she can see, accept, and love you when you tell the truth about yourself.

"Several weeks ago," said Marilyn, "you suggested that I be more truthful about myself with my husband. Remember that?"

"Sure," said Angela.

"Well, I've tried it, but it doesn't work."

"Give me an example," said Angela.

"Okay. The other day I was supposed to meet him at the bank at two o'clock to sign some papers. I was only ten minutes late, but you'd think I'd committed a major crime. He went on and on about it, complaining that I'd made him late for some meeting at work. He said I'm always making him late for something. He wasn't very nice. Usually, I get mad when he does that, and I defend myself by making excuses or telling him about the times *he's* been late. But those conversations are always awful, so I decided to try what you suggested. I said, 'You're right. I'm late pretty often, and I don't think about how that's going to inconvenience you. I need to be more careful about that.'"

"What did he say?"

"He kept criticizing me—talked about other times I'd been late, and said it was about time I was responsible. He didn't accept me at all, so why should I tell him the truth and just get more of the same old stuff from him?"

"When I suggested you tell the truth to Bob," said Angela, "I didn't mean just once or twice. Do you really want to change your relationship with him?"

"Of course."

"Then you'll have to give him *a lot* of opportunities to see and accept you. You'll have to tell the truth about yourself many times, even when it doesn't go very well."

"I tried it some other times, too—about other things—but it

didn't go a bit better." Tears began to flow as Marilyn experienced the pain of realizing that Bob really didn't seem to care about her. "This is impossible. He never sees what I need. He only complains and thinks about what *he* wants. It hurts when he does this. I don't know how long I can keep it up."

"At this point in his life, Bob may not be *able* to love you. If he can't, you still need to practice being honest with him. It's a happier way to live no matter what he does in return, and if you keep telling the truth, you might discover that he can *learn* to be accepting. Your being honest gives him those learning opportunities. But you can't *expect* him to love you. Expectations ruin everything. You can only tell the truth and see what happens."

"So what if he never changes?" asked Marilyn. "How long can I go on like this?"

"How do you feel," asked Angela, "when you talk to *me* about your mistakes? You've told me some pretty unflattering things about yourself—that you spend too much, you're often critical toward Bob, and you get mad whenever you can't have things your way. When you told me those things, how did I treat you?"

"Oh, you've been very accepting, and I love that."

"That's what Real Love is. I'm not a saint, but I *have* gotten enough unconditional love in my life that I can accept you and care about you without wanting something for myself. I can't do that all the time, and I can't do it with everybody, but I can do it with you right now. As you keep telling the truth about yourself, you'll find many other people who can also accept and love you, and eventually you'll get enough Real Love that you'll be happier—all the time, even with Bob. Bit by bit, you'll be able to share your love with him. That might take time, but it's worth it."

"But Bob is my husband. He's *supposed* to love me, and you're suggesting I get that from other people instead?"

"It would be wonderful," said Angela, "if you could always get the Real Love you need from your spouse, but if your husband doesn't feel loved himself—as a result of a lifetime of experiences with conditional love from other people, including you—he has no Real Love to give. He can't give what he doesn't have. When you quit expecting from him what he can't give, two great things will happen: First, you'll lose your disappointment and irritation toward him. Second, you'll be able to concentrate more on feeling the Real Love other people have to offer you."

Marilyn believed the illusion taught in movies, on television, and by everybody she knew, that she could find somebody who would *make* her happy. Most of us believe that. We're looking for the handsome prince or beautiful princess who will fill our emptiness and turn our lives around. When we find someone who seems to make us happy, we marry that person, and he or she promises—in the wedding vows and in other ways—to deliver the happiness we expect. After all that waiting, and all those expectations, we can become quite disappointed when that promise isn't kept.

Fortunately, you do *not* have to be loved by your spouse in order to be happy. Your happiness does not depend on the love of any one person. The effect of Real Love from *any* source is powerful, and we need to do whatever it takes to find it. Marilyn continued to tell the truth about herself with Angela and other people, and as she filled up with Real Love, she felt like she was accumulating the twenty million dollars we talked about in the last chapter. Once she had what she wanted most, she discovered several things:

- She was happy. All she'd ever wanted was to feel unconditionally loved, and she was getting that from a number of people—not perfectly or constantly, but in doses of acceptance here and there.
- She wasn't nearly as demanding toward Bob. She didn't need to be, since she had the Real Love she'd always wanted.
- Because she wasn't as empty and afraid as she'd been, she didn't feel as threatened when Bob was critical and unloving.
- With less fear in her life, Marilyn found it much easier to keep telling Bob the truth about herself, even when he didn't accept her.

When you have enough Real Love—it doesn't really matter from *whom*—you don't feel a need to insist on acceptance from any one person, like your spouse. But doesn't your spouse have a *responsibility* to love you? Of course. Actually, we *all* have a responsibility to love one another, but we must also remember that

- just because people have a *responsibility* to love doesn't give them an *ability* to be loving. People simply can't give what they don't have.
- just because people have a responsibility to love us doesn't give us a right to *expect* them to love us, as stated in the Law of Expectations.

If your spouse can't love you in the way you need, find Real Love from others, and then you'll be able to take that love back to your partner, which is what he or she needs most. Even if your spouse doesn't entirely accept or return the love you offer, *you* will be much happier, because loving is simply the happiest way to live. Regardless of what he or she does, *you* must learn to love your spouse before you can be truly happy. Some people can even find happiness in a marriage where their partner never does develop a significant capacity for unconditional loving, and I'll talk more about that in Chapter Nine.

Finding a Wise Man

I have a friend who hunts wild turkeys. I asked him how he finds them, since I've been in the woods many times and have rarely seen them. He said he sits in one place, makes the sounds of a turkey with a mechanical device, and they come to him. They're attracted to the sounds he makes.

We find wise men in a similar way. We don't have to search for them. We just tell the truth, and wise men are naturally attracted to it. Simply tell the truth about yourself and you'll find the people who can see you and accept you. Those are the wise men in your life, and you'll be able to sense who those people are.

We have many opportunities to tell the truth and find the wise men we need. With our friends, we often talk about the activities in our lives—we describe events, complain about injustices, and voice our opinions about many things—but we rarely tell the truth about *ourselves*. With practice, we can learn to be honest about ourselves. Let's observe some real examples of people learning to be truthful:

- When Daniel makes mistakes at work, he offers excuses or shifts the blame onto coworkers. As a result, he feels like he's always hiding, which makes him feel alone. That approach affects his marriage in a negative way, too. After learning about the potential benefits of telling the truth about himself, he decides to try it out. One day when the boss asks him about a mistake he's made, Daniel says, "That was all my fault. I didn't start that project as soon as I should have, so I finished it in a hurry and made some careless mistakes. I'll correct those by the end of the day." You'd think his boss would be more angry after Daniel admits his carelessness, but he's not. He's pleased with Daniel's honesty and gives him even more important assignments, knowing he can trust him. And Daniel feels more accepted by his boss and coworkers.
- After an angry conversation with her husband, Nancy is talking to her friend about it. In the past, she's always been critical of him and blamed him for how she feels, but on this occasion she says, "My husband said something I didn't like this morning, and I really got irritated. I do that a lot—I can be pretty demanding when I don't get what I want."
- Talking to a friend, Andrew says, "For the past couple of years I've really had a hard time with my son. He's been difficult at home and at school, and I've done everything I could think of—lectured him, restricted him, yelled at him—but nothing's helped. But I'm beginning to see that the biggest problem here is *me*. It's true that he needs to change some things in his life, but he also needs me to love him unconditionally

while he learns those things, and I haven't been doing that. When he screws up, I get irritated at him, and then he can see that I *don't* love him unconditionally. Until lately, I didn't understand how much that's hurt him. I need to learn how to be a better father."

These kinds of conversations don't require that you bare your whole soul to anyone, and they're not complicated psychological analyses. Just tell the truth about who you really are. As you do that, some people won't have the slightest idea what you're talking about and won't want to participate in such a discussion. You haven't lost anything by trying, however. Keep trying with other people, and you *will* find some who will be fascinated at your honesty and will want to hear more.

Sometimes, as you tell the truth about yourself, people will react in ways that are not helpful to you. Imagine, for example, that you're talking with a friend about your being selfish and demanding with your spouse—as Nancy did with her friend above—and your friend says, "I think you're being too hard on yourself. If your husband talks to you like that, you have a *right* to be angry. If you don't get mad, how will you keep him from doing it again?" This person is more interested in defending you or attacking your spouse than she is in seeing or accepting you with your flaws and selfishness, which is what you need. Perhaps she wants to be your ally and gain your acceptance by offering you sympathy. Or she might be trying to justify the way she treats *her* husband. You don't need sympathy, however, nor do you need an ally in attacking your husband. In a case like this, it may be wise to change the subject back to something less personal, and then later you can keep making attempts to be truthful with other people.

In the process of telling the truth about yourself, sometimes you will need to mention the mistakes of your spouse or other people but only to provide a *context* or background for talking about your own mistakes. You might say, for example, "Yesterday when my wife said something unkind to me, I got angry, like I usually do," and then you can continue a discussion about *your* selfishness and Getting and Protecting Behaviors.

Wise men are all around us—our friends, coworkers, and family members—and we will find them as we tell the truth. I encourage you to be rigorously honest about your feelings and behavior, and consider sharing the following with some of the people you know:

- When you get angry, admit that you're attacking people for the purpose of protecting yourself or getting something from them.
- When you withdraw from a difficult situation, admit that you're running.
- When you hide your true feelings or you outright lie about a mistake you've made, admit that you're lying.
- When you're complaining about some terrible injustice—about how something just wasn't "fair," or how someone should have done something for you—tell the truth about acting like a victim.

Start off by telling the truth about these behaviors at least to yourself, and then to people who you think might be able to accept you. In some cases, we might even share the truth about ourselves with those who are professionally trained: psychologists, psychiatrists, ministers, and the like.

What We Need in Order to Tell the Truth—Faith

If the benefits of telling the truth about ourselves are so enormous—if we feel like we have twenty million dollars all the time as we acquire Real Love—why don't we do it more often? Why do we continue using Getting and Protecting Behaviors when we know they can result only in unhappiness? Partly, we just don't know any better—we use these behaviors because it's what we've always done, and what we've seen everyone around us do—but even after learning about truth-telling, we tend to avoid it like we would a colonoscopy. We've had countless past experiences where people have not accepted us when they've learned the truth about us, so we're understandably terrified that we'll experience that same painful lack of acceptance each time we're truthful about who we are. Instead of telling the truth, therefore, we keep using those Getting and Protecting Behaviors that have caused us so much pain.

Telling the truth about yourself requires faith—a *decision* to try something different even when you don't know what the results will be. If you really want to feel the power of Real Love, you simply have to share who you are and take the risk of people not liking you. It's really not such a big risk, however. If you already don't feel unconditionally loved, that's the worst possible feeling. If you share yourself with other people and they don't accept you, you'll only experience a *continuation* of the emptiness you already feel. That price seems small when you consider that telling the truth creates the possibility that you will find the Real Love you've always wanted, which is priceless.

Many of us are reluctant to tell the truth about ourselves unless we're first certain that we'll be accepted, but insisting on that condition will only keep us feeling alone and unloved. When a farmer takes seeds into the field, he has no assurance which seeds will sprout. If he insists on proof that each seed will germinate before he plants it, he'll get no crop at all. The only sensible way for him to find out which seeds will grow is simply to plant all of them. Certainly, some of the seeds won't grow, but that's of no consequence. What matters is that *some* seeds will grow and produce a crop.

As you tell the truth about yourself, you're planting seeds. You can find out which ones will grow—which people will accept you—only if you plant them. The more you plant, the more opportunities you create to grow an abundant, life-giving harvest. If you keep the seeds in your pocket, waiting for proof and perfect safety, you'll get no harvest at all.

Loyalty to Your Partner

When you've lived with insufficient love for a lifetime, unconditional acceptance and Real Love from *anyone* feels great, and you'll
have a tendency to develop a strong attachment to the people who
genuinely love you. Although that connection can be life-giving, it
also creates two potential problems. First, when you find people
who accept and love you, sometimes the behavior of your spouse
can seem even more unloving by contrast and thereby become a
greater source of disappointment to you. You may then feel even
more alienated from your spouse. Second, as you feel loved by other
people, your spouse may feel excluded, betrayed, and even jealous.

There is little in a marriage more important than a deep sense
of loyalty between both partners, and you must do everything
possible to preserve that. This does not mean, however, that you
can't tell the truth about yourself to people outside your marriage
and experience their acceptance. On pages 66–68 we talked about
Marilyn, who learned to find Real Love from other people after
finding that her husband, Bob, was incapable of giving that to
her. She addressed the issue of loyalty to her partner as she talked
again with her friend Angela.

"Feeling accepted by some of the women I've talked to has
made a big difference to me. I'm much happier, and people are
noticing it. Even Bob can see the difference, and the other day he
said, 'What's up with you? You seem to be smiling a lot more
these days.' So I told him I was telling the truth about myself to
other people so I could feel more accepted. He asked what I
meant by that, so I gave him some examples of me talking about
my mistakes. He wanted to know who I was talking to, and if I
talked about *him*. I said I did sometimes, but mostly so I could describe how *I'd* been unkind or unloving. Then he blew up and
said he didn't want me talking to you or anyone else ever again."

"That's understandable," said Angela. "He's just afraid of looking bad. Most people are."

"So what am I supposed to do? Stop talking to people and go
back to being miserable all the time?"

"What would you do if you were getting treatment for cancer, but Bob didn't like it?"

"I'd get the treatment anyway."

"Is your happiness any less important to you than your physical health?"

"No, it's not."

"Have you felt happier since you've started talking about yourself to these people who are loving you?"

"It's unbelievable. I'm happier than I've ever been, and I don't want to lose that—but Bob really doesn't like it."

"I am not telling you what to do in your relationship with your husband—that's none of my business—but *if* you want to keep feeling loved, and you want to get that by associating with people who can love you, you might just tell him that. Say, 'Bob, I love you very much, and I want to learn how to love you even better. When I talk about myself with the people I told you about, they help me a lot. I feel more loved, and I'm learning how to be more loving with you. So I hope you can support me in this.' When he knows you're trying to do something to make your marriage stronger—which will help *him*—he'll probably stop resisting you."

"What if he doesn't?"

"Then you *could* stop meeting with the people who love you, *or* you could nicely tell him that this is too important to you—like the cancer treatment we talked about—and you're going to keep doing it. Then don't keep it a secret from him. Tell him when you talk to people. Tell him as much as he wants to know—who you talk to, what you talk about, whatever. You're not reporting to him or asking his permission—like you were a child—you're just being thoughtful and telling him what you're doing so he won't be as frightened by it."

Finding the Real Love you need is critical in the process of finding your own happiness and enriching your marriage. As you get loved by people other than your spouse, you can do several things to minimize the potential negative aspects of getting love outside your marriage. First, tell your partner what you're doing.

Don't hide the fact that you're trying to change your life, and that you're talking with other people who can help you. If your spouse wants to know what you talk about, share that. Some spouses will feel threatened even when you're open about what you're doing, but honesty is still the best way to go.

Second, remember that when you're looking outside your marriage for the Real Love you need, you're only trying to *add* to the love you have in your marriage, not trying to *replace* it. Your goals are to become happier yourself and to share with your spouse the love you find with others. Some people find Real Love outside their marriages and then become bitter and accusing toward their spouses, saying or thinking, "See, now I have to go somewhere else to find what I should have gotten from you all along." That's not healthy.

Third, remember that your first loyalty is to your spouse. Never do anything that could lead to infidelity, either sexual or emotional. Marilyn practiced telling the truth about herself with several women, and she also talked to two men she'd known for years. She always told Bob when she spent time with other men, and she never met with them alone. We'll talk much more about sexual and emotional infidelity—its causes, how to prevent it, and how to respond to it—in Chapter Eight.

Loving Groups

Your efforts to find Real Love and to learn how to share it with others will be far more successful if you intentionally associate as often as possible with people who have the same interest. When two or more people are consciously making an effort to tell the truth about themselves and be wise men for each other, I call them a group of wise men, or a group of wise men and women, or—more often—simply a *group*. A group is not a place. It's not therapy. It's not a cult. It doesn't make arrogant claims to fix people. It's not exclusive, does not require loyalty or money from its members, and is not characterized by a formal organization. A group is just a loose association of people with a common interest in finding and sharing

Real Love. You don't have to *join* a group; if you're deliberately in-volved in the process of giving and receiving Real Love, you're al-ready in a group, whatever your numbers or location.

A group exists only to increase the opportunities of its mem-bers to be seen and loved. For most people, a group becomes a loving family, healing the wounds of the past and changing lives forever. I refer to groups of *wise men* not because everyone in the group is perfectly loving—or *anyone* in the group, for that matter—but because these men and women are *consciously trying* to see and love others. Throughout the book I will mention peo-ple turning to a group—friends who care about them—for the acceptance and love they need.

The Effect on Your Marriage of the Real Love You Get from Others

The love you get from other people can have a very positive effect on your marriage. For many years, when Bob was being grumpy, unkind, or otherwise inconvenient, Marilyn responded with the Getting and Protecting Behaviors that only made things worse for both of them. As Marilyn felt more loved by her friends, however—and as she understood that Bob was just drowning—she became much more accepting and loving toward Bob. As he felt her love, he became less empty and afraid himself, and he gradually lost his need to criticize her and withdraw from her. Real Love is infectious.

Because you have greater expectations of your spouse than of anyone else, you will usually feel more fear, frustration, and anger with him or her than with other people. What your husband says and does can often provoke a far more intense reaction from you than if someone else had said or done the same thing. On those occasions, you may not be able—because of your emptiness and fear—to tell the truth about yourself to your spouse. You may need Real Love from others to eliminate your emptiness and fear and enable you to respond to your spouse in a loving way.

When should you be having these interactions with wise men

and women and creating the opportunities to feel accepted and loved? You could wait until you're in the middle of a conflict and then call a loving friend for the support you need, but there are considerable drawbacks to that approach, which I can illustrate by telling you a story.

Years ago I built a bridge over the creek that runs through my backyard. Every few years, when the rainfall is heavy, the creek will rise and flood over the banks, and for that reason I made the bridge very sturdy—heavy beams, thick support pillars, and a great deal of concrete in the foundation. Several of my friends thought I had put far too much effort and material into the construction, but I was convinced it was necessary. Subsequently, the creek rose above the level of the bridge many times, but the bridge never wavered.

Years later, two of my neighbors built bridges over the same creek. One of them, Dennis, came to see my bridge, and although he asked me many questions about its design, he decided to put much less concrete and vertical support in his bridge.

Three months after Dennis constructed his bridge, there was an unusually heavy rain that flooded the creek. After the water subsided, I went outside to clean off the logs and branches that had accumulated on my bridge, and when I looked downstream, I saw that Dennis's bridge was gone. It had floated downstream and washed up alongside the other neighbor's bridge, which had also been destroyed.

Dennis made several discoveries during this event:

- When the creek was flowing fast and heavy, there was nothing he could do to strengthen his bridge. He could only watch it be destroyed, wait until the water dropped, and rebuild.
- For several weeks, he couldn't get from his house to the lake on the other side, where he had a dock and fishing boat.
- Building the stronger bridge in the first place would have required a lot less work than the combination of building the old and the new one.

I often see a similar pattern in marriages. Stephanie called me one day to say that she and her husband, Brian, had just had a terrible argument. "It was awful," she said. "We both said a lot of unkind things, and now I don't know what to do. I know he doesn't want to talk to me. In fact, he just got in the car and drove off."

After telling her the story of the bridge over my creek, I said, "In a minute, I'll suggest some things you can *try* to say when he gets home, but for now you might consider that the bridge between you is washed out. Sometimes you just have to wait for the water to go down. You have to wait for him to get over being angry, and for you to lose *your* anger. But if you don't give up, you'll be able to build the bridge again. Real Love is a powerful thing."

"I hate it when this happens," she said.

"Then *prevent* it from happening. Remember that my bridge held firm in the flood only because I had put enough effort into building it *before* the flood came. You can do the same kind of building in your marriage. Usually, though, you wait until there's a crisis—until the water is rising over the bridge—before you call me or anybody else to talk. Then it's often too late, and once again you have to live with the consequences of the bridge washing away. Rebuilding takes a lot of time and effort. It's much easier to build a strong bridge *before* the flood, by calling people in your group—people who accept and love you—to get the love you need from them. When you feel loved by other people—and when you practice loving *them*, too—your bridge won't wash away when the floods come. When you feel loved, you won't collapse into Getting and Protecting Behaviors when Brian says something unkind to you. Your bridge will still be standing, and you'll be able to cross over it to give him the love he needs. That is a wonderful experience."

Don't wait for a crisis before you call people and get the love you need. Call and meet with wise men and women as often as possible. Create an inner strength and peace that will enable you to stay loving and happy when your spouse is using Getting and Protecting Behaviors. Accumulate the twenty million dollars that will make it possible for you to scarcely notice when your partner takes two dollars from you. Prevention of a crisis is much more effective than crisis management.

Group Meetings

People can give and accept Real Love while talking on the phone, waiting for a bus, jogging in the park, standing in a supermarket line, sitting in a car on the way to work, and so on—no formal setting is required. Once you find people interested in telling the truth and experiencing Real Love, however, you can accelerate the creation of these experiences by arranging regular times and places to meet with these developing wise men. In these planned group meetings you can share who you are with more people in less time, and you can learn more as you listen to the many experiences of others who are feeling the effect of Real Love in their lives. You'll also have more opportunities to accept and love other people. The effect of association with one wise man can be life-changing. Group meetings simply make it possible to multiply that effect. To learn much more about groups and group meetings, see the Additional Resources on page 325.

The Power of Real Love

You will always be surrounded by people who are empty, afraid, and flawed to varying degrees, and they will therefore behave in thoughtless and even unkind ways toward you. On each of these occasions it will feel like they're taking two emotional dollars from you, as we discussed in Chapter Two. You then have two choices:

- You can attack people, lie to them, act like a victim, run, and otherwise control people and events in an attempt to avoid all inconvenience and injury. Good luck. No matter how hard you try, there is no wall high enough or thick enough to keep out everyone who might take two dollars from you.

- You could tell the truth about yourself and be filled with Real Love, the greatest gift of all. With that twenty million dollars, people will still take two dollars from you on occasion—many occasions, actually—but it won't be a big deal, because you won't become empty and afraid.

Is there any question which of these choices is the wiser? Do you really want to constantly build a wall around you that's never truly effective, or would you rather have twenty million dollars and not worry about what people might do to you or what they might not give you? Feeling unconditionally loved—by anyone—is a magnificent experience. Real Love fills up our emptiness, heals our wounds, and gives us the profound and lasting sense of peace, safety, and joy we've always wanted.

Gratitude—Magnifying the Real Love and Happiness You Have
For several weeks Sylvia had been telling the truth about herself and feeling the Real Love offered by a few of her friends. She continued to complain, however, about the behavior of her husband, Roberto. As she talked to me about Roberto on one occasion, I asked, "What do you really want?"

When she repeated some of the things she wanted him to do—and things she wanted him to *stop* doing—I said, "Those are the details. What is the most important thing you want?"

Remembering what she'd been reading and learning, she said, "For him to love me."

"Almost," I said. "What you really want is to be happy, and you'll get that when you have enough Real Love—from *anyone*, not just from your husband. Are you feeling loved by the members of your group, the women you've been talking to about yourself?"

"Well, yes," she said, "but Roberto—"

"This isn't about him," I said. "All your life you've never felt enough Real Love, and now—when you're actually getting it from some friends—you're wasting it by expecting more from your husband. You're making two mistakes here: First, you're expecting him to love you. We've talked about that. He has the right to make his own choices, even when you don't like them, and you don't have the right to expect him to do anything, especially love you. Second, while you focus on your expectations, you also can't feel the Real Love you *are* getting—in other words, you're not being grateful for the love you're getting from your friends."

"But I *am* grateful."

"Your friends are giving you twenty million dollars, but it's obvious that you don't appreciate that—which is not intentional on your part—because you keep talking about the two dollars that Roberto *isn't* giving you, or the two dollars he actually takes from you sometimes. You already have twenty million dollars, but when you focus on Roberto, you're *forgetting* you have it."

Gratitude is not a trick of positive thinking. It's a *choice* we make to simply acknowledge and remember the truth about what we have. When we make that choice, we greatly multiply the effect of the Real Love we have and the happiness we enjoy. When we're ungrateful, we forget that we already have twenty million dollars, or we fail to see it in the first place.

When you choose to be grateful, you immediately feel more loved. You also lose your expectations that certain individuals— like your spouse—will give you what you want. After our conversation, Sylvia made a conscious choice to see and remember the Real Love she was getting—a conscious choice to be grateful— and when she did that, she felt happier and didn't *need* to demand that Roberto give her what she wanted all the time. She slowly lost her expectations of him, and then she also began to see even more evidence of the love he *was* giving her. With gratitude—and without expectations—she noticed that there were many occasions when he did demonstrate a concern for her happiness. She recognized that he really was doing his best to love her, even though his love was often imperfect. She had not been able to see all that when she was ungrateful and was focusing on what she *wasn't* getting.

When you choose to see the love you've received, you can enjoy the happiness that follows, you can carry that love with you wherever your go, and you'll lose your need to make demands of any particular person. When you're grateful, you appreciate everything you receive as a gift. You don't keep score. You don't have expectations. You don't cling for more time and attention.

In genuine gratitude there is a large element of surprise. Without expectations, you'll feel surprised and delighted any time your spouse does something for you. You won't feel like you deserved it or earned it, and that really contributes to a feeling of unconditional love.

Sharing Real Love

On pages 66–68, we listened to Marilyn as she talked about her husband, Bob. She was concerned that he didn't really care about her happiness, and she was right—Bob was primarily concerned about protecting himself and filling his own emptiness. He *wanted* to be more loving—as we all do—but he'd never received enough Real Love himself to be able to share it with anyone else, including his own wife. Although she judged that she was the more wounded party in their relationship, Marilyn wasn't unconditionally loving toward Bob, either. Like Bob, she couldn't give what she didn't have.

We can summarize the process of learning to love other people—including our spouses—in the following linear diagram:

Loved → Seeing → Accepting → Loving

Without sufficient Real Love, you will be empty and afraid, and you'll tend to see your spouse only in terms of what he or she might do for you or to you. In that condition, you can't possibly accept your spouse unconditionally. As you learn to tell the truth about yourself, however—to your spouse and to others— and feel unconditionally *loved* (the first step in the diagram), you'll gradually lose your emptiness and fear. Without the need to manipulate your husband to fill your emptiness, or to protect yourself from him, you'll begin to *see* who he really is. You'll see that he doesn't have the primary intent of hurting you or withholding what you want. He just needs to feel unconditionally loved, and when he doesn't have enough of that, he uses the Getting and Protecting Behaviors that inconvenience—sometimes to the point of injury—the people around him, including you. When you truly understand that, you'll find it relatively easy to *accept* your spouse, even when he or she doesn't behave in a way you'd like. You'll be understanding of his or her Getting and Protecting Behaviors, instead of feeling hurt and irritated by them. After you see and accept your spouse as he is, you'll naturally develop a concern for his happiness, which is the definition of Real Love.

Loving Is a Miracle—and a Choice

We can compare loving your spouse to sharing a bucket of water with him or her. When your own bucket is empty—when you don't feel loved—you simply don't have anything to give. Even when you want to love and help your partner, you *can't*—there's nothing in the bucket to pour out. But when you do what it takes to get loved yourself—as other people pour what they have into *your* bucket—you can begin to share what you have, and the more you have, the more you have to give. When your bucket is full to overflowing, loving your spouse becomes effortless.

Loving people, however, is somewhat different from pouring water from a bucket. As you share Real Love with your spouse, you'll often find—at the end of the day, or at the conclusion of a single interaction—that you have more love than you started with. As you are more *loving,* you also feel more *loved,* even if your spouse—or whoever else you're loving—gives you nothing in return. In some miraculous way, your bucket fills up as you empty it. The more Real Love you share, the more you'll have. This doesn't work, of course, if you're merely *acting* as though you're loving. Your bucket will fill up only as you share your attention and concern with others for *their* benefit, without expectation of anything in return—the definition of Real Love.

We can see, therefore, that the process of Loved → Seeing → Accepting → Loving is not linear, but circular, as depicted in the following diagram.

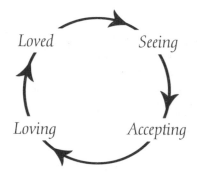

Feeling loved leads to seeing, accepting, and loving, and when we're loving, we also *feel* more Real Love, which perpetuates and amplifies this healthy cycle. For that reason, I can't propose strongly enough that the fullest measure of happiness comes from sharing your love with others at every opportunity. You could sit back and wait for other people to love *you* and fill up your bucket to overflowing—certainly you would then have love to share with others—but you can do much more. You can greatly accelerate the process of loving others—especially your spouse—by consciously choosing to love them *before* your own bucket is full.

The Synergistic Elements of Loving

This suggestion that we need to make conscious decisions to love other people even when we don't feel completely loved ourselves might seem to contradict my earlier statements that our ability to love others is largely determined by how unconditionally loved we feel. There is no contradiction here. Our ability to love others is influenced by several elements simultaneously:

- Intellectual understanding
- Receiving Real Love
- Making a choice to love

When we have an *intellectual understanding* that our spouses use Getting and Protecting Behaviors only because they're drowning—because they lack sufficient Real Love—it becomes much easier to accept them unconditionally and to feel a desire to give them the love they need instead of being offended by them and reacting with Getting and Protecting Behaviors of our own. But when we're drowning ourselves—when *we* don't have sufficient Real Love, either—our understanding alone is often not enough to keep us from using the Getting and Protecting Behaviors we believe will temporarily keep our own heads above water. We also need to *receive Real Love*, which eliminates the emptiness and fear that interfere with our ability to see and accept our spouses. Our ability to love is also enhanced when we make a *conscious choice* to love.

Each of these elements—intellectual understanding, feeling loved, and choosing to love—is important but also has its limitations when operating alone. Fortunately, they all work together to yield an effect far greater than any one of them could create by itself.

In addition to their combining in a synergistic way that greatly magnifies our ability to love, each element also makes an enormous contribution to the individual effect of the others. We all know intellectually, for example, that we *should* choose to be loving. It's always a happier and better way to live than manipulating people and protecting ourselves from them. Without sufficient Real Love ourselves, however, we're starving to death and down to our last two dollars. In that condition, we're severely limited in our ability to choose to remain happy and loving when a thief steals our money. Receiving Real Love, therefore, greatly enhances our ability to make loving choices. Even when we lack Real Love, however, we still have a measure of self-control, and *to some extent* we can still choose to withhold our Getting and Protecting Behaviors and make efforts to be loving. As we make decisions (self-control) to love other people even when our bucket is not full, we experience the miracle of feeling more Real Love ourselves. So choosing to love others contributes to feeling loved, and feeling more loved contributes to our ability to love others. Additionally, our ability to love and feel loved are both amplified by our intellectual understanding of Real Love and Getting and Protecting Behaviors.

With each decision we make, what is the relative influence of self-control, understanding, and the amount of Real Love we feel? Exactly how strong is our ability to simply *choose* a loving behavior even when we've experienced relatively little Real Love? To what degree can our understanding and willpower overcome the obviously crippling effects of insufficient Real Love? I don't know anyone who can answer these questions with any certainty, and even if they could, our course of action would be little changed: We learn to love our spouses most effectively as we diligently apply ourselves to all three elements we've discussed.

Loving Acts

Accepting people means that when they behave badly, you don't get afraid or angry or react to control them with other Getting and Protecting Behaviors. *Loving* people is a more active concern for their happiness and is often accompanied by some kind of action. Loving is a result of seeing and accepting and consciously making loving choices. Loving *includes* accepting.

Our spouses need to hear that we love them, and the most important "words" we use are our *behaviors*. We need to speak our love often and with the greatest possible vocabulary—with a broad range of loving acts. Most of us, regrettably, haven't seen love spoken in many ways, nor with much sincerity, so our vocabulary is limited. Let's broaden our expression as we discuss some of the many ways we can demonstrate our love to our spouses:

- Listen.
- Look.
- Touch.
- Talk.
- Tell the truth about yourself.
- Apologize.
- Say "I love you."
- Perform random acts of kindness.
- Cooperate.
- Ask.
- Find.
- Consciously choose to accept and forgive.
- Love without expectations.
- Give your time.

Listen

Many techniques have been described for effective listening and communication, but they often fail to produce significant and lasting positive changes in relationships because they ignore the powerful, primal need we all have for Real Love. One element of communication that is often taught, for example, is our need to acknowledge what we've heard, and even to echo or reflect back to the speaker what he or she has said. Certainly, that *is* a potentially useful approach, but it will rarely lead to the most effective communication if the need for Real Love is disregarded.

To illustrate this concept, imagine that you've spent considerable time and money to purchase a gift for me. You wrap it yourself and bring it to my office, where I'm working at my desk. Taking the gift from your hand, I turn it over a couple of times and write on a piece of paper, "Received: one box, $4 \times 5 \times 8.5$ inches, wrapped with blue paper and bow, April 17, 2:00 p.m." Then I photocopy the note, give the original document to you, toss the box onto a pile of objects in the corner of the room, and turn back to my work.

How would you feel? Although I acknowledged receipt of the gift, and even described it accurately, you certainly don't feel appreciated, because you were giving me much more than an object wrapped in a bow. You were giving me a piece of *you,* and I failed miserably to acknowledge and accept that.

Every time your spouse speaks to you, he or she is offering you a very personal gift—literally a part of who he or she is—and how you listen is naturally perceived as a strong indication of how you receive that precious gift. Genuine listening is much more than simply receiving and acknowledging words with a mechanical communications technique. When we really listen, we communicate to our spouses that we *care about them.* When you listen, you're telling your spouse that he or she is important to you. Real listening is an expression of love.

In any conversation, your spouse's greatest need is to feel unconditionally accepted and loved. If you fail to communicate that acceptance, he or she will almost certainly feel more empty and afraid, triggering the Getting and Protecting Behaviors that make genuine communication impossible. The principal goal of listening is to communicate Real Love, as illustrated in an experience I had while observing Karen listen to her husband, Jeremy.

As a mechanical engineer specializing in robotics design, Jeremy spent his days working with complex equations, metallurgy, and production problems. After he came home from work one evening, I watched him talk excitedly with Karen about some of the things he'd done that day. Much of what he talked about was highly technical and beyond the understanding of someone without an extensive background in math and science, which I knew that Karen didn't have, so I wondered what she was getting out of the conversation.

Later in the evening, when Jeremy was out of the room, I asked her, "Do you understand all that engineering and robotics stuff Jeremy says to you?"

"Hardly a word of it," she said.

"You looked absolutely fascinated with the discussion, and it's obvious that Jeremy really enjoyed talking to you. How can you be so interested in something you don't understand?"

"I'm not really interested in engineering," she said, "but I *am* interested in *Jeremy*, so I'm interested in anything that's important to him. I'm not really listening to a discussion about engineering. I'm listening to *him*."

Karen couldn't accurately reflect back to Jeremy the specifics of what he said, but that wasn't important. She did understand the real purpose of listening, and as a result, Jeremy loved to talk to her and be with her.

There are few things you can offer your spouse that provide greater evidence of your love than to genuinely listen to him or her. As you truly listen, you are seeing and accepting your spouse. You're saying that she is important, worthwhile, and entitled to be the center of your attention. When you do not listen well, on the other hand, you're telling her that she doesn't matter, that the expressions of her soul are meaningless to you, and that you do not truly care about her. The consequences of not listening well are devastating. As I've talked with hundreds of couples over the years, I have observed that the ability to listen may be the single quality that most distinguishes those who have successful marriages from those who do not. Again, however, listening is not just a communications technique but rather the natural product of the listener really caring about the happiness of the speaker.

Although Real Love is the key ingredient to real listening, I will nonetheless describe here some of the mechanical characteristics of listening, and from these we can all learn better to listen to our spouses in ways that are accepting and productive.

Be Quiet

Many people don't really listen—they're only looking for an opportunity to speak themselves, and they frequently jump into the conversation without the slightest regard for their partners. Although we often do need to make responses, one of the most powerful indications we give that we're listening is that our upper and lower lips are sealed together. Let your spouse speak until he or she is finished. If you're not sure whether he or she has more to say, simply ask: "There's something I'd like to say, but I don't want to interrupt you. Are you finished with that subject?"

Express Your Acceptance Nonverbally

Some studies suggest that as much as 93 percent of human communication is nonverbal. At least half of that is transmitted by way of facial expression, while other modes include tone of voice, arm and leg position, foot and hand movement, and overall body posture and motion. As you raise your brows, shift your eyes, furrow your forehead, sigh, shuffle your feet, cross your arms, and change your tone of voice, your spouse can easily recognize your lack of acceptance and/or interest. Then she will usually change what she's saying either to protect herself or to get something she wants: acceptance, cooperation, and so on. When she does that, you're no longer having a conversation with *her;* you're interacting with a defensive posture or manipulation. You're hearing what she thinks you want her to be, and your conversation becomes an empty lie or a contest.

When Karen listened to Jeremy, she was leaning slightly forward in her chair, obviously involved physically in the conversation and giving no indication that she was eager to be somewhere else. Expressions of interest danced enthusiastically across her face. I'm not advocating that you attempt to fabricate these nonverbal signs of acceptance with your spouse—you won't be able to fake it for long. If you don't feel accepting toward your spouse, you *will* communicate that feeling. What I am suggesting is that you be aware of these nonverbal signs that you don't really care, and when you sense them in yourself, recognize that you're not communicating the acceptance your partner needs.

Avoid Verbal Criticism

Every time your wife speaks, she's sharing who she is, creating opportunities for you to see, accept, and love her. If you criticize her when she speaks, she'll stop talking, or she'll defend herself, and your relationship will be seriously damaged. We claim to have an interest in listening to our spouses, but then when they speak, we often reveal that our real goal is to argue with them, trap them in their words, and even beat them down with the evidence they've provided with their own mouths. When they speak, for example, often the first word out of our mouths is *but*. To be sure, we may have something brilliant to add to the conversation, but when we say the word *but*, we might as well say, "I'm not really listening to you. My real goal is to be right." When we criticize and contradict people, we feel powerful or look good by comparison, and our partners feel it when we use them in that way.

Certainly there are times when you need to suggest a course different from what your spouse has offered, or when you need to correct a piece of misinformation, but without Real Love, you'll almost certainly detract from your spouse's message and will contribute to his or her not feeling accepted.

Restate What You Hear—"Eight"

Although the central need for acceptance must never be forgotten, on many occasions your spouse also needs you to understand and respond to the *content* of what he or she is saying. If your wife gives you a description of a task that must be done in a particular way, for example, she needs more from you than a sense of warm, fuzzy acceptance. She needs you to indicate that you understand *what* she's saying, so she'll have a glimmer of hope that the job will be done as she's described.

While it's obvious that understanding the content of a speaker's message is important for the accomplishment of tasks, understanding content is also important as a way of communicating acceptance and concern. One way to demonstrate to your spouse that you understand what he or she is saying is to restate what you hear, as shown here by Andrew and his wife, Lynn.

"I feel so mad right now," says Lynn. "I've asked you a million times to put food back in the fridge after you eat, but today I found a jug of milk you left downstairs when you were watching television. It was warm and spoiled, and now I can't use it for the custard I wanted to make."

In the past, whenever Lynn talked about something Andrew had done wrong, he made excuses, frowned, grunted, retaliated with critical comments about *her* behavior, or walked out of the room, none of which had a soothing effect on Lynn. But he's been learning about Real Love and how to listen, so this time he looks directly at her, nods his head as she speaks, and says, "I'm sorry."

Of course, Lynn is pleased that he's not lying, attacking, acting like a victim, or running, but still his response is less than completely satisfying, because she's heard him apologize many times before with no subsequent change in his behavior. Wisely, however, she doesn't press her point, having learned a bit about Real Love herself.

A few weeks later, Lynn again makes a comment about something Andrew left out of the fridge, and this time he's armed with even greater understanding and compassion. "I know I should have put that meat back where I got it," he says, "and I can see you're angry at me. I'm sorry." This is an example of what many people call *active listening*. Andrew has repeated back to Lynn what she said—including the emotion she expressed—and he's done it in his own words. This is certainly better than just an apology—and far superior to responding with Getting and Protecting Behaviors—but so far Andrew has demonstrated only an ability to *repeat* her message, which is not the same as expressing a complete *understanding* of it.

With more time and experience, Andrew begins to understand what acceptance and listening really are. The next time Lynn is irritated about something he left out of the fridge, he goes a significant step farther than before. "Yes, I did that," he says. "I wasn't thinking about you when I left the milk downstairs. I do a lot of things like that, actually, where I don't think about you and inconvenience you—like yesterday when I used your cell phone and didn't put it back in your purse. I know you had to look around for quite a while before you found it. And sometimes I leave my clothes on the floor and hope you'll pick them up. When I do those things, you must feel like I don't care much about you."

Lynn immediately feels thoroughly seen, because Andrew has heard not only what she was saying about the food but has given additional examples of his overall thoughtlessness. More significantly, he has addressed her real concern—that he doesn't care about her. She was really talking about that fear, not a container of milk or a piece of food. The effect on Lynn was profound.

Andrew provides an example of a principle I call "Eight." Suppose I say to you, "Two, four, six . . . ," and then I wait to see if you understand what I'm saying. You respond, "Two, four, six." Certainly you've demonstrated an ability to *repeat* what I said, but you have not shown that you *understand* what I'm really saying. On the other hand, if you simply respond, "Eight," I know you understand what I've said. When your spouse speaks, he or she is almost always saying, "Two, four, six," and it's quite fulfilling when you say, "Eight."

Ask Questions
As you increase your involvement in any conversation with your spouse, he or she will sense more interest from you and will feel more accepted. One way to increase your involvement is to ask questions. As she walks in the door, for example, don't just keep reading the paper or watching television. Ask her how she's feeling and where she's been. Don't respond with grunts or one-word answers. Ask for more details if it's obvious she wants to provide them. When she says, "I'm tired," ask her to tell you more about that. It's not the additional details that matter but your indication of interest in her life.

Be careful about asking confrontational questions. For example, the words "Where have you been?" can demonstrate either a genuine concern or an accusation, depending on the tone of voice and other nonverbal clues. We often ask questions that are intended only to express our doubts and objections, which will not help our partners to feel accepted.

Agree Where Possible

When Lynn said Andrew had left the food out a *million* times, he could have argued about that number and been offended by her exaggeration. Instead, he *agreed* that he had indeed been inconsiderate on many occasions, and then their conversation became quite productive. People make many mistakes as they speak, and although it's easy to identify them, it's almost always more useful to identify what you agree with.

Look

From an early age we've noticed the intimacy of eye contact. When people look straight into your eyes for more than a few seconds, you can feel them reaching into your soul. If you believe they love you, you'll feel connected and accepted. If, on the other hand, you have any doubt about their acceptance of you, you'll likely feel accused of something—you'll feel criticized, attacked, and even violated. Studies have shown that most of us become uncomfortable if people look directly into our eyes for more than just a few seconds, or even less.

When your wife is speaking, don't busy yourself with other things. Look directly into her eyes as you listen. If you haven't done this very often, she might wonder what's going on, but she'll come to love the connection established by your eyes. In fact, if you really want to provoke an intimate moment, just catch her eye and hold your gaze. She might ask you, "What?" or turn her eyes away. Hold your gaze and approach her. By the time you reach her, she'll be ready for you to hug her and express your affection for her. There are few activities more intimate than eye contact.

Touch

Physical touching is another intimate experience. If you know someone loves you, and that person touches you on the hand, shoulder, or face, you'll feel even more accepted and connected in a way that far transcends the physical contact. If you doubt the love of the person touching you, however, you'll probably feel threatened.

We have a thirst to be touched by people who care about us. We love this physical communication of affection. Women commonly complain that their husbands never touch them other than during sex, or as a prelude to it. They're describing their need for the affection that touching communicates.

You have many opportunities to touch your spouse:

- Instead of talking to your wife from across the room, sit close and touch her hand while you speak.
- If your husband is watching television, don't just pass through the room or sit in another chair. Reach out and touch his neck as you walk by. Or stop and place your hands on his shoulders for a full minute. Or sit next to him and put your hand on his leg.
- During dinner, reach out and gently squeeze her knee.
- Put your arm around his waist when you're standing next to him.
- Touch her on the cheek when she's describing a tender experience.
- Put your hand on the back of his neck while he's driving.
- Hug him every chance you get.
- Hug her every chance you get.
- Just before you go to sleep, reach out with your foot or hand and touch her.
- Rub his or her feet while you're sitting on the couch together.

Hugging deserves a special mention. Many people haven't been hugged with genuine affection, so they're unfamiliar with it. Others are too afraid to fully participate in a hug. When people are uneasy, they turn their bodies slightly away from the people their hugging, essentially hugging with a single shoulder or hip. Or they do the A-frame hug, with their feet some distance from their partner while patting them on the shoulder, their two bodies creating the shape of an "A." Or there's the manly hug, executed quickly and with enough physical force to eliminate any suggestion of tenderness. Don't miss out on the intimate communication that's possible with a loving hug. Stand as close to your spouse as you can, with your feet touching. Face her directly and touch her with as much of your body as possible—with as much space between you as there is between two pieces of paper pressed together in a book—and squeeze her gently, tenderly. Now stay there. Don't be in a hurry—you're not trying to *accomplish* something. You're telling her you love her.

Touching is a powerful tool for expressing affection. Use it. If you touch your partner only when you want sex, however, he or she will regard touching only as an introduction to something *you* want instead of a communication of your genuine affection for him or her. We'll talk a lot more about sex in Chapter Eight.

Talk

Lynn often complained that Andrew never talked to her, and one day he discussed that subject with me. "She's always whining that I don't talk to her," he said.

"*Do you talk to her?*" I asked.

"Well, sometimes, but I don't always have something to say."

"You don't sleep all day, so you must fill your day with *something*. Tell her a little about what you did that day, or the day before."

"Mostly I just do the same old stuff. It's not interesting."

"I promise you, it will be interesting to *her*. And there are *thoughts* running through your head all day, too. Just share some of those with her."

Every time we open our mouths to speak to our spouses, we have an opportunity to tell them they *matter* to us enough to share who we are with them. It's a loving act we need to repeat often.

Tell the Truth About Yourself

On pages 56–65 I discuss telling the truth about yourself to your spouse. When you talk about your mistakes, flaws, and fears, you're exposing much more of who you really are than if you only talk about things like your activities at work, what you've read in the newspaper, and so on. You're saying to your spouse, I trust you enough—I love you enough—to share with you even the things I'm afraid of or embarrassed about: my selfishness, my laziness, my lack of responsibility, my Getting and Protecting Behaviors.

Apologize

When you make a mistake, don't minimize it, or hide it, or make excuses. Just tell the truth about it and apologize for the inconvenience and pain you've caused. As you do that, you're communicating your concern for your spouse's happiness, and that's what Real Love is.

Say "I love you."

Although this chapter has many examples of expressing affection with our behavior, we also need to remember the power of expressing our love with words. Many of us haven't often heard loving words, so we're uncomfortable saying "I love you." Some of us have heard these words only when we did something the speaker liked, which has led us to conclude—usually accurately—that "I love you" is just a way to manipulate people. If your spouse tells you he loves you only when you're having sex, for example, "I love you" will really be an indication that he likes it when you give him what he wants, not a genuine concern for *your* happiness. On other occasions, you may hear "I love you," but then ten minutes later the same person is irritated at you for something you did, leading you to conclude that "I love you" doesn't mean much.

Despite these many negative aspects to the verbal expression of love, "I love you" can still have a powerful effect. Especially when you say these words for no particular reason, they can feel like an unconditional gift. We have many opportunities to use them:

- When you're watching television, lean over and say, "I love you." Our spouses appreciate it when we stop what we're doing to pay attention to them.

- When your husband makes a mistake that inconveniences you, tell him you love him. That's when he needs it the most. Do not say, "I love you *anyway*."
- Before you leave for work, write a love note and leave it where she'll find it.
- When he's leaving the room, call out his name, and when he's looking at you, point your finger at him and silently mouth the words "I love you." When you've done this enough times, you can do a shorthand version by simply pointing your finger and mouthing the word "you" or by pointing and saying nothing at all.
- Call her at work just to say you love her. Do that without bringing up anything you want her to do.
- E-mail him at work—several times—and tell him you love him.
- When you're watching a tender moment together in a movie, lean over and say to her, "I love you even more than that."
- When you're eating your favorite meal, say, "This is great . . . but I love you even more than meat loaf."

Perform Random Acts of Kindness

Each time you do something for your spouse, you're communicating with your behavior that you care about him or her. You're sacrificing time and effort to say "I love you." You can't do this too often. Following are some examples of random acts of kindness you might use to communicate "I love you" to your partner:

- When she walks in the room, that should be a cause for celebration. Don't just sit there and let this opportunity pass. Show her how happy you are to see her. Get up from your chair, walk over to her, give her a hug, and tell her you love her.
- Make his favorite dessert.
- Ask her to go on a walk with you.
- Ask him if there are any particular drinks or snack foods he'd like to have while he watches the football game this Saturday. And would he like to invite anybody else over?

- Set up a time with her every week—a date—when you and she will be completely alone with each other for at least a couple of hours.
- When he has an errand to run, ask him if you could do it for him while he stays home and relaxes or does something else he wants to do.
- Suppose you've committed to do something with your wife at a certain time. When someone calls and asks you to do something else during that time, tell the caller you can't—you have an important previous engagement.
- Offer to drive when he's tired.
- Ask him if there's anything sexual he'd like from you.
- Massage her feet, or shoulders, or whatever she'd like.
- When he doesn't feel well, ask him if he'd like to lie down and let you take care of him for a while.
- Take her out shopping to get something new to wear. Tell her you don't care how long it takes.
- When he gets angry, tell him how you could have been more sensitive toward him, no matter how wrong he is.
- Bring her some flowers. They don't have to be expensive—it could be a single flower from the roadside, or from a grocery store. Put them in a vase yourself.
- When he fails to take out the garbage, take it out yourself and don't mention that you did it.
- Learn how to cook something you know she likes. If you're absolutely hopeless in the kitchen, bring her something she likes from a restaurant or deli.
- Mow the lawn for him.
- Tell her you'd like to set aside an entire day where you both do whatever she'd like. Then don't object to a single suggestion she makes.
- When you're running an errand, ask her if she'd like to come with you, just so you can be together.
- When you don't like how he's driving, or you're sure he's going in the wrong direction, don't say anything.

Cooperate

One day I offered to help Donna sweep and mop the kitchen and dining room floors. As I worked, she kept telling me how to do it. For a moment—maybe two moments—I thought, *You've got to be kidding. I've operated on thousands of patients, climbed mountains, run businesses, and swept hundreds of floors, and you think I need instruction in floor sweeping?* But then I realized that I had an opportunity to simply do it the way she wanted, as a sign of my affection for her—it didn't matter how I usually swept the floor, or what I thought about her method.

When you and your spouse are doing something together, it's unavoidable that you'll sometimes want to do it differently. On most occasions, it simply doesn't matter which way it's done. As you cooperate with his or her requests or preferences, you'll introduce yet another level of harmony in your relationship.

Ask

As I said earlier, most communication is nonverbal. If you begin to look for these nonverbal clues, you'll have many opportunities to ask questions that will indicate a sincere interest in your spouse's feelings and activities, as we see with Blaine and Amanda.

As Blaine and Amanda are returning home in the car from a party at Blaine's parents' house, Blaine notices that Amanda is quiet and is leaning slightly away from him. He knows she's mad at him about something, and frankly, he'd rather let her sulk about it in silence. He's not in the mood for any kind of confrontation. But he's been learning about the power of expressing love even when he doesn't have much to offer, so he decides to explore how she's feeling. "You don't seem very happy," he says. "Do you want to talk about it?"

"No," she says.

It would be easy for Blaine to leave her alone, but he gently persists. "You don't have to talk about it, but if you want to, I'd be happy to listen."

His making an offer twice to listen to her is enough to convince her of his sincere intentions, and she says, "Whenever we go to your parents' house, you don't pay any attention to me at all. You entertain everybody else in the house, but you completely ignore me, like I'm not even there."

Blaine can think of a dozen brilliant defenses, all quite reasonable, for how he behaved: He doesn't get to see his family very often, and when he does, they're quite possessive of his time. Amanda hasn't paid *him* much attention tonight, either. And so on. But again he decides to do the loving thing, and he responds to her need for acceptance instead of defending himself. "Whenever we go over there," he says, "I feel this pressure to make everybody happy. If I don't do all the right things, somebody's feelings will be hurt, and then they'll be mad at me. So I spend all my time making my family happy. I don't like it, but I'm afraid not to. And in the process, I ignore you. I'm sorry about that."

Blaine and Amanda then work out something that will satisfy Amanda's need for attention and will allow Blaine to pay attention to his family. When we ask our spouses how they're feeling, we create opportunities for them to share themselves and feel accepted by us.

Find

As Blaine learned more about Real Love and how to share it with Amanda, he began to share it with her in ways that had never occurred to him before. Amanda called me one day and said, "I just have to tell you how much our lives have changed since we started learning about Real Love."

"I'm happy for you," I said. "Give me an example."

"After work, Blaine used to come home and go straight to the television or the computer. We hardly ever talked, unless I spoke to him first, and even then he just answered with grunts or single words. But now it's really different. As soon as he gets home, he comes and *finds* me, wherever I am. He asks about my day and tells me about his. Can you imagine how that feels, when the first thing he wants to do when he comes home is be with *me*?"

It's not hard to imagine how Amanda feels. What could you possibly do in a day that would be more important than enriching the relationship you have with your spouse? Don't wait for those loving interactions to just happen when it's convenient—*initiate* them, as often as possible. Make a decision that you'll get up from whatever you're doing at least once a day and find your spouse. Throw your arms around her and say, "I've been looking all over the house for you. I just wanted to tell you I love you." That simple act will bring great rewards—for both of you.

Consciously Choose to Accept and Forgive

Because he or she is imperfect, your spouse will sometimes— perhaps often—use the Getting and Protecting Behaviors that inconvenience you. In every case, you have a choice to make. You can respond with your own Getting and Protecting Behaviors— which *never* make you or your partner happy—or you can choose to remember that your partner is simply drowning, a condition we discussed on pages 31–36. When you remember that, your hurt and anger will vanish. You'll find it easy to accept and forgive him or her, just as you would accept and forgive a man for splashing you after you learned he was drowning. We *choose* how we see the behavior of our partners, and with that choice we also determine how we'll respond.

If you choose to hang on to your partner's past offenses, you're choosing to be miserable and injure your relationship. Forgiveness is easy when you see the cause of your partner's behavior and accept that he or she really does get to make mistakes. When you choose to actively care about his happiness, and build a genuinely loving relationship with him, forgiveness becomes the only sensible choice.

Love Without Expectations

One day after Bob had said something especially unkind to Marilyn, she reacted with more than her usual anger, and he realized he'd better do something if he wanted to make any kind of peace.

When he came home from work the next day, he brought her some flowers, and she forgave him. They'd repeated many variations of this pattern on other occasions when there was contention between them. When Bob bought her something, or did something she really liked, she saw this as evidence of his love for her, and harmony was restored. The positive effect, however, was always short-lived, because Bob was doing these things for her to get something for *himself*—peace, forgiveness, her attention, and so on—which did not fill Marilyn's need for *unconditional* love.

Our spouses can sense when we give them our time, attention, and affection with an expectation of getting something in return. They feel the disappointment and anger we express—often subtly—when our expectations are not fulfilled, and then they can't feel unconditionally loved by us. We must be honest about identifying our disappointment and anger, because only then can we recognize the expectations that destroy the possibility of Real Love.

Give Your Time

It could be argued that we have nothing more precious than time, and when you demonstrate with your behavior—not just your talk—that you'd rather spend time with her than with anyone else, you're strongly communicating your love. She won't feel loved, however, if you share your time only when there's nothing else to do—who likes to be an afterthought? One way to communicate your priority is to set aside regular times to be with her. When you do that, she has hours and days to look forward to your time together, and the anticipation can create a heightened feeling of attention and love for her. There are many ways you can regularly set aside time for your spouse. Let me suggest a few:

- Go on a date with your spouse every week, where you spend at least two or three hours together and will not be interrupted by other things, including children. This time is an important opportunity to do many of the loving acts we've already discussed: talking, listening, touching, telling the truth about yourself, and so on. These dates do not have to be expensive. You can read together in a bookstore or library, for example, or go to a park, go on a walk, or do many other things that are free.

- Say to her, "Every night this week, I'd like to go to bed fifteen minutes earlier than usual and spend that time talking to you before we go to sleep. Would you be willing to do that?" With rare exceptions, there should never be days when you don't take time with your spouse to talk about how you feel and what you're doing.
- Plan a weekend away together as often as possible. With children and limited finances, these mini-vacations can be more difficult, but we can usually manage to accomplish what we really want to do. Weekends can be creatively planned for little expense. You could stay at home, for example, take the children to stay with friends, and turn off the phones.
- Have a meeting once a week, where you talk about the plans, goals, appointments, tasks that need to be done, times that children need rides, and other activities that need to be discussed for the coming week and beyond. This will eliminate many sources of potential conflict.

Once you've set aside these times, respect them. You wouldn't lightly cancel a business meeting. Don't lightly change the times you've promised to your spouse.

Many men and women claim they couldn't begin to regularly set aside time together—there simply isn't enough time in their day. Unless you're in prison, the amount of time you spend with your spouse is a *choice*. You can always choose to spend time with the most important person in your life. If other things are interfering with that time, do what it takes to change those things. You might claim, for example, that your job takes all your time. Certainly, our jobs are important, but they'll never give us the kind of profound joy that comes from a loving marriage. If your job is interfering with the time you want to spend with your spouse, make a decision that you will spend less time at work. Once you've made that firm commitment, you'll discover the ways to make it happen: changing your job description, living with less pay, sometimes even changing jobs. No success in this life can compensate for a marriage that's less than deeply fulfilling. I've known many couples who have made financial sacrifices in order to build their marriages and families, and they have not regretted their decisions.

☙

The potential list of loving acts we can share with our spouses is endless. Be creative. If you were going to invest all your money in the stock market, you'd certainly take the time to research the companies whose stock you're buying. Building a marriage is at least as important as building a stock portfolio. Take the time to sit down and think of ways you can express your love to your spouse.

When to Offer Your Love

If you demonstrate to your spouse that you love him or her in the above ways only when she's doing what you want, that won't mean very much. In effect, you'll be paying her for being nice, and that doesn't lead to feeling unconditionally loved. What your spouse needs most is to see all these evidences of love when she's *not* being loving—when she's using Getting and Protecting Behaviors. If your spouse is being grouchy, unkind, and thoughtless, that's exactly when he or she needs you to listen to her, look at her, touch her gently, ask her how she's doing, apologize for your mistakes, give her your time, and perform random acts of kindness.

On some occasions, you'll notice that your partner will be too irritated and touchy to accept your offers of love, even when your intentions are the best. Imagine, for example, that your husband walks in the door with a sour expression on his face. You ask him how he's doing, and he doesn't answer you, nor does he respond to your looking directly at him. He even shrugs you off when you try to touch him. Do not take this personally, do not feel offended, and *do not give up*. Remember that he's drowning, and that you just haven't come across the right way to throw him a rope. Bring him something to drink. Ask if there's something you can do for him. If he's really annoyed, he might not have an answer to your question, so you might gently touch him and say, "I know you're not feeling great right now. Would you like me to sit quietly with you, or would you like me to come back in fifteen minutes and see how you're doing?" You're communicating complete acceptance and not pressuring him to do anything or accept anything you're offering. You're giving him a chance to feel accepted and think of something you can do to help when you return.

Exercises

Exercise One

Write down three of your irresponsible behaviors. Here are some examples:

- It's my job to take out the garbage, but I often fail to do it, and then she has to ask me about it.
- When it's my job to prepare dinner, I wait till the last minute, put as little effort into it as possible, and don't really care much whether the meal is nutritious or tastes great.
- It's just as much my job to teach and discipline the kids as it is hers, but I usually just let the kids argue or misbehave until she takes care of it.

Now sit down with your spouse and share what you've written. You need only to tell the truth about your mistakes; you don't need to grovel, or feel guilty, or promise never to be irresponsible again, which would be unrealistic. Where appropriate, you could also apologize for the inconvenience and pain you've caused.

Exercise Two

Write down a list of your warts, especially your Getting and Protecting Behaviors. Here are some examples:

- I can be pretty irresponsible and lazy (running, unloving).
- When my husband doesn't do just what I want, I get irritated, almost every time (attacking).
- When she's mad at me, I blow up at her (attacking).
- When he doesn't remember my birthday or anniversary, I act hurt and sulk (acting like a victim, running).
- I almost never tell her how I really feel when I'm sad or discouraged (lying, running).
- When he has to go out of town for several days in a row, I complain about it (clinging, acting like a victim).

Don't minimize these behaviors. Write down how they affect your partner, your marriage, and your own happiness. Now recognize that you're not *bad* for doing these things. You just haven't had enough Real Love in your life, and now you can do something about that.

♡

Exercise Three

Sit down with your spouse and tell him or her about some of your Getting and Protecting Behaviors. Apologize for the inconvenience and pain you've caused.

♡

Exercise Four

Choose a friend and make a commitment to yourself that you will share with that person some of your Getting and Protecting Behaviors. Then do it. Be specific. Describe a recent interaction with your spouse where you were angry (attacking), or lied, or acted like a victim, or ran. If that friend isn't really interested in seeing the truth about you—if he or she can't listen without criticizing you, or criticizing your spouse, or sympathizing with you—continue telling the truth about yourself until you do find people who see and accept you.

ॐ

Exercise Five

Using pages 87–107 as a guide, choose a different loving act to practice with your spouse *every day*. Write down what you plan to do each day, and the next day record what you did, how your spouse reacted, and how you felt.

ॐ

Exercise Six

Write a list of things your partner has done in the past week that benefited you in some way: He or she fixed meals, went to work to earn a living for the family, picked up your clothes, ran errands, took out the garbage, didn't make a comment about some of the mistakes you made, and so on.

Rather than dismiss these actions as just part of the daily grind, make a decision to view them as evidence that he or she cares about your well-being, which is the essence of Real Love. To be sure, your partner still makes mistakes and communicates disappointment and anger on occasion, but this list is an indication of his or her attempts to love you. Stay with this mental exercise until you feel genuinely grateful for these acts of love. Carry this gratitude around with you—physically carry the list you wrote—and see how it changes the way you behave toward your partner.

4

The Great Wars

How to Eliminate Conflict from Your Marriage

I magine that for the past hour, you've been sitting in a great restaurant with good friends, enjoying your favorite food, music, and conversation. You're having the time of your life—a truly memorable experience—when suddenly the doors of the restaurant burst open and three men with guns charge into the room. For the next five minutes the room is filled with the sounds of screams and destruction as the intruders shoot holes in the ceiling, throw tables to the floor, and haul away everything they can get their hands on. A man next to you is knocked to the floor, and one of the robbers takes your wallet and watch before fleeing into the street.

As you leave the restaurant, which of the two experiences do you remember most vividly: the sixty minutes of delightful food and conversation, or the five minutes of terror? The negative effect of some experiences can completely overwhelm the impression made by many positive ones. Seldom do we feel more confusion and pain than when we're trying unsuccessfully to resolve a conflict with a spouse. We must learn how to resolve these conflicts, because while we're learning the process of feeling loved and loving others, one significant conflict can wipe out the effect of a dozen steps taken in the direction of a loving relationship.

By *conflict* I do not mean disagreement or differences. I mean any interaction that involves Getting and Protecting Behaviors—most often anger. Without these behaviors, we can disagree with our spouses about many things without the slightest conflict.

Conflict is so common around us—between spouses, friends, businesses, coworkers, drivers on the highway, parents and children, and even entire nations—that we have come to regard this destructive condition as unavoidable, even normal. Many of us actually *enjoy* conflict, because it gives us an opportunity to gain the upper hand over someone and feel a rush of power. For most of us, however, conflict is painful, and we variously respond with attempts to control, manage, and minimize it. Sometimes we run from it, or we may simply resign ourselves to it, with a shrug of our shoulders. It is possible, however, and infinitely preferable, to eliminate conflict—gradually, to be sure—from our personal lives and from our marriages, which we can accomplish as we understand and apply the following nine guidelines:

1. Realize that it's always about Real Love.
2. Listen.
3. Never speak in anger.
4. Tell the truth about yourself.
5. Tell the truth about your partner.
6. Recognize what you really want.
7. Remember the Law of Choice.
8. Determine *how* you and your partner can both get what you want.
9. Refuse to be in conflict.

1. Realize That It's Always About Real Love

One early winter day I went outside to blow some leaves off the lawn and discovered that the leaf blower wouldn't start. My wife had mentioned some difficulty with starting it in cold weather, so I put it in a warm room in the house for a couple of hours, but it still wouldn't start. I filled it with gas, changed the air filter, and even kicked it a couple of times, but no matter how many times I pulled on the starting cord, the engine would not come to life. Finally, my wife walked by while I was sweating over my little project, and she asked if I had the switch turned to the *on* position. Sure enough, the engine was turned off, and after I flipped the switch, it roared to life at the next pull of the cord.

Until we know the real reason for any problem—a leaf blower that won't start or a conflict in a marriage—all our efforts to fix it are often doomed to failure. We'll see this concept illustrated in a conversation between Linda and her husband, Richard. On a warm Saturday afternoon, Richard bounded into the house, grabbed Linda by the arm, and dragged her outside, saying, "You've just got to see this!"

Reaching the driveway, Richard proudly gestured at the gleaming new pickup truck that was parked there, looked at Linda with eager anticipation, and said, "Well, what do you think?"

With her hands on her hips, and her eyes wide, she said, "How could you?!"

Richard's excitement was gone in an instant. "What do you mean?" he asked.

"How could you buy a truck without talking to me about it first?"

"But we did talk about it."

"We did not."

"Yes, we did," he said. "Remember, I told you my truck was getting pretty old, and I was thinking about getting another one. And you agreed with me."

"Sure, I agreed that it was getting old, but I didn't say, 'Let's run out and get another one today'! You didn't say you were actually going to *get* a new one! I can't believe this. We just finished paying the other one off!" As she spoke, the pitch and volume of her voice were rising.

"It's been nearly a year since we paid it off, and it had almost 80,000 miles on it. It was old. I spend a lot of time on the road, and I ought to be able to drive something I like."

"Sure, everybody'd *like* a new car. That would be great, but you didn't *need* this. We can't afford it."

"Did I say anything when you got two new dresses last week, or when you spent enough on your hair to feed a small family for a month? You didn't exactly need all that, either."

It's not difficult to imagine where the conversation went from there, as their communications had done many times before.

When Linda later described the argument to a friend, she said, "We're always arguing about money." Linda honestly believed their arguments were about money, and she believed that if they only had more of it, their arguments would disappear.

When couples are asked to list the causes of conflict in their marriages, the answers given most often are money, sex, household duties, and children. Some people reflect more deeply and suggest that their conflicts are a result of poor communication, a lack of commitment to the marriage, or a gradual change of interests. Couples spend a great deal of time and effort working on—and arguing about—these problems, and they often go to counselors who prescribe communication techniques and other devices.

On pages 2–3, I suggested that heart attacks are not caused by any specific event but by a lifetime of choices and predisposing conditions. Similarly, Getting and Protecting Behaviors—which are the essential elements of any conflict—are not caused by specific events or issues. They're a response to the emptiness and fear caused by a longstanding lack of Real Love. Conflict isn't a result of poor communication, lack of commitment, or disagreements about money, sex, household duties, and children. Conflict occurs only as people struggle over the scraps of Imitation Love that become so valuable in the absence of Real Love. When two people are starving to death, a crust of bread suddenly becomes very important, an object worth fighting about. In the presence of a mountain of food, however, the reason to fight simply disappears. Money, sex, household duties, and children are simply the *arenas* where we fight about the lack of Real Love and Imitation Love in our lives. Poor communication and lack of commitment are not the *cause* of conflict. Rather, they are *caused* by a lack of Real Love and always coexist with conflict.

In short, conflict is always about Real Love—which isn't just *one* of the things we need to be happy; it's *the* thing we need—and until we see that, we can manage conflict, temporarily control it, and manipulate it to our advantage, but we can't eliminate it.

Although Richard and Linda thought their argument was about money, an understanding of Real Love enables us to see the real cause. Neither of them had ever felt much unconditional love, not as children or as adults. When they met, they both expected the other to deliver the happiness they'd always wanted. They needed Real Love, but since neither of them had it to give, they settled for the Imitation Love they both had to offer. They fell in love because of the abundance of Imitation Love they traded, and when the effect of that "love" wore off, they were sorely disappointed. They both had an innate desire to be loving toward each other, but without receiving Real Love themselves, and without a consistent example of unconditional love from others, there was no way they could love each other in the way they both needed.

Within this background of insufficient Real Love, let's look at the individual elements of their conflict. We'll begin with Richard's purchase of the new truck. He claimed that he bought it because the other one had gotten old and just wasn't as comfortable as he wanted, but a large part of his motivation was a response to the lack of Real Love in his life. Feeling unloved and alone, he was always looking for some external source of excitement and pleasure—entertainment, sex, food, sports—to fill his emptiness. Buying a new truck gave him a jolt of excitement and a sense of power, and when he showed it to Linda, he hoped she would praise his choice and thereby give him yet another morsel of Imitation Love.

But Linda didn't give him what he wanted. Not only did she withhold the praise he was looking for; she attacked him, because she didn't have enough Real Love in *her* life, either. In that condition she was primarily concerned about where *her* next dose of Imitation Love would come from, and she sensed that her choices of Imitation Love might be limited if the family resources were consumed by new truck payments. She also felt powerless when she learned that he had made the purchase without consulting her, interpreting his behavior—correctly, it turns out—as a reflection of his lack of concern for her. When Linda attacked Richard, she relieved her sense of helplessness with the feeling of power that always comes from being angry, and she also hoped her anger might motivate him to change his decision. He responded with anger of his own, however, and their conversation deteriorated into an unhappy exchange of Getting and Protecting Behaviors.

Both partners wanted Real Love. Without it, they desperately used whatever Getting and Protecting Behaviors they had to get the Imitation Love that would temporarily make them feel better. In this conflict, it became apparent to both of them that they wouldn't get either Real Love *or* Imitation Love, which only heightened their emptiness, fear, and Getting and Protecting Behaviors. It was an impossible situation.

Don't Get Distracted by the Details

As you experience conflict with your spouse, you will be tempted to argue about *details*—who did what, who got the most, who did the worst thing, and the hundred brilliant justifications for what was done, as Richard and Linda did—but focusing on the details is absolutely worthless when you're empty and afraid, and when you're using Getting and Protecting Behaviors. You can talk about details forever, and although you may arrive at some kind of compromise, or truce, or surrender, you will not move toward the kind of happiness you really want unless you address the need you both have to receive and give Real Love. When you're drowning—when you don't feel loved, and when you're using Getting and Protecting Behaviors to keep your head above water—you don't need discussions about the depth of the water, nor do you need to ferret out and punish the people you believe are responsible for your predicament. *You need air.*

We need to learn to tell the truth about ourselves and find the Real Love that will pull us out of the water. We need the Real Love that will eliminate the emptiness and fear that lead to the Getting and Protecting Behaviors that fuel every conflict. That is the long-term solution to conflict, but what can be done to resolve the conflicts we're experiencing right now—before we're filled with Real Love? That's what we'll be talking about for the remainder of this chapter.

Don't Get Discouraged

Once you understand that it's the lack of Real Love that lies at the foundation of all conflict, you might for a time become discouraged at seeing how unloving and selfish you often are. Every time you use Getting and Protecting Behaviors with your spouse, you're declaring that you are empty, afraid, and not capable of loving unconditionally. Don't be discouraged by that. Just remember that in the process of learning to feel loved and loving, you will inevitably make many, many mistakes. No punishment is necessary. Simply admit your mistakes and move on with a renewed determination to recognize your mistakes more quickly the next time. Eventually, as you have more Real Love in your life, you'll begin to lovingly and consistently see the needs of your spouse rather than manipulating him or her, or protecting yourself.

2. Listen

In the last chapter I discussed the importance of listening, and in this section we'll discuss some additional guidelines that will enable you to listen effectively to your spouse, which really means to *see* your partner as he or she really is. I will refer to whoever is speaking or communicating nonverbally (smiling, crying, withdrawing, sulking) as the *speaker.* The other partner is the *listener.*

The First Rule of Seeing: One Speaker

During any truly productive interaction, there can be only one speaker. When both of you compete to speak, no one is effectively heard or seen, which makes feeling loved impossible.

The Second Rule of Seeing: Whoever Speaks First Is the Speaker

What happens when both of you want to talk at the same time? Who is the speaker then? Whoever speaks first. This doesn't prevent either of you from having your say. It simply determines the *order* of speaking and ensures that you'll both be heard.

One morning, as Richard was preparing to go to work, he discovered he didn't have a single ironed shirt in the closet. He and Linda had long ago divided up the household chores, and he was irritated that she often didn't hold up her end of the agreement, which included the ironing. *Dang it,* he thought, *I do my part. Why can't she do hers?* Stomping into the next room, where Linda was eating breakfast, he said, "Are you ever going to do the ironing? I have to leave for work in five minutes, and I don't have a shirt!"

"You think I have time to do it now?" she said.

"You'll have to. You brought this on yourself. I'm not the one who put off the ironing all week."

"Oh, like *you* don't put things off? How long have you been promising to clean out the garage?"

"What does that have to do with ironing shirts?"

Of course, their conversation only went downhill from there. Later, as Linda talked to me about it, she said, "We have arguments like that all the time. I don't know what to do about it."

"What do you both want most?" I asked.

"To feel loved."

"And that will require that you both create opportunities to feel seen and accepted by each other. Neither of you can feel seen if you're both trying to talk at the same time. Whoever speaks first needs to be heard until he or she finishes."

"So when he stomps into the room and says unkind things to me, I'm supposed to just listen to him?"

"Sure. How does it work when you're both trying to talk at the same time?"

"Not very well," she admitted.

"So it doesn't matter who is right or wrong. What you want is an opportunity for both of you to feel seen, and that means only one person can speak at a time—in this case, the first person to speak."

"So what am I supposed to say when he says something like that?"

"Remember that he's the speaker, and your primary job is to listen to him. Sometimes you need to respond to what he's saying, but not to argue, only to communicate that you really understand him and accept him. Let's apply this to the argument you just described. Is it your job to do the ironing?"

"Yes, I guess it is. I've always done it. He doesn't know how. And I agreed years ago that I'd do it."

"It appears that you don't like the arrangement, but that's something you'll have to work out later. For now, it is your job, so you could say, 'You're right, I didn't do the ironing, and I should have. I'll iron one right now.' You might be inconvenienced, and possibly even a little late for work, but that's the only thing you could say and do that would communicate that you really heard what he was saying."

"But what about all the stuff *he* puts off doing?" she asked "And what about the accusing way he always talks to me about things like this? Can't I talk about that?"

"Sure you can, but not in the same conversation where he is the speaker, and I strongly recommend that you wait hours or days before bringing up the subjects you want to talk about. If you talk about his mistakes right after he's talked about yours, he'll feel like you didn't really listen—that you were just waiting until you could speak yourself."

Let me be clear that Richard was unkind, unloving, and wrong when he spoke angrily to Linda, and I discussed that with her. Had he been there talking to me, I would have spoken to him about his anger, but he wasn't. Linda was there with me, and she needed to see how following the Second Rule of Seeing could make a great contribution to her ability to listen to her husband and help him feel accepted and loved. That approach has a much more positive effect in conversations and relationships than insisting on being right and trying to speak at the same time as our partners.

Allowing your partner to be the speaker won't keep you from saying everything you want. The first two Rules of Seeing simply make it possible for everyone to be genuinely heard and seen.

The Third Rule of Seeing: The Speaker Describes Himself

Continuing my conversation with Linda, I said, "You can do even more to really listen to Richard. You need to understand the real messages that underlie most of what he says. Whenever he's irritated, for example, the subject isn't really shirts needing to be ironed. His anger is always a Getting and Protecting Behavior that tells you he's reacting to feeling empty and afraid. He's telling you he doesn't feel loved, even though he doesn't realize that that's what he's saying. If you can see that and respond to it, you will give him an opportunity to feel seen and accepted."

"So what would I say to show that I understand what you just said?" she asked.

"You could say, 'Richard, I should have ironed your shirts, but I didn't. There are a lot of other things you've asked me to do that I haven't done, either. Sometimes you must feel like I don't care about you, and you know, sometimes I *am* pretty selfish. I choose to do what *I* want instead of paying attention to what *you* need. I'm learning to do better with that. Thanks for being patient with me while I learn."

"Wow, that would be hard to say."

"Harder than the arguments you have now?"

"I get the point."

None of this is to imply that Linda is Richard's slave and has to do everything he wants. This is a description only of how she could respond in a situation where she has made a mistake. Working out a division of labor, making agreements, making requests, and refusing requests will be described later in this and subsequent chapters.

The Fourth Rule of Seeing: If You Can't Be a Wise Man, Get One

"So what can I do," Linda continued, "when I'm too mad to say something like that to him? What if I just want to snap back at him?"

"If you can't give him the acceptance he needs, it would be nice if you could refer him to someone else—a wise man—who could give him that love. But that isn't always practical. He probably wouldn't appreciate it if you said, 'Obviously, you're not feeling loved. I can't give you that right now, but you could call Gerald and see if he can love you.' But you *can* iron the shirt and later you can call someone who has demonstrated an ability to see and accept you—a wise man or woman from your loving group, for example—and tell the truth about how you were irresponsible and unloving. When you feel the acceptance of that person, you'll be getting the Real Love you need to take back to your husband. You'll become the wise woman he needs."

When you can't be a wise man for your spouse—which is what he or she really needs—you can at least get one for yourself, after which you'll be capable of being more accepting and loving toward your spouse.

Confusion About Who Is the Speaker

Sometimes it's not clear who the speaker is. Earlier we discussed the interaction between Linda and Richard about his buying the new truck. Linda could have maintained that she was the speaker, because Richard invited her to speak when he said, "Well, what do you think?" But the fact is, Richard spoke first—when he excitedly asked her to look at his new toy—and what he was really asking for was her acceptance.

Does that mean she was obligated to accept his decision to buy the truck, which had serious financial implications for both of them? No, but she still needed to communicate her acceptance of *him*, in great part simply by not being irritated. She also could have oohed and ahhed about how great the truck looked, and she could have asked him to describe its features or to take her for a ride in it.

But what about the financial issue? Did she have to ignore that? Of course not, but she couldn't bring it up until Richard was finished speaking. It's important to understand that people are not done speaking just because they're done *talking*. They're finished speaking when they've been sufficiently *seen and heard*. When we understand that, we're much slower to interrupt the seeing and accepting process with our own agendas. I suggested to Linda that she not discuss the financial implications of the truck until later in the day, or even the next day. If she had brought up the finances too soon, he would only have felt attacked. You can talk to your spouse about anything you want, but you'll be much wiser if you accept and love your partner while he or she is speaking, and if you learn how to slowly and lovingly take your turn as speaker.

If you have any doubt about whether your partner is finished speaking, ask. You could say, for example, "I have something I want to talk about, but I don't want to interrupt what you're saying about the kids. Are you finished with that subject?"

On some occasions, even when we speak first—and, technically, can therefore claim the role of speaker—we need to be willing to give up that role and allow our spouses to speak. One day, when Richard began to speak to Linda about a mistake she'd made, he noticed that she wasn't happy and didn't seem to be listening to him. He could easily have demanded to continue speaking. After all, he had spoken first and could claim the right to be the speaker. He also could have been irritated that she wasn't listening very well. But he had made the decision that he wanted a loving relationship more than anything else, so he silently gave up the speaker role and said, "It looks like there's something bothering you. You want to talk about it?"

Linda was stunned. She had been bursting to talk about something unpleasant that had happened at work that day, and she was grateful to feel his understanding and acceptance. Imagine how the conversation would have gone if Richard had insisted on being the speaker. He didn't give up the right to discuss the topic on his mind—he just decided to bring it up later in the day, when Linda would be more capable of listening.

The Second Rule of Seeing—Whoever speaks first is the speaker—is just a guideline to help you establish who should speak. If you speak first, but you perceive that your partner can't hear you, or that he or she needs to be seen and heard more than you do, give your spouse the position of speaker.

One Topic at a Time
When Richard came home late one evening from work, Linda was irritated as she talked to him about his never calling to tell her where he was. He wisely listened and acknowledged his mistake, but then Linda began to talk about a number of other issues she was unhappy with—money, the kids, household responsibilities—and Richard began to feel overwhelmed.

Don't abuse your position as speaker. While your spouse may be capable of listening to a discussion about one or two mistakes, he or she may not be capable of handling a long list of issues. When you sense impatience or resistance on the part of your spouse, realize that you can always talk again later. It's usually best to stick with one topic at a time. You don't have to deal with everything right now.

If you're the listener, you also need to say something when you get to the point where you can't effectively hear anymore. As Richard, for example, began to feel intimidated by the long list of problems Linda was presenting above, he said, "I really am being selfish when I don't call you from work. It would only take a minute to tell you I'm going to be late, but I don't think about how it will affect you, and I'm going to do better about that. I know you have some other things you want to talk about, too, but I do better when we discuss one thing at a time. Right now, let's talk about me not calling you when I'm late at work, and then we can get together later tonight to talk about the other things. Would that be all right?"

3. Never Speak in Anger

We've learned that with anger, we feel stronger and less helpless, and we can often get people to do what we want, because anger provokes fear in the people around us. As Marcel Proust said, "To kindness, to knowledge, we make promises only; pain we obey." Our anger causes pain and fear in our spouses, and then they often leap to do whatever it takes to please us and eliminate our anger.

Because we've learned that anger can be quite effective, it's tempting to use it with our spouses. When your spouse doesn't have enough Real Love, however—which is the case in most marriages—he or she is empty and afraid. When you get angry, your partner hears you speaking only four words: "I don't love you." And he's right. When you're angry, you're expressing a greater concern for your own welfare than for his. You are telling him you don't love him—at least not unconditionally, which is the only kind of love that counts—and that can only worsen his emptiness and provoke greater fear than he already has. He's then virtually certain to react with Getting and Protecting Behaviors, which will make loving communication impossible.

With anger you may achieve some kind of strained agreement with your spouse, but you will never truly resolve a conflict. When you're angry, therefore, I recommend the five steps to eliminate anger, which are discussed in greater detail in Chapter Nine of *Real Love*. I recommend that you write these five steps on an index card and put it in your pocket or purse. Pull it out and read it several times a day, especially when you're angry. If you do that, you will change your life:

- Be quiet.
- Be wrong.
- Feel loved (remember that you're loved).
- Get loved.
- Be loving.

Be Quiet

When you're angry, there is nothing you can say that will make you or your spouse feel loved, loving, and happy. Nothing. In the presence of accusations and misinformation, it may sometimes be necessary to point out inaccuracies and injustices that involve your spouse, but if you're irritated, you will make the situation worse, no matter how cleverly you respond and how *right* you believe you are. I've tried hundreds of ways to express my anger at people in a productive way, and I've watched hundreds of others do the same. I can say with absolute certainty that when we're angry at people, we cannot communicate as effectively with them.

This does not mean you can't talk about your anger, but *while* you're angry at your spouse, do not express your anger *to him or her*. You'll damage your relationship and your happiness, and you'll make it very difficult to arrive at the best solution to any specific conflict. You *can*, however, express your anger *to another person*, not to someone who will only sympathize with you and thereby perpetuate your anger, but to someone who can help you see the selfishness of your anger and then *accept you*.

This also does not mean you have to agree with or give in to your spouse when you're angry. That's just being a doormat, which isn't healthy. Throughout the chapter we'll discuss many things you *can* do to resolve conflicts, but all these principles and actions are more effective when you're not expressing anger at your spouse.

When I say you need to be quiet when you're angry, I don't mean that you just need to stop *talking*. You also need to avoid the many nonverbal forms of communicating a lack of acceptance that we talked about on page 91. Obviously, you can't avoid all these forms of expressing anger unless you're actually *not* angry. If you're angry, you *will* express it in some way. You won't be able to fake it for long, if at all.

Be Wrong

On pages 25–26, I suggested that any feeling or behavior that detracts from feeling loved, loving, and happy is wrong. When you're angry, you're trying to protect yourself and get what *you* want. You're unloving, blind, trying to control your partner, and expecting him or her to make you happy. Because anger always detracts from feeling loved, loving, and happy, it is always wrong, and once you recognize that, it's much more difficult to stay angry or insist on whatever course of action you're pursuing.

When I say anger is wrong, I am not saying you *shouldn't* be angry, nor that you should hide the anger you feel—we've already talked about expressing anger to other people in order to create opportunities to feel accepted. Anger is wrong because it simply doesn't work—it's not a loving way to live, and it keeps us from achieving our greatest goal, which is happiness.

You can always find something wrong with the behavior of your partner. That's easy, but it's also irrelevant. It simply does not matter how wrong your spouse is if *you* are angry. You cannot change the interaction or the relationship in a positive way until you admit the error of *your* anger.

Every time we're angry, there are two ways we can go. First, we can blame our partner and demand that he or she change. Or, second, we can admit that we're wrong and do what's necessary to find the Real Love that will eliminate our anger. We often choose blaming because it *seems* easier in the moment. But does it ever work? Does it ever eliminate the anger that poisons our happiness and our relationships? When we see the utter futility of blaming and anger, it's much easier to admit that we're wrong and to take truly productive steps to change ourselves.

Feel Loved (Remember That You're Loved)

Feeling unconditionally loved really is like having twenty million emotional dollars. With Real Love nothing else matters; without it nothing else is enough. Sometimes, however, we do have a few million in the bank but simply *forget* we have it when confronted by a particularly stressful situation, like when our spouses are vigorously attacking us. On those occasions, we have what we need, but we temporarily lose access to it. If we make a conscious decision to *remember* that there *are* people who genuinely love us, we can often gain immediate access to our millions, lose our emptiness and fear, and thereby lose our need to use anger as a Getting and Protecting Behavior. It is not possible to feel loved and angry at the same time. Of course, this step is only effective if we've previously told the truth about ourselves and actually felt Real Love.

Get Loved

Sometimes you may take the three steps above—be quiet, be wrong, feel loved—but you still won't have enough Real Love in the bank to handle a situation with your spouse. On those occasions, you can tell the truth about yourself to *other people* who are capable of accepting and loving you. With that Real Love in the bank, you'll no longer be controlled by your emptiness and fear, and then you'll be able to handle the situation that had previously overwhelmed you. This process can be illustrated by another interaction between Richard and Linda, the same couple that argued earlier about the ironing.

Late one evening, as Richard angrily confronted Linda about something she'd done, she began to feel increasingly irritated. She thought of a dozen brilliant, biting things to prove that she was right and he was wrong, but she remembered how badly conversations had always gone when she'd said those things, so she made a decision to practice being loving rather than insist on being right. Quietly, she pulled from her purse an index card, upon which she had written the five steps to eliminate anger. First, she resolved not to express her anger verbally at Richard, although she recognized that she was probably showing it in many nonverbal ways. Second, she realized that no matter what Richard was saying, no matter how unkindly he was behaving, *her* anger was selfish, unloving, and wrong. Third, she remembered the many occasions when she had felt unconditionally accepted and loved by friends as she had told the truth about herself.

Despite all those efforts, however, she was still irritated, so she took the fourth step. She said, "Richard, I have to make a phone call right now, but I'll be back in just a few minutes. Is that all right?"

Then she went into the next room and called her friend Elise. "Sometimes I just want to scream," she said. "He can be so demanding and critical—about everything."

"When Richard gets angry at you like that, what is he really telling you?"

"That he doesn't care about me."

"Right. At least in that moment, he cares a lot more about what *he* wants than about what *you* need. Anger is a Getting and Protecting Behavior, and we use it to get what we want and to protect ourselves. Anger is always selfish. So you're right, he's telling you he doesn't care about you. But he's also telling you something about *himself*, unrelated to you. What is it?"

"I'm not sure."

"Why do people use Getting and Protecting Behaviors?"

"Because they're empty and afraid?"

"Sure, and why would Richard be empty and afraid?"

Linda sighed and smiled. "Because he doesn't feel loved."

"So when he's angry, he's not only telling you he doesn't care about you. He's telling you he needs to be loved himself. And then how do you respond to that need?"

Chuckling now, Linda said, "I get angry at him, which only makes him feel worse. Then he protects himself by getting even more angry. It doesn't make much sense, does it?"

"No, it's kind of crazy, really," said Elise.

"So how can I love him if I don't feel loved myself?"

"Do you feel less angry at him right now?"

"I don't feel angry at all."

"That's because you're getting the love you need. I'm not doing anything fancy here. I'm just accepting you and caring about you while you're being angry and unloving, and you can feel that. Nice feeling, isn't it?"

When Linda went back to her conversation with Richard, she was carrying with her the love she had received from Elise, and with that love, she was able to listen to Richard and respond to him in a loving way.

Be Loving

One morning, Richard asked Linda to mail a package for him at the post office. She agreed, but when he got home that evening, he was furious to discover that his package was still on the dining room counter. Pulling from his pocket an index card tattered at the edges, he was reminded to be quiet—he didn't call her on the cell phone and say the unkind things running through his mind—and he understood that he was wrong to be angry. He also remembered that there were people who cared about him, but he was still angry, so he called his friend Glenn and said, "Dang it, I needed that package to go out today, and she knew that. But she didn't do it."

Glenn briefly acknowledged that Linda had been inconsiderate and had inconvenienced Richard, but then he talked to Richard about the selfishness of *his* anger, and he was accepting and loving toward Richard as they spoke. Still, Richard couldn't let go of his fixation on the inconvenience of the situation and the offense he felt. So Glenn finally said, "Are there any dishes in the sink?"

"What are you talking about?" asked Richard.

"Go look and see if there are any dishes in the sink."

Richard took the portable phone into the kitchen and said, "Sure, a few."

"Wash them and put them away," said Glenn.

"Is this like a joke? What does this have to do with her not mailing the package?"

"You can see that your anger isn't helping you or your

relationship. Right now you're getting the acceptance you need, and you're remembering that you have other people who care about you. But you're still angry, so I'm suggesting that you'd feel more loved and loving if you did something loving for Linda. As you wash the dishes—as you consciously choose to do something for her—you might be able to start thinking about *her* happiness and remember the importance of a loving relationship with her instead of fussing about what you didn't get for yourself."

Richard washed the dishes. He also cleaned up the rest of the kitchen, and by the time Linda got home, he wasn't angry at all. As soon as she walked in the door, she gasped, both because she realized she hadn't mailed the package and because she saw what Richard had done in the kitchen. They had a wonderful conversation, quite different than they would have had if Richard hadn't taken the five steps to eliminate anger.

Doing something loving for your spouse when you're angry at her may be the last thing you feel like doing, but as we discussed in Chapter Three, sharing love with others can often have the miraculous effect of multiplying the Real Love we have, even if the people we love give us nothing in return. If, therefore, you make a conscious decision to behave in a loving way toward your spouse when you're angry at her, you'll often find that the resulting love you feel will eliminate your anger.

Sometimes you don't have to do something loving for your spouse to eliminate your anger at him or her. You might, for example, be a hundred miles apart and have no immediate way to demonstrate your love. But if you do something loving for *someone else*, the love you subsequently feel can eliminate the anger you feel toward your spouse. Real Love from any source is healing and energizing.

4. Tell the Truth About Yourself

Most conflicts are characterized by multiple and often contradictory details that seem to weave an impossibly tangled web. Both parties offer numerous and irrefutable proofs that they are right and the other person is wrong. It can all be quite confusing.

How can you keep from falling into this awful web and making everything worse as you struggle with all the threads in a conflict? Just tell the truth. But about what? When you're in a conflict, you tend to believe that every word you utter is the truth, but so does your partner, and since your views are contradictory, it's not possible that both of you are right.

We need to be careful about our claims that something is true. Following are a few examples of what you might believe to be facts, as well as the consequences of maintaining that belief:

- "You never do anything with me." Even if that's true, your partner will likely feel attacked, and conflict will then be guaranteed. But is it really true? Does your partner *never* do anything with you, or does it just *seem* like that when you have great expectations that are not being filled?
- "I've told you four times to do that." Maybe you did, or perhaps you told her once directly, hinted at it twice, and told her a fourth time only in your mind. And would it make any difference if you *were* right? What if you *did* tell her four times? Conflict is still guaranteed if either of two circumstances exists: First, she doesn't feel loved. In that condition, even if she does remember all four occasions, she'll deny it just to protect herself from your attack. Second, she simply doesn't remember the four instances. If you insist on being right in that situation, you'll worsen the conflict, because she will sincerely believe she's right and will find it very difficult to back down from that position.
- When people criticize our performance, we often say, "But I did what you asked." Is it a fact, however, that we did what we were asked, or is it only our perception of what happened? Perhaps we did less than was asked, but because we were afraid of disapproval, we deluded ourselves into thinking we did more than we did. We tend to see things as we want them

to be. Or maybe we did exactly what we were *asked,* but not what was *needed* or desired. In other words, we kept the letter of the law, but not the spirit. If, for example, you accomplished a specific task, but you did it with resentment, took a great deal longer than was reasonable, and produced an end result of less than superior quality, then "I did what you asked" is really a lie.

- "I was only trying to help." Perhaps you did have some desire to be helpful, but often that desire is partly driven by selfish motivations, like getting praise, power, and safety for ourselves. On those occasions, our "help" is tainted, and the consequences of our selfishness often outweigh the benefits of our assistance.

- "You don't care about me." That may be a fact, but when you're empty and afraid, you can't clearly see the feelings and motivations of other people. It may be that you're simply demanding a certain amount of time and acceptance from him, and when he doesn't deliver, you say he doesn't care about you in order to justify your fears and anger.

We can see from these examples that we often have difficulty identifying the truth about events, the feelings and behavior of others, and our own motivations. We're confused because we want to see these things in a way that makes us right. To vigorously insist, therefore, on our being right in a given situation can be a shaky proposition indeed.

So what *can* we productively tell the truth about? We can talk about our own emptiness and fear, our Getting and Protecting Behaviors, our selfish expectations, and our mistakes. We talked about how to do this in Chapter Three. We need to admit when we're *wrong,* sometimes to our spouse but on other occasions to a wise man. Sometimes it's enough to admit to *ourselves* that we're wrong. We can also talk about what we *believe* to be true about our spouse and what we want (more about that later in the book).

Tell the Truth About Yourself to Your Spouse When You're in Conflict

Jennifer and her husband, Daniel, often argued about money. He said she spent too much, and of course she disagreed. It was a frequent source of contention. One evening she called me to talk about it.

"Daniel was paying the credit card bill," she said, "and he started snapping at me about everything on the bill. 'What's this?!' he said. 'Why did you buy that?' He was really being ugly."

We talked about the specific things she bought, and she agreed—reluctantly—that none of them were really necessities.

"So let's look at what's happening here: You're buying things *you* want, which affect the finances that concern *him,* and then you let him find out about them only as he's paying the bills. He becomes afraid—both because of the money you're spending and because you're telling him you don't care about him—and he protects himself by getting angry at you. Then you react by getting angry that he would dare to protect himself when he's afraid. I'm not excusing his anger, but do you see your contribution to all this?"

Jennifer lets out a sigh. "I didn't before, but I think I'm starting to see it now. What can I do about it?"

"You can tell the truth about *yourself.* Go tell him you've been wrong to be angry, and you've been selfish as you've spent money without thinking of the consequences to the family finances. Tell him you'll be more thoughtful in the future. Can you imagine how Daniel will feel when you do that, and how it will affect your relationship?"

"I agree I need to be more responsible about money, but after all the unkind things he's said to me, I don't see how I can tell him I was wrong."

"Oh, I understand that—really, I do—but I've also learned from considerable experience that being right is a pretty shallow pleasure compared with being happy. You need to decide which is more important to you, being right or having a loving marriage and being genuinely happy."

Two weeks later, Jennifer called and said, "You were right, it *is* better to be happy than right. Yesterday Daniel started to criticize me about something I bought for my daughter, and I started to argue with him about how she needs it. It was turning into the usual argument—you know, both of us being right and angry—when I remembered what you said about choosing to be happy or right. I decided I just didn't want to be angry and miserable anymore, so I said, 'Daniel, I should have talked to you about buying this before I did it. You've asked me to do that a hundred times before, and I haven't done it. This is all my fault.' When I said that, Daniel stopped talking, stopped frowning, and relaxed. Finally, he said, 'Well, I shouldn't have gotten angry. I'm sorry.' The argument was *over*. Can you believe it? And it all happened because I said I was wrong."

One obstacle to our admitting that we're wrong is our self-created Wrongness Point System. In each conflict, we unconsciously assign Wrongness Points to the person we're talking to. You might decide, for example, that your spouse is eighty points wrong in a particular situation, and you are twenty points wrong. Of course, the Ultimate Judge in the Universe for the Wrongness Point System is *you*. Comparing eighty points to twenty, your final judgment is that your spouse is wrong and you are right, and naturally you then feel justified in pointing that out to him or her.

Although that system may seem to make sense at the time, have you ever seen it work out well? When you're telling your partner that he or she is wrong, have you ever felt more loved, loving, and genuinely happy? Impossible. The only way you can feel more loved and loving is to describe *your* twenty points of wrongness—regardless of how wrong you believe your partner to be. If you do that, you'll discover enormous benefits on most occasions:

- The argument will usually be over. If you and I are arguing, and I tell you how I'm wrong, what's left for you to say? Eliminating conflict with the person you love most is far more important than being right.

- You'll create an opportunity to feel loved while you're wrong, which is the essence of Real Love.
- It's very likely your partner will then describe how he or she is wrong, and then you can get to the solution of the conflict rather quickly.

Despite the advantages of admitting that we're wrong, however, we have such a hard time doing it. We hate to look foolish. We hate that our partners might feel smugly superior to us. But being wrong only creates an opportunity for us to learn, to feel loved, and to grow. It's far better than continuing an argument with your partner and guaranteeing that you'll feel unloved and unhappy. The cost of being right far exceeds its rewards.

Quibbling

Even when we do admit we're wrong, we tend to make subtle excuses and point fingers at our spouses. When you tell the truth about yourself to your spouse, you need to be very clear about it and avoid involving him or her in any way. Imagine, for example, if Jennifer—from the preceding example—had said any of the following as she told the truth about herself to Daniel:

- "I shouldn't have bought that stuff the other day without telling you, but sometimes you do the same thing." (Daniel would have heard only that she was attacking him.)
- "I admit, I'm not perfect about helping you with the finances." (Admitting to a flaw in a vague, general way is fairly useless. We need to specifically describe what we did wrong.)
- "I know I should have told you, but you don't have to get angry about it." (Another attack directed at Daniel.)

Tell the Truth About Yourself to a Wise Man or Woman

Jennifer called me a week later and asked, "Remember how well I handled that argument with Daniel last week?"

"Sure."

"I haven't done very well since then. I don't know what happens. We start disagreeing about something, and I get angry and just keep going when I know I should be quiet. When it's all over, I'm sorry I did it—but then it's too late."

"Pretty foolish when we keep doing things that make us so unhappy, isn't it?"

"It really is, but at the time, I don't know how to do it differently."

"Do you want a suggestion?" I asked.

"Sure."

"You get angry because you still expect Daniel to love you—but he doesn't, not unconditionally, not consistently. We get angry when our expectations don't get filled, so remind yourself that he *can't* give you what you're expecting. Continuing to expect it then becomes foolish. But that doesn't mean you have to live without the love you need. You just need to get it from people who already have it. So when you feel angry, you can call someone right then and get a moment of the acceptance you need."

"Right in the middle of an argument?"

I described how she could call a friend at any time—even in the middle of an argument with Daniel—and get the love she needed, as Linda had done with her friend Elise on pages 127–128. "I know that might seem a little strange the first time you do that," I continued, "but *anything* is better than continuing a conflict that's destroying your happiness and your relationship. Do whatever it takes to eliminate the conflict in a healthy way."

Tell the Truth to Yourself

There may be occasions when you won't have the courage to tell the truth about yourself to the person you're arguing with, and you may not have access to a wise man. But at least you can admit *to yourself* what's really happening in a conflict. First, you need to admit that you're *having* a conflict, which means that you're empty and afraid and using Getting and Protecting Behaviors. It's those feelings and behaviors that characterize a conflict—without them, you can't have a conflict, only differences or disagreements, which are easy to resolve or ignore.

You're having a conflict only because you're having expectations that your partner will be different than she is. You want her to be more loving, or to agree with you, or to behave in a way more convenient for you. And your expectations arise from your emptiness and fear. When you're empty and afraid, you naturally expect your partner to fill your emptiness and to do nothing that would inconvenience or frighten you.

Most of us have been empty and afraid—and using Getting and Protecting Behaviors—for so long that we can scarcely recognize them anymore. Let's illuminate some of the signs that will reveal the truth about our feelings and behavior. When you're in a conversation or other situation,

- do you find your voice getting higher in pitch and volume?
- do you feel anxious? Are you afraid that you're not being heard or that you won't get what you're looking for?
- is your mouth getting dry? Are you shifting your feet, clenching your hands, biting your nails, folding your arms tightly?
- are you thinking about how you can *convince* your partner to agree with you?
- are you feeling pushed or cornered, like you're being forced to agree with your partner or to make a decision you don't like?
- are you really listening to what your partner is saying, or are you trying to come up with a rebuttal to what you're hearing?
- are you feeling disappointed or irritated?
- do you want to hide?
- do you feel like crying?
- do you feel ashamed?

These are all signs of emptiness and fear, and in that condition you will almost certainly use Getting and Protecting Behaviors. If you don't look for these feelings and behaviors, you often won't see them. I've seen people deny their anger, for example, while their voices were raised, their veins were bulging, and their eyes were about to pop out of their heads.

You need to recognize that when you're empty and afraid, you can't be loving. When you're angry—or lying or using other Getting and Protecting Behaviors—you can't be happy or build a loving relationship. When you remember that, it's difficult to remain angry, and you may be able to make a conscious choice to see and accept your partner.

5. Tell the Truth About Your Partner

Everyone makes lots of mistakes, so it's easy to find fault with your partner. But it's rarely productive to focus on the mistakes themselves. What you need to see is that when your partner uses Getting and Protecting Behaviors, he is drowning, and to save himself he's using the behaviors that often inconvenience and hurt other people—including you. When you understand that your husband or wife is drowning, how could you be hurt or angry? Who could be offended by the splashing of a drowning man? Or be angry at him? But we do that all the time. We're actually irritated because our spouses are empty and afraid and are reaching out to save themselves with Getting and Protecting Behaviors. In most cases you need to tell the truth about your partner's drowning only to yourself, not to him or her, as illustrated on one occasion by my wife, Donna.

One day I was busy with writing deadlines, coordinating publicity, and other things, and I approached Donna to ask her if she'd accomplished one of the tasks I'd asked her to do. After sitting back at my desk for a few moments, I realized that I had spoken to her with impatience, annoyed that she hadn't finished the job earlier in the day. I went back into the room where she was working and said, "When I asked you about that assignment, I was impatient and irritated. I shouldn't have done that."

She looked up from her work, smiled, and said, "I just assumed you were temporarily insane."

We both laughed. She saw the truth about my behavior, that I was using a Getting and Protecting Behavior because I was feeling empty and afraid. In the face of numerous pressures, I had forgotten about the Real Love in my life and in my marriage. It was enough that she saw this truth for herself. She did not have to stop me and point out what I was doing. Right while your partner is drowning, he or she will often be less than grateful to hear your description of his or her Getting and Protecting Behaviors.

Sometimes we do need to point out to our partners the mistakes they're making—including their Getting and Protecting Behaviors—and we'll discuss how to do that in Chapter Seven. It is most important, however, that we simply see the truth about their emptiness and fear, and their need to be loved.

6. Recognize What You Really Want

There once was a man who owned a beautiful apple tree. Although he enjoyed the delicious fruit he picked from it every day, he harbored a nagging wish that he could reach the apples in the top branches of the tree. One day, unable to resist his greed any longer, he cut the tree down and gorged himself on the fruit in the upper branches. Of course, he never again ate apples from the tree.

In every interaction you have with your spouse, you're making a choice: You can enjoy the love and happiness available to you, or you can insist on more than you're offered—you can cut down the tree. Paula learned this as she talked to me about her husband, Aaron.

Aaron made a mess everywhere he went in the house. You could tell where he'd been by the trail of food, plates, peelings, underwear, and auto parts he left behind him. Whenever he was finished using something, he dropped it right where he was, and Paula was becoming more irritated about it every day.

"I'm sick of living with this pig," she said.

"So you'd like him to clean up after himself, right?"

"Of course."

"Is that what you want *most*? For him to be neater?"

Paula was confused by my question. Like most of us, she spent her days distracted by one individual desire after another. She hadn't stopped to prioritize them.

"We have to be careful about what we want," I suggested, "because that will often determine what we get—and don't get. Which do you want more, a clean house or a loving and fulfilling relationship with Aaron?"

Paula naturally argued for a while about her right to have both—which is possible, by the way—but eventually she concluded that if she had to choose just one, she'd pick a loving relationship over a clean house.

"What we all want most," I said, "is to be genuinely happy, and that comes from receiving and giving Real Love. We can desire a great number of other things, but if we interfere with the process of feeling and sharing love, we can't be happy. Look at what's happening in your marriage now. You're trying to control his behavior and make him neater. You nag him and get irritated with him. Does that *ever* make you happy? Does it ever make you feel *closer* to your husband? Does it ever make *him* happy?"

"No, I guess it doesn't."

"This is pretty simple. If you can learn to unconditionally accept and love your husband, you can still figure out ways to have a clean house, but if you keep demanding that he be neater—controlling him and being angry at him—you will make it impossible to have a loving relationship with him. You have to make Real Love the first priority always."

I described to Paula how to find Real Love, and the steps to eliminate conflict, which we discussed earlier in this chapter. Paula began to see that she was cutting down the apple tree instead of nourishing it for the fruit it might bear increasingly for a lifetime.

Always ask yourself what you really want in your marriage. Do you want to win this argument, *or* do you want to establish a long-term relationship that will benefit both of you? Do you want to be victorious in this contest of wills *or* have a happy marriage? Do you want to be loving and happy, *or* right and miserable? Do you want to cut down the apple tree, *or* do you want to nourish it, prune it, and enjoy its fruit for many years? Always remember that what you really want is to have the genuine happiness that comes from Real Love. Pay attention to that goal first and always, and then work on the other things you want.

7. Remember the Law of Choice

"But I just don't understand," said Paula, "why he gets to keep doing this to me. I hate cleaning up after him. I really do have other things to do, you know, and he doesn't seem to care."

"I understand that," I responded, and I explained the Law of Choice, which we discussed in Chapter Two. "He really does get to make his own choices, even when those choices inconvenience *you*. You can't have a real relationship with someone whose choices you control. I know that sometimes you *think* you'd like that, but then he'd just become an object in your hands—an extension of you—and you'd be alone."

"So what choices do *I* get?" she wondered aloud. "Why should I be stuck with this?"

"You're not stuck," I assured her, and I explained the three choices from Chapter Two: Live with it and like it, live with it and hate it, or leave it.

She decided she didn't want to divorce him over his underwear on the floor, and she realized it was foolish to live with him and resent him forever, so she was left with "live with it and like it."

"So I'm supposed to *like* having food and dishes all over the house?"

"No, not at all. You can't sugarcoat the fact that his being messy is inconvenient and thoughtless. It really is. But you *can* learn to live with *him*—and your marriage—and like it. As you learn to feel more loved, and love him unconditionally, it simply won't matter to you as much that he leaves his things around the house. When you have twenty million dollars, losing two dollars here and there really isn't a big deal."

"Okay," she said, "I understand that I need to feel more loved and be more loving, but it sounds like I'm still stuck with these messes he makes."

"No, you just *feel* stuck. It's just that while you're insisting on one particular solution here, you're not seeing some of the other choices you could make. When he leaves stuff all over the house, what do you do?"

"I have to pick it all up."

"Who says so? Who says you *have* to pick it up? Who forces you to pick up his things?"

"Well, nobody, but if I don't pick it up, who will?"

"Probably no one, and that's one of your choices—that nobody picks up his stuff. You feel stuck only because you feel like you *have* to clean up after him. You don't. He has chosen to be messy, but you can still make any choice you want. You can choose not to clean up those messes. You didn't sign on as the house slave, did you?"

"But then the house would be a mess, and I couldn't stand that."

"Seems to me like things couldn't be much worse than they are now, with you resenting him and being unhappy. What have you got to lose by doing something different?"

Paula quit picking up Aaron's things, and after a week or so he asked where his underwear was. "I don't know," she said, "but I think I saw some under those engine parts in the dining room."

"How come they're not in my drawers, where they belong?"

"When I do the laundry, I always put your clothes away in your closet or drawers, but this week I haven't seen any of your laundry."

Aaron looked at Paula in utter confusion. "What do you mean you haven't *seen* my laundry?"

"In the past, we've talked about the fact that all laundry has to go in the laundry basket, and I haven't seen any of your laundry in the basket all week."

It is critical to understand that as Paula said this to Aaron, she wasn't angry. She wasn't punishing him or trying to control him. She was simply making a different choice. She was still choosing to help him—by doing his laundry, among other things—but she was choosing not to pick his things up all over the house.

We try to control other people only because we're afraid that otherwise we won't get anything we want. That's an illusion. You do not have the right to control the choices of your partner, but that still leaves you with many choices of your own.

8. Determine *How* You and Your Partner Can Both Get What You Want

Not long after their conversation above, Aaron called and asked if we could meet. I suggested he bring Paula with him, and we met later that week in my office.

Aaron described what had been going on in their home, and he concluded with, "The house is really turning into a pigsty, and for some reason Paula has decided that she's not going to do anything about it."

"What do you want most?" I asked.

Aaron didn't understand what I meant—most people don't think about what they want most in life—so I explained to him the genuine happiness that comes from Real Love, much as I had explained it to Paula earlier.

"So how am I supposed to feel loved when she won't even keep the house clean?" he said.

"You can feel loved and happy," I said, "*and* you can also have a clean house. You can have it all. What we're here to talk about is *how* you can have all that. A relationship is the natural result of people making independent decisions. Once people have made those independent decisions, their relationship is determined. I assume you both want to feel loved and happy, right?"

After they both nodded their heads, I explained how conflict destroys the happiness in relationships, and I discussed the principles of eliminating conflict, as written above. Pointing at each of them, I said, "Let's look at the decisions you've both made and see how they've contributed to either the creation or elimination of conflict. We're not criticizing anyone here, and we're not trying to change anybody. We're just describing what's been happening, so you can make better decisions in the future." I then discussed with them the guidelines for eliminating conflict, which we've been discussing in this chapter of the book.

- Realize that it's always about Real Love. For years Paula had nagged at Aaron to be neater, each time telling him—without realizing it—that she cared about herself more than about him. On the other hand, each time Aaron left something on the floor, that dirty plate or pair of underwear shouted to Paula, "I don't love you." Their conflict wasn't about house-keeping. It was about not feeling loved.

- Listen. Neither of them was allowing the other to be the speaker. They were both competing to get what they wanted, and as a result neither of them felt cared about.

- Never speak in anger. Because they were both lacking in Real Love—and were therefore empty and afraid—they were con-stantly using Getting and Protecting Behaviors, especially anger. This only made them both feel even more empty and afraid and more likely to use the Getting and Protecting Be-haviors that were destroying their marriage.

- Tell the truth about yourself. Neither partner had ever told the truth about his or her emptiness, fear, or Getting and Pro-tecting Behaviors, which guaranteed that they'd continue to feel and behave in those ways. Their hiding of the truth also made it impossible for them to feel unconditionally loved by each other. In their defense, they didn't *see* the truth about themselves—they were not lying intentionally.

- Tell the truth about your partner. Certainly, they were telling the truth about the other's mistakes and selfishness, but they were not telling the truth about the other's needs and fears—nor were they seeing the positive behaviors of their partner.

- Recognize what you really want. Because they'd had little or no experience with Real Love, they didn't even know that was available to them. So they settled for far less. Paula believed she just wanted a clean house and to be able to control how that was accomplished, and Aaron believed he only wanted the nagging to stop.

- Remember the Law of Choice. All their lives, Aaron and Paula had seen people try to control one another, and they had learned to do the same. They were trampling on the Law of Choice every day, and as a result each of them felt controlled, not loved.

- Determine how you and your partner can both get what you want. When neither partner understands what he or she really wants, and when they're headed in different directions while ignoring all the principles above, it's impossible for them to get anywhere together.

Now let's examine what happened when they both agreed that they'd be willing to apply the principles of eliminating conflict, and would consider making different independent decisions.

- Recognize what you really want. Aaron and Paula admitted that what they wanted most was a loving relationship, and once they'd made that overarching decision, implementing the other principles became much easier.

- Realize that it's always about Real Love. They decided to do whatever it took to create Real Love in their marriage, no longer settling for the Imitation Love of power, praise, controlling each other, and so on.

- Listen. We talked about how to listen, and they both understood how easy that becomes when we're genuinely concerned about the happiness of our partners.

- Never speak in anger. They could easily see in their own relationship the destructive power of anger, and they resolved to use the five steps to eliminate anger (pages 124–129).
- Tell the truth about yourself. When they decided they were willing to tell the truth about themselves, I suggested they start right then. Aaron said, "I've been pretty selfish about throwing my stuff around, and then I've gotten angry when you've tried to talk to me about it." Paula said, "I've wanted a loving relationship with you, but in order to get what I want—like you picking up your stuff—and to hurt you, I've used anger and sulking, but that's only hurt our marriage."
- Tell the truth about your partner. "Every time I leave something on the floor," Aaron said, "you hear me telling you I don't care about you as much as I do about my own convenience. That just makes you feel more unloved, and then you get angry just to protect yourself and to feel less helpless." Imagine how Paula felt to hear that Aaron really understood her. She said, "And then when I nag you, you just want to pull away from me even more. Why wouldn't you?"
- Remember the Law of Choice. They both recognized that the other person had the right to make his or her own choices, even when they weren't convenient. "I really do see that," said Paula, "but I know I'll forget sometimes and try to get you to do what I want."
- Determine how you and your partner can both get what you want. With these two partners willing to take all the above steps toward eliminating conflict, the tension between them virtually vanished. In the absence of emptiness and fear, they were able to see rather easily how they could get the housework done. Aaron agreed to pick up after himself, and he admitted that he'd have a hard time with that in the beginning—he'd just never done it. Paula offered to pick up things here and there when he forgot—not because she *had* to but because she loved him—and he agreed that he'd listen to

her when she told him that she was having to pick up his things more than occasionally. They also worked out a way to involve the kids much more in the housekeeping—so the kids could learn responsibility, and so the parents wouldn't have so much to do around the house.

The course of action Paula and Aaron worked out was just one of many possible solutions to their problem. If Aaron had found picking up his own messes particularly distasteful—for whatever reasons—Paula could have agreed to do that for him, while Aaron helped by running errands, taking the children to activities, and so on.

Conflict is a natural condition. When we don't have enough of the Real Love we need more than anything else, we're empty, and then it's natural that we become demanding toward the people we think should make us feel better by doing what we want. If they don't give us what we want, we quickly find fault with them and conclude they don't care about us. From the time we were children we were taught to identify and focus on the mistakes of others—after all, that was what people did with us. Teachers pointed out our errors on tests and essays. Parents pointed out when we *didn't* do what they wanted. In an atmosphere of emptiness and fault-finding, reaching agreements is very difficult.

When people are not empty and afraid, however, and when they're not using Getting and Protecting Behaviors, they don't have a need to find fault with others, and most issues are then fairly easy to work out. After their discussion, Paula didn't get every bit of help from Aaron that she once would have demanded, and Aaron ended up doing more work than he once had planned, but despite not getting everything they wanted, their agreement about the division of labor around the house became relatively easy when they followed the principles we've discussed, and when they tried to unconditionally care about each other's happiness. We'll talk much more about making requests and agreements in Chapter Six.

Aaron and Paula found it useful for me to be there and help them with their realizations and decisions, but often people can do all that for themselves. Don't even think, however, about talking to your spouse as Aaron and Paula did with each other if you don't feel some measure of Real Love yourself. If you try to have such a discussion when you're empty and afraid, the conversation *will* go badly.

What if your partner doesn't *want* to talk about a particular issue that's troubling you? Recognize that he or she gets to make that choice. If your spouse isn't ready to talk, it would be foolish to push her. Take the steps to find Real Love for yourself, and as you share that with your partner, he or she will feel accepted and safe. In the absence of emptiness and fear, people are much more likely to be able to listen to you talk about any subject. When your spouse feels accepted, she can also begin to communicate to you how she really feels and what she really thinks instead of saying only what would make her feel right, safe, or accepted.

9. Refuse to Be in Conflict

The best way to respond to the Getting and Protecting Behaviors of your partner is to be unconditionally loving and to use the principles we've discussed above. On some occasions, however, you may not feel loved and loving enough to take the steps that usually eliminate a conflict. When you are not properly prepared—when you don't feel loved and loving—you will bring Getting and Protecting Behaviors to an interaction, and with those you can only wound your relationship. On other occasions, you might feel loving, but you sense that your partner is too frightened and defensive to feel loved—no matter what you do.

In either of those situations, conflict would be inevitable, but you can make a simple choice that you will not participate in the conflict. Conflict is a choice. If you are incapable of loving, or your partner is incapable of receiving your love, do not continue the interaction. You can't determine the behavior of your spouse, but he can't have a conflict without your participation. If you refuse to use Getting and Protecting Behaviors, your partner can still choose to be angry or otherwise manipulative, but the conflict will die for a lack of fuel from you.

Occasionally, your spouse might continue to attack you even though you refuse to participate in the conflict. Do not give in to your natural tendency to defend yourself. Make a conscious decision to emotionally—and sometimes physically—remove yourself from the situation. Although this appears to be the Protecting Behavior of running, it's actually quite different. Running is motivated by fear, is designed to protect yourself, and is usually a knee-jerk response. When you strategically withdraw from a conflict, by contrast, you're making a deliberate choice to avoid injury to your partner, yourself, and your relationship.

What exactly can you say when you want to withdraw? Following are a few examples:

1. "My mistake." Admit that you're wrong. When our partners are angry and criticizing us, we have a natural tendency to defend ourselves. As soon as you demonstrate an insistence on being right, your partner will sense that you're also saying that he or she is *wrong*. People do not like to hear that they're wrong—because then they feel powerless and less lovable—so they naturally defend themselves from that accusation, direct or implied. You can defuse all that if you simply say, "My mistake." But what if you're certain you're right? Get over it. You can always find something you're wrong about. For example:

   - If you were defending your position and not genuinely listening to your partner, you were wrong.
   - If you were irritated, you were wrong.

- If you didn't notice that your partner was empty and afraid—and therefore unable to discuss the issue you were eager to pursue—you were wrong.

If you have a need to be right—and therefore resist admitting your mistakes—you will spark and perpetuate conflicts everywhere you go.

2. "I'm not responding well to you right now, and that's not your fault. Let me collect my thoughts here and come up with a way to address what you're saying in a better way."
3. "I'm just not loving enough to continue this conversation. Can I come back to you in a few hours [or minutes, or the next day] and talk some more?"

Notice that in the above examples, you are taking complete responsibility for withdrawing from the conflict. You must avoid any hint of blaming your partner for your withdrawal, even though it may seem quite justified. It can be very tempting to say, "I just can't talk to you when you're like this," but now you're not simply withdrawing from a conflict; you're attacking your partner.

You'd think that our partners would be pleased on the occasions we withdraw from a conflict, thereby putting out the fire, but they often resist our withdrawal because they have a lot to gain from the conflict. With their Getting and Protecting Behaviors they seek safety, power, and the sense of worth that comes from being right. When we decide not to participate in a conflict, we're taking from them the morsels of the Imitation Love they want, and they often don't like that. They might insist on continuing the conflict that feeds their need for a sense of power. Your partner might call you names or otherwise become abusive. You might have to repeat the above responses more than once. Sometimes the best response is to say nothing at all. That might be uncomfortable at first, but eventually, if you refuse to be involved in the conflict, your partner will run out of steam. You might even have to leave the room, or the house.

Caught in the Middle

Even before Charles married Sarah, he could see that her parents were going to be a problem. They had opinions about *everything:* where Charles and Sarah should live, when they should have a baby, what Charles should do with his career, and so on. The advice never stopped, and eventually Charles began to avoid them. He made excuses—busy with work, tired, not feeling well—for not attending birthday dinners, Sunday gatherings, and other family events. Sarah was getting tired of her family pressuring her about seeing them more often, and one day she talked to me about it. Notice that Sarah and I are illustrating all nine principles of eliminating conflict.

"This is really getting to be a problem," she said. "He hates my family and doesn't want to be around them. That puts me in a terrible spot, because I still want to visit them sometimes, but I don't want to go without him. My family is always inviting us somewhere, and when I try to talk him into going, he gets mad about it. He says I don't understand how awful it is for him to be around them. They only live a couple of hours away, but I never get to see them now, and I'm tired of bringing it up to him—it just causes fights—and I'm tired of defending him to my family. They're really starting to criticize him now. I feel like I'm in the middle and can't do anything right."

"You only feel like you're in the middle," I said, "because you *allow* yourself to be there. You don't have to get involved in this conflict at all."

"But my family—"

"You're getting confused by all the details. What does your family really want?"

"They want us to visit more often, but—"

"They want what we all want. They want to feel accepted and loved by you and Charles. You can't control whether Charles accepts them, so let that go. Let's talk about what you *can* do to help both your family and Charles feel accepted. First, your family. The next time they invite you to do something with them, accept their offer and tell them you're looking forward to it. Tell Charles you're going, and add that he can go if he wants. If he chooses to stay home, and if they press you about why he's not coming, just tell them he's staying home. You're not in the middle of this. You don't have to justify his choices to them."

"I don't think Charles is going to like this," she said.

"He's made *his* choice not to spend time with them, and he has the right to make that choice. Now you can choose to do what *you* want. Remember that what Charles wants most is Real Love. I'm guessing that what's hardest on him in this situation is not your family, but you. When your family complains about him, what do you do? You try to get him to change his mind and spend time with them, which means you're not really listening to him or accepting him."

"I guess I'm not," she said, "and sometimes I get irritated at him when we're talking about this."

"So really listen to him and tell him you understand why he wouldn't want to visit your family. Tell him you're never going to persuade him to visit them again, and tell him the truth about yourself—that you haven't been very accepting of him about his choice. Then say, 'Charles, I really love you—more than anybody. I don't want you to feel uncomfortable visiting my family, and if you don't want to spend time with them, I accept that completely. But *I* want to see them sometimes, so how can we work it out so we both get what we want here?' If he can't think of anything, you can offer several options:

- You can visit them without him from time to time, with no pressure on him to go with you.
- He could go with you occasionally, and if it would help him feel more comfortable, you could agree to leave whenever he wants, without arguing or delay.

• You could invite your family over to your house on occasion, at times when Charles won't be there."

"When you push Charles about your family," I continued, "he feels the same kind of criticism from you that he hates to get from your family. No wonder he doesn't want to go over there. If he senses that *you* accept him, he just might be willing to spend some time with them, and if not, at least he probably won't mind if you go alone. Through all of this, remember that you only feel pressured because of your own need to please everybody. When you see that you're not in charge of making everybody happy, you won't feel like you're in the middle."

Preventing Conflict

Sarah took the steps to find and share Real Love—with her husband and with others—and one day she called me. "It's taken time and effort," she said, "but I can't begin to tell you how different our lives are. Remember how we used to argue about my parents? Now we never argue about that. In fact, we almost never argue about anything. Feeling loved makes a big difference."

When two people feel unconditionally loved and loving, they have the greatest treasure on earth, and with that treasure they have no need to defend themselves or manipulate other people. They have no *reason* ever to participate in a conflict. The best way to deal with conflict is to prevent it entirely. Keep telling the truth about yourself, find the Real Love you need, and enjoy the miracle of conflict disappearing from your life.

Avoid Creating Conflict

I have watched hundreds of couples generate conflicts over matters of no importance. For example, one spouse will say to the other, "Why are you turning here? It's faster if you go down Westminster Highway." Or, "Are you going to wear that?" Your spouse will often do things differently than you do—driving, cleaning, record keeping, talking to the kids, and so on. Occasionally, you *might* offer suggestions about how he or she could do something different to achieve greater ease, efficiency, or safety, but most of the time you need to ask yourself the following questions before you speak:

- Is this any of my business? Every day most of us make comments to other people about things that have nothing whatever to do with us. We offer our opinions about the clothes they wear, what they eat, the way they style their hair, and so on. When you do that with your husband, you're telling him that how he chooses to do things—who he *is*, actually—is unacceptable to you, and he hears that message loudly. When that is the consequence, is it really worth making a comment about something that doesn't directly affect you or hurt someone else?

- Does this really *matter*? Even when your wife's behavior does affect you, on some occasions it is still foolish to speak up, because the issue at hand simply isn't important. Most couples argue over meaningless things. Let's say your wife leaves the cap off the toothpaste, for example, which leaves you with that nasty, dried glob the next time *you* use it. That does affect you, but is it really worth pointing out over and over? Would it not be much wiser to simply get your own tube, and let her do whatever she wants with hers? Is it really worth having an argument over fifty cents of wasted toothpaste a year? As another example, you might be inclined to offer a faster route to your destination when your husband is driving the car, but if he doesn't like that, does it really matter that your way might save you sixty seconds of travel time? Is sixty seconds worth the conflict you'll introduce into your relationship?

- Am I being unconditionally loving? Your husband's greatest need is to feel unconditionally loved—especially by you— and filling that need is far more important than any piece of advice you'll ever give him. You might have a much better way for him to do something, and you might have a legitimate request to make of him, but none of that will matter if you offer your advice or ask your question with a tone of accusation or impatience. If you're feeling disappointed or angry, you can only hurt your marriage. Do you really want to do that?

One way to communicate a lack of Real Love is to show a lack of trust for your husband. If he gets home late from work for example, do you feel compelled to ask him why he's late? I'll give you a hint: If he wants to tell you why he's late, he will. If you push him about it, the results will *rarely* be positive, as you've probably noticed. Does that mean you can never ask him about something he's done? Of course not. If he's late consistently, you might ask him—at a time other than right when he's walking in the door late—if there's a reason he's been late a lot. And you must ask him with no degree of impatience whatever.

When you do ask about his being late, it will be much better received if you ask out of a genuine concern for *him* rather than for yourself. You might say, for example, "It seems like you've had a lot of late days lately. Is everything all right? Anything you want to talk about?"

· Is she capable of hearing what I'm about to say? Even when it affects you, and it matters, and you're being loving, it is foolish to speak when you know your wife can't hear you. If she's obviously angry when she walks in the door, do you really think she's going to hear anything you have to say? Why bother to say anything you know will be perceived by her as threatening? Even if you're loving, she'll take it as an attack, and you'll instantly be in the middle of one of those awful arguments.

If you'll follow these guidelines, your arguments will decrease dramatically, and you'll begin to create the kind of loving and fulfilling marriage you've always wanted.

You can also help to avoid conflict by not asking for someone's opinion when you don't really want it. Sarah, for example, often asked Charles what he thought about her clothing, the color of paint she'd picked out for a room, and so on. But she'd *already made up her mind* and wasn't really looking for his opinion, only confirmation that she'd bought or done the right thing. Then when Charles offered a different view from her own, she argued with him to prove that her choice was best. She should have said, "I've made up my mind here and just want you to tell me I was brilliant." If you're not looking for honest feedback, don't ask for it.

Ask a Question and Describe Your Feelings, Don't Make an Accusation or Demand

Sarah told me that when she tried to talk to Charles, he often kept reading the newspaper or a magazine, and she added, "I hate that. It's really rude. But when I tell him I don't like it, he just gets defensive and argues with me."

"If you *hate* it," I said, "it's a virtual certainty that when you talk to him about it, he can feel your anger, and then he reacts to *that* instead of addressing what you're saying. Even if you don't talk to him about it in anger, though, he'll likely become defensive, because when you tell him what you don't like, he'll feel obligated to change himself to please you. He feels accused and controlled."

"So how can I get him to stop reading when I'm talking to him?"

"Don't try to *get* him to do anything, but you can try to help him see what he's communicating with his behavior, and you can tell him how you feel about it. For example, you could say, 'Charles, I'm not trying to get you to change what you do. I *am* trying to talk about something that I think is interfering with both of us feeling more loved and happy. Would you be willing to talk with me about that?' It's almost a guarantee that he'll be willing to stop what he's doing at that point and talk to you."

"What if he doesn't?" asked Sarah.

"If he keeps reading, you can ask him when would be a good

time for him to talk with you later. When you finally talk, tell him that when he's reading, you feel like he's saying, 'I don't care about you or what you're saying.' Emphasize that you're not trying to get him to change, just describing how you feel when he does that. Then ask some questions to help you understand what to do when he's reading. You could, for example, ask him any of the following questions:

- "When you're reading, would you prefer that I not talk to you at all?"
- "Sometimes I don't need you to listen as completely as at other times. When I really need you to pay attention, can I say to you, 'Charles, I really need you to hear this part. Can you put the paper down for a moment while I tell you this?'"
- "Would it be better for you if we set aside a time—after work or at bedtime—when we can talk without interruptions for fifteen minutes?"

Where possible, don't tell you're partner what he or she is doing wrong. Describe how you feel about it, and ask questions to arrive at a solution that will make both of you happy.

Offer Unsolicited Love

In most cases you and your spouse will have conflicts only when you don't feel loved, when you feel empty and afraid. Conflicts can best be prevented, therefore, if both of you will share Real Love with each other as often as possible. You could share, for example, the loving acts discussed in Chapter Three.

On the occasions when your partner is already upset, however, extending yourself toward him or her can be difficult, so we need to discuss how to be loving in those circumstances.

Imagine that your husband is unusually quiet, or gives other evidence that he's upset. He's telling you that he's empty, and in that condition, many seemingly innocent things you do may become threatening and irritating to him. You can often avoid a future conflict by proactively addressing his feelings in the following ways:

- Ask general questions.
- Ask specific questions.
- Make specific offers.
- Leave him alone.

Ask General Questions

You might say, "You look unhappy. Is something wrong?" This will give him an opportunity to communicate what's bothering him. Remember, however, that when he's upset—when he's empty and afraid—he's also likely to protect himself, with lying, attacking, or withdrawing. In his fear, he may not be able to answer your question.

It is critical to observe the tone of voice you use—and other nonverbal forms of communication—when you speak to him. If you're the least bit impatient when you say, "What's wrong?" he will hear that as an accusation, as though you had said, "What's wrong with *you*—again." Of course, that *is* what you're saying, and then he'll feel defensive. He'll also feel responsible for making you feel less upset, which will create an emotional burden for him that he won't like.

Ask Specific Questions

If your partner is unable to answer your general questions, be more specific. You could ask, "Did something happen at work today?" Or, "Is there something I've done? If so, I really would like to hear about it." Do not ask these specific questions to pry but only to help your partner share his burden with you, to create an opportunity for him to feel loved by you.

Make Specific Offers

Again, when people are upset, they're likely to protect themselves, so your partner may be too occupied with protecting himself to be able to answer your questions. In that case, you can often help by simply offering a gift, which is usually less threatening than a question. You could say, "Can I get you a glass of water? Or something else to drink?" Or you could sit next to him while he's sulking on the couch, put your hand on his knee, and say, "I'll just sit here with you for a few minutes, but if you don't want me to, I'll leave."

If you make such offers without accusation or expectation of a positive response, it's likely that your partner will feel your love, and that can make a big difference.

Leave Him Alone

If he is sufficiently irritated, he will only respond with Protecting Behaviors when you speak to him, no matter how lovingly. Sometimes it's best just to leave him alone, but only until the fires cool and you can ask the questions and make the offers discussed above. Allowing him to cool off is different from avoiding him because you're not willing to deal with his difficult behavior. The latter approach is simply running on your part.

Just Answer the Question

One day Charles came into the house in a foul mood and said to Sarah, "Why are my tools scattered all over the driveway?"

Sarah was offended, and she responded by saying, "How should I know? They're not my tools. I've been working all day, too, and you come home expecting me to know what's happening with your tools?" That started an argument about a number of issues, and they both avoided each other all evening.

The next day, Sarah called me for some advice about how she could have handled the situation better, and I said, "Next time, just answer his question." Instead of answering his question, Sarah had defended herself from his attack by launching one of her own, and that never leads to a productive conversation.

I described to Sarah how she might have responded to Charles, and one week later, he brought up the same subject, saying, "My tools are in the driveway again. What's going on?"

On this occasion, however, Sarah remembered to answer his question instead of responding to his attack. "I don't know," she said without a trace of irritation. "I noticed them out there earlier, but I didn't ask anyone about it, because I was busy with other things." She also remembered that Charles could be angry only if he were drowning, so she went a step further to help him out of the water. "Yesterday I heard Billy say something about his bike being broken, so he might have used your tools to fix his bike. Ten-year-olds aren't very good at putting things back. Relax and have a bite to eat with me. Then you can ask him about the tools. Or, if you'd like, I'll ask him for you."

When your spouse approaches you with anger, he or she is using that Getting and Protecting Behavior only because he's empty. He's telling you he doesn't feel loved and is incapable of being loving in that moment. If you respond with your own Getting and Protecting Behaviors, you'll add to his feelings of being unloved, and he'll respond with even more of the same behaviors. When your spouse asks a question or makes an accusation in anger, simply respond to the *content*, rather than defending yourself from the attack.

Resolving the "Little" Conflicts

Dwayne and Robin didn't argue often, but when they did, it was like a nuclear war. They each saved up dozens of offenses to bash the other with, and the damage they each inflicted was considerable. I suggested to Robin that by the time they got into a major conflict, it was often too late to stop it, so it might be wise to start resolving the conflicts while they were little.

Soon after that, Dwayne got home from work an hour late, and Robin was angry that she hadn't known where he was. She began to beat him with accounts of the many times he'd done this before, but then she stopped and realized that she was only perpetuating the arguments they always had. "Wait a minute," she said. "Forget the past. I don't want to beat you about that anymore. I just want to tell you that when you get home late, and you don't tell me where you are, I feel like you don't care about me. I feel alone and afraid. You don't have to stop it, and you're not to blame for my being angry. I just need to tell you what I'm thinking and feeling when you do this. If I were more loving, it wouldn't bother me at all."

"When I'm late," Dwayne said, "like when I'm running an errand or something, I really don't stop to think about how it would affect you. I need to do better."

They both had an accepting, loving conversation after that. When a hundred "little" disappointments and conflicts go unresolved, they *become* a big deal. We use these little conflicts to justify our judgments that something serious is wrong, and to justify our overblown reactions. When you feel disappointment and irritation at your spouse, you need to resolve that conflict, sometimes with your partner and sometimes just by telling the truth about your feelings to a wise man or woman.

Little conflicts won't build into big ones if you and your spouse will make an unshakeable commitment to spend at least fifteen minutes each day talking about how you felt and what you did that day. Share your disappointments, failures, successes, and what you learned. Couples who do this consistently will eventually eliminate serious conflicts in their marriage. Going on a date once a week, and talking about how you feel, will also be an enormous asset.

Getting Feedback

Don't wait for a full-blown conflict to develop. When you see that your spouse is beginning to react badly to something you're saying, simply ask about it. You could say, for example, "It looks like you're feeling disappointed/irritated/confused about what I'm saying. Is there a way I could have said this better, so you would feel less threatened/annoyed by it?"

Making the Primary Decision First and Once

A couple, Jack and Sandra, came to see me, and it soon became obvious that they lived in a virtually continuous state of conflict over a wide variety of issues. Following is a small sampling of their disputes:

- Jack often left the house for hours at a time, without telling Sandra where he was going.
- Sandra recently loaned her brother some money, over Jack's vehement objections.
- They disagreed about how much allowance the children should be given.
- Jack's mother often said unkind things to and about Sandra, and Sandra was furious that Jack usually defended his mother.
- Sandra's cat sometimes urinated in Jack's study, and she felt hurt when Jack took his rage out on her.

On a number of occasions they had seen counselors and managed to painfully work out compromises for a number of similar issues, but whatever problems they "solved" were immediately replaced by others. The issues seemed to multiply.

After maybe fifteen minutes in our first meeting, I asked them, "Would you two like to have a deliriously happy marriage, or would you prefer to argue with each other forever?"

It was apparent from their reaction that they thought I was asking a trick question, but I repeated it, and eventually they did answer that they both wanted a happy marriage.

I knew that Jack owned and successfully operated his own business, so I asked him, "What is the mission statement of your business?"

"To provide a high-quality product to my customers," he said, "and to give them the kind of service that will make them want to return to our business again and again."

"Are those just words, or do you actually run your business by that goal?"

"I mean it," he said, "and so do my employees."

"But what if it's Tuesday?" I asked.

"What do you mean?"

"When Tuesdays arrive, do you have to come up with a different mission statement, or is it constant throughout the week?"

Jack thought my question odd, but he answered, "It's the same every day of the week, and every week of the year."

"But what if you have a difficult customer? Then do you change the mission statement?"

"No," he said. "In fact, that's when our mission statement is most important."

"What about when you have an employee who doesn't *feel* like giving great service. Then do you change it?"

"Of course not."

"So you created your mission statement *once,* and it became a foundation to guide you through all the many other decisions you've had to make. Is that right?"

"Exactly."

"Why is it that you don't do the same with your marriage?"

"I don't understand."

"What is the mission statement—the guiding foundation—of your marriage?"

"I guess I'd never thought about it," he said.

"It would have to include loving her, wouldn't you think?"

"Of course."

"And there are different levels of love. If Sandra knew that you loved her roughly the same as you do, say, the mailman, do you think that would be enough?"

"Probably not."

"If Sandra doesn't know that she is the most important person in the world to you—and if she doesn't know that your marriage is the most important relationship you have—what are the odds that you will achieve that deliriously happy marriage you just told me you wanted?"

"Probably not good."

"So that might be at least part of a good mission statement for your marriage, don't you think? That Sandra will be the most important person in your life, and your marriage will be the most important relationship?"

"Yes, I suppose it would."

"So far," I said, "you have demonstrated in hundreds of ways with your behavior that you are not yet willing to make that statement or set those goals. You *say* she's important to you, but over and over, as new circumstances come up, you demonstrate that you have little or no real commitment to her."

Jack was really listening now, so I continued. "You've acknowledged that your marriage can't be what you want unless you place Sandra and your marriage first. But then you're distracted by every little thing that comes along. As you said, you don't change your business mission statement just because it's Tuesday, or because other circumstance changes. Make the same kind of commitment to Sandra and your marriage. Make that decision *first* and *once*. If you'll do that, you'll create a foundation upon which to make all other decisions."

I then had a similar discussion with Sandra, and they both finally made the Primary Decision in their marriage, which for any happy couple is to place their spouse and marriage first in their priorities. Parenthetically, I am not telling anyone to change the place that God may have in their priorities—only to make his or her spouse and marriage first among *human* relationships.

After Jack and Sandra made their Primary Decision, they both found it much simpler to address the issues that had previously seemed unbearably complicated and painful:

- Jack often left the house for hours at a time, without telling Sandra where he was going. Jack realized that if Sandra were truly the first priority to him, and if he were really trying to demonstrate a concern for her happiness, he would never go anywhere without telling her. At first he argued that he didn't like feeling obligated to "report" to her, but that objection disappeared when he remembered his higher goal of making her and his marriage first in his life. He understood that he

164 · *Real Love in Marriage*

wouldn't be reporting or asking permission, only sharing his life with his partner—and how could that not be a good thing?

- Sandra recently loaned her brother some money, over Jack's vehement objections. Sandra saw when she made a decision about money without talking to her husband, she was clearly telling him that he was not the first priority in her life. She decided to make the Primary Decision first, after which it was obvious that she never again wanted to make a decision about money that could interfere with the happiness in her marriage.

- They disagreed about how much allowance the children should be given. They realized that no individual task or issue was worth interfering with the harmony in their marriage. So they resolved to tell the children that until both Jack and Sandra had worked out this issue and were in complete harmony, there would be no discussions with the children about allowances.

- Jack's mother often said unkind things to and about Sandra, and Sandra was furious that Jack usually defended his mother. Jack told Sandra that she was the most important person in his life—more important than his mother—and he apologized for defending his mother and for not really listening to Sandra. Immediately, Sandra felt more loved, and the tension over that issue disappeared.

- Sandra's cat sometimes urinated in Jack's study, and she felt hurt when he took his rage out on her. Whereas Sandra had previously defended the cat, she now saw that she was violating the Primary Decision and told Jack that she would do whatever it took to resolve this issue in a way that would demonstrate her commitment to him. The details of the solution were actually unimportant.

As Jack and Sandra made the Primary Decision—to put each other first—all the other decisions became relatively simple and easy. I recommend the same for you. Don't keep making difficult decisions over and over. It's unnecessarily confusing and exhausting. Make the important decision first, and make it *one* time. You'll be glad you did.

In the most important relationship in your life, how big a wedge are you willing to allow to grow between you and your partner? Countless millions of us have learned that a wedge of any size in a marriage tends to grow into a larger wedge, and in no time at all the division is painful and often seemingly irreparable. You don't want anything to ever get between you and your spouse—not money, not the children, not in-laws, not work, not anything—and you will accomplish that goal if you will make the decision that your spouse and your marriage are first in your life.

Resolving Differences

Without conflict—without emptiness, fear, and Getting and Protecting Behaviors—resolving differences is relatively easy. We'll talk more about this in Chapters Six and Seven.

Mental Illness

Imagine that you have a serious illness and a high fever. In that condition, the chemistry of your brain is dramatically altered, which will cause you to say and do things differently from how you normally would. You'll be confused, for example, and unlikely to show any concern for the people around you. You might even say unkind things to them. You won't *intentionally* be unloving, but with a high fever, you simply won't be able to make loving choices.

There are many clinical disorders—depression, for example, which afflicts as many as 19 million Americans—that alter the chemistry of the brain and therefore make it very hard for those who are affected to behave in healthy ways. If you are consistently taking the steps of finding and sharing Real Love but still experience chronic symptoms of depression—depressed mood, loss of interest in activities, sleep problems, difficulty concentrating, agitation, restlessness—it might be advisable for you to seek the advice of a physician. Of course, the same observations apply to your spouse. If he or she continues to experience the symptoms of depression after consistent efforts to find and share Real Love, seek medical help.

We're not looking here to use depression or any other mental illness as an excuse for our behavior. We're only looking for explanations and treatment. An insufficient supply of Real Love will often cause or worsen depression. On the other hand, genetically determined clinical depression can significantly worsen feelings of being unloved and can make it impossible for people to feel the love they're offered. Each condition—depression and a lack of Real Love—contributes to the other.

In individual cases it can be difficult to determine whether people need medical assistance in addition to Real Love. With most people I first recommend taking the steps to find Real Love, and if that is ineffective after they've really done all they can—telling the truth about themselves regularly to those who can love them—I suggest they see a physician.

Some people stubbornly resist the idea that they might need medical assistance for their problems. They're frightened of the social and personal stigma still attached to any form of mental illness. They "hate to take a pill" or want to just "handle" their own problems. These are not productive attitudes. Just as we don't try to handle diabetes or a heart attack without medical help, sometimes we can't handle alterations in our brain chemistry without help. When that help is available, resisting it can lead to a great deal of unnecessary suffering.

Premenstrual Syndrome (PMS)

In the two to five days prior to menstruation, more than a third of women experience significant physical and emotional symptoms, among which are irritability, anxiety, anger, tension, panic attacks, aggression, mood swings, depression, tearfulness, poor concentration, fear of not being understood, and mental confusion. Making loving judgments and decisions is hard enough without the complicating burdens and distractions of PMS. When you're premenstrual, you'll be tempted during difficult interactions with your husband and others to judge that things are worse than they are. For that reason, during those days it is not wise to make major judgments or decisions about your life or your marriage.

An understanding of PMS is intended neither to give women an excuse for their behavior nor to give men an opportunity to label or attack their wives. PMS is just a common additional stress in many marriages that needs to be identified and discussed by both partners. The proper goal of understanding this condition is to enable both partners to respond more effectively. Develop a language between the two of you for PMS. You might tell your husband, for example, that you're having a "bad day" or "difficult time," or you're just "not yourself." Or "It's PMS again." Men, go out of your way to be especially accepting and kind to your wives—but not condescending.

Other Contributors to Conflict

I have mentioned mental illness and premenstrual syndrome as just two of the more common examples of factors that can contribute to conflict in a marriage or any other relationship. There are many other potential contributors, and they all have their effect as they detract from the Real Love available to the individuals involved in the relationship.

Consider that in any given moment we have only a finite supply of Real Love. When that supply is great—when we have twenty million dollars (pages 36–38)—we can tolerate many inconveniences and even unkindnesses from other people, including from our spouses. When we're down to our last two dollars, however, the slightest offense is then enough to deprive us of happiness.

As you're trying to build up your supply of Real Love, you'll find that many things can "steal" that supply from you:

- Being physically tired
- Being physically ill: a cold, diabetes, heart disease, arthritis—anything
- Several inconveniences in a row
- A bad day or long day at work
- A crying child
- A death in the family

Under the best of conditions you might have enough Real Love in your life to respond in a loving way to any number of stressful situations, but each of the factors listed above has the effect of draining away some of your Real Love. This depletion can sometimes happen gradually and subtly, such that we're not even aware that anything is wrong until we're completely drained and unable to respond in a productive way to any kind of stress.

You can gain great power from an understanding of Real Love as a finite quantity that can be depleted. With that understanding,

- you won't be as mystified or frustrated by your natural fluctuations in the capacity to respond lovingly to people. We all have "good days" and "bad days," and many of us have a tendency to blame ourselves for those shifts from one condition to the other. On many occasions we're just experiencing the natural effects of Real Love being depleted by the external factors we've discussed.
- you'll wisely avoid some situations where you're virtually assured of responding poorly. If you're tired and sick, for example, you'll recognize the draining effects of those conditions and will avoid having conversations with your spouse about subjects that have consistently proven difficult in the past.
- you'll wisely avoid some situations where your spouse is virtually assured of responding poorly. If your spouse has a cold and has just finished a long day at work, for example, you'll

know that his or her reserves of Real Love are probably low, and you'll not choose that time to discuss subjects that have consistently proven difficult in the past.

- you can be much more compassionate toward the fluctuations in your spouse's ability to behave in loving ways toward you. When he or she is unusually critical or short-tempered, for example, you can remember that there are very likely other factors involved—like the ones listed above—and that his or her behavior isn't just about you.

Exercises

Exercise One

1. Write down the following nine principles we've discussed that will eliminate conflict from your life. Allow for several lines of writing between each one:

   - Realize that it's always about Real Love.
   - Listen (the Four Rules of Seeing).
   - Never speak in anger.
   - Tell the truth about yourself.
   - Tell the truth about your partner.
   - Recognize what you really want.
   - Remember the Law of Choice.
   - Determine *how* you and your partner can get what you want.
   - Refuse to be in conflict.

2. Choose a conflict you regularly experience with your spouse—about sex, money, housekeeping, the children— and write that at the top of the page.

3. With rigorous honesty, after each of the above principles write how you are *not* following that principle, and how that is affecting your relationship.

4. Share your list and comments with a friend you think will be capable of accepting and loving you with your flaws.

🍂

Exercise Two

1. Write the nine principles again, and this time write beside each one what you can do to implement that principle the next time you have a conflict over the issue you chose in Exercise One.

2. Share your list and comments with a loving friend and get his or her feedback about what you've proposed.

3. Take the list with you and say to your spouse, "I'd like to talk to you about [the issue that has resulted in conflict in the past]. I haven't done a good job of communicating with you about this in the past, and I'd like to try to do it differently." Then implement the nine principles as you talk and listen. If necessary, keep referring to the list you created.

5

❧

The Unique Union

How Marriage Is Different from Other Relationships

With your spouse you have experienced some of the happiest moments of your life. On the other hand, with that same person you have probably experienced some of your worst disappointments and moments of anguish.

Despite the enormous potential for happiness in marriage—precisely why we got married in the first place—most of us are confused about what marriage is and how to make it succeed, as demonstrated by the fact that 50–60 percent of us will end our marriages in divorce. The great majority of those marriages that survive, moreover, simply endure instead of providing both partners the kind of joy and fulfillment they really want. As we learn more about what marriage really is and can be, we'll become much better prepared to eliminate the disappointment and irritation, and to find instead the rich rewards that are unique to marriage.

The Expectations of Marriage: Natural but Deadly

Some of the reasons for disappointment and frustration in marriage are illustrated as Marcia talks to me about her husband, Shawn.

"I just don't get it," she says. "When we first got married, you couldn't pry us apart. We did everything together. Now he hardly wants to do anything with me. He just watches television by himself, and when I suggest that we go out and do something, he's always too tired. This is not how I thought marriage would turn out."

"You seem irritated."

"Of course I am. Who wouldn't be?"

"*I* don't spend much time with you—certainly less than Shawn does—and I never go out with you. Why aren't you irritated with *me*?"

"Oh, come on. That's different. You're not my husband."

Marcia was more angry at Shawn than at me because she had much greater *expectations* of him. We get disappointed and angry only when people don't behave as we expect. If you expect nothing at all from someone, his or her behavior simply can't be a source of disappointment to you. We tend to experience greater anger with our spouses than with others because the expectations we have of our spouses are very high. Let's examine why that is.

Most of us received very little Real Love in childhood and adolescence. To eliminate our emptiness and fear, we constantly looked for people who would give us the Imitation Love that temporarily made us feel better. We fell in love with our spouses because they gave us a sufficient supply of Imitation Love, and we married them in the hope that they would continue to give us the satisfaction we thought was genuine happiness.

When two people get married, they exchange promises that boil down to this: "I will always love you more than I love anyone else." That's what each partner *says,* but as I said in Chapter Two, each person *hears* the other say much more:

> "I promise to make you happy—always. I will heal your past wounds and satisfy your present needs and expectations— even when you don't express them. I will lift you up when you're discouraged. I will accept and love you no matter what mistakes you make. I give to you all that I have or ever will have. And I will never leave you."

Neither partner is consciously aware of making these many promises, but each partner still hears them and desperately insists they be fulfilled. When we feel empty and unloved, we understandably expect the people around us—especially those who claim to love us—to give us what we want and make us feel better. In the case of a spouse, where we've exchanged solemn promises of love, we feel especially justified in having those expectations.

In most marriages, however, neither partner has the Real Love his or her partner needs, so they both struggle constantly with the impossible task of trying to make the other happy. Because our principal motivation for getting married is our powerful expectation that our partners will love us and make us happy, our disappointment and anger are then colossal when we don't achieve those goals.

When our partners don't fulfill our expectations, we respond by insisting even more urgently, which begins a pattern of mutual manipulation or outright resistance but certainly doesn't produce the Real Love we want. Although our attitude is understandable, we often use our marriage vows as a whip to force our spouses to give us what we want, an approach that can only be frustrating and cause great unhappiness. Even in marriage, expectations are usually selfish, because the Law of Choice still applies.

The Real Purpose of Marriage

So what *is* marriage? *Marriage is a commitment* we make to stay with our partners while *we learn* to unconditionally love them. It's an agreement to stay in a relationship for a lifetime, even when our partners are not loving. It's also a commitment to limit the sharing of some things (living together, sex, financial resources, and so on) to one partner.

After hearing this definition, many people wonder, "Since almost all partners are not unconditionally loving, why in the world would I *want* to get married in the first place and make a lifetime commitment to share my body, my financial resources, and so on with only one person? It doesn't sound like marriage is such a great idea." Indeed, if we view marriage as an opportunity to squeeze all the Imitation Love we can get out of another person, marriage usually *doesn't* turn out very well, since the effects of Imitation Love always wear off, and the trading of it becomes unfair. But when we see marriage as an opportunity to learn to love another person unconditionally, making such a commitment to one person is quite rewarding. Sex, praise, financial resources, and everything else we have become tools with which we express affection for our partner. When we reserve some of those tools exclusively for one person, we're able to communicate a more profound level of loving with that partner.

The Power of Commitment

Bees fly 55,000 miles—more than twice around the world—and visit 2,000,000 flowers, to produce a single pound of honey. Thomas Edison made more than 9,000 failed attempts before he created the lightbulb. Most worthwhile goals are accomplished only after considerable time and persistence. It is often the case, moreover, that half an effort yields not half the desired result, but nothing at all. If Edison had abandoned his efforts after 4,500 attempts, he would not have invented half a lightbulb. Similarly, success in marriage requires everything we have, and if we're not committed to persist until we achieve the love and fulfillment we want, we will almost certainly fail. Half measures will not do. Without a full commitment, we tend to give up and withdraw whenever we become uncomfortable, and since marriage is guaranteed to produce moments of disappointment, irritation, and frustration, a marriage without commitment is certain to fall apart. Viewing marriage as a lifetime commitment helps us to persist in the process of learning to love our partner. Alex learned about this as he talked to me about his wife, Erica.

"Our marriage is over," he said. "We've grown farther and farther apart, and Erica finally moved some of her stuff into an apartment a week ago. She's filed for divorce, and I don't think there's anything we can do to save this now." Then he described many of their arguments—which were filled with the usual mutual accusations—and he took great pains to describe how Erica was always the primary problem in all their conflicts.

I explained the concept of Real Love and showed Alex how it was the lack of love in both their lives that had caused the demise of their marriage, not anything Erica had done or not done.

"That makes a lot of sense," Alex said. "I can see now why we did a lot of the things we did, but I don't see how this will help us now. She's moving out, and I've pretty much given up, too."

"If you knew your marriage could be loving and fulfilling—everything you ever hoped it could be, and more—would you walk away from it?"

"No, but it's too late for that now."

"How do you know that? All you really know is that in the absence of Real Love, your marriage is failing. Without Real Love it *can't* succeed. You have no idea what will happen if you learn to feel unconditionally loved and share that with Erica. Don't you want to find out what's possible?"

"I don't think you know how bad it's gotten. She's actually sold her wedding ring, and she's just hateful when she talks to me now. I don't know if I could be happy with her again."

"Erica is not the reason you're unhappy. You felt unloved and empty long before you met her. And then you expected her to make you happy, but she couldn't do that because she'd never been unconditionally loved, either. She didn't make you unhappy—you came to your marriage already in that condition. She just couldn't fulfill your expectations that she would change your whole life."

Alex was beginning to feel less angry and more receptive. I continued. "When you married Erica, you made a commitment to keep trying to love her, even when it became difficult. You have an important opportunity here to *learn* how to love her. If you leave her now, you'll learn nothing, and you'll just repeat the same mistakes in your next relationship."

When our conversation was over, Alex drove home and found his wife and a couple of her friends loading more of her things into a truck. She was not in a charitable mood, and told him to back off. He told her he wasn't there to make anything more difficult for her and just wanted to apologize. That got her attention.

"For a long time," he said, "I've been blaming you for our arguments and blaming you when I was angry. I was wrong to do that. I can also see that all you ever wanted me to do was love you unconditionally, and I've never done that. I just didn't know how, but now I'm talking with some men who seem to know what it means to love people unconditionally, and I'm going to try to learn how to do that. It may take me a while, but I'm determined. I'm not doing this to get you to stay, or to get you to do anything. I just want to learn how to love you better. I think it can make a big difference in our marriage, but it's still up to you whether you want to put up with me while I'm learning."

Erica stopped her friends from moving anything more into the truck. She stayed home, and she talked with Alex all night. Months later, I got a phone call from Alex.

"I feel like my whole life is different now," he said. "We're both still making lots of mistakes, but we're committed to learning what it takes to accept and love each other. Because we're committed, we don't run away when things get hard. We stay there and try to listen better, and we try to tell the truth about ourselves better. We almost never argue anymore, and we're happier than we've ever been."

When you find Real Love for yourself and take it back to your marriage, you may not see the dramatic results that Alex and Erica experienced. Changes in your marriage may take a long time, and that's exactly when you need the commitment of marriage to give you the motivation to persist through the difficulties until you experience the joy you want. Brenda learned about the rewards of persistence in her marriage with Gary.

Brenda and Gary had fallen out of love years before, and although their marriage was quite unhappy, they continued to stay together—as many couples do—out of fear and a sense of obligation to the children. The principal form of Imitation Love they exchanged was safety. He learned which of his Getting and

Protecting Behaviors were most threatening to her, and he mostly avoided those in exchange for her not doing the things that made him feel anxious. They avoided "pushing each other's buttons." They were not consciously aware of this exchange, but what they enjoyed was really a cease-fire, not a fulfilling marriage. They had become little more than roommates living in the same house.

Brenda learned about Real Love and began to experience the sensation of being unconditionally loved as she told the truth about herself to a group of her friends. They called one another on the phone almost every day, and they also met weekly to share the truth about themselves and feel accepted.

As Brenda felt more loved, she noticed that she no longer had the uncontrollable urge to respond with Getting and Protecting Behaviors when Gary was thoughtless and unkind. She began to demonstrate her concern for his happiness by genuinely accepting him and sharing with him some of the loving acts described on pages 87–107. She had heard some of the women in her group tell stories about how much their marriages had changed, and naturally she was eager to see those same changes in her own marriage.

Even when she was loving toward Gary, however, it didn't seem to make any difference. He was still withdrawn and sullen most of the time. In any other relationship, she would have withdrawn and spent her time with people who could be more loving, but she realized she had made a commitment to learn how to love this man *no matter how he responded*. She realized that it's not Real Love until we give it even when we're getting nothing in return. Armed with that realization and commitment, she continued to act in a loving way toward Gary.

When I spoke to her, she had been loving him for about a year, and so far she hadn't seen any significant response from him. "So why do you stay with him?" I asked. I wasn't suggesting that she leave, just probing for the reasons that kept her going, and hoping to confirm those reasons in her mind.

"Because when we got married, I said I'd stick with him and learn how to make this work," she answered. "Even though he's not responding very well to what I'm offering him, *I* am so much happier myself. Being loving is just a much happier way to live, you know?"

Your spouse may respond slowly to Real Love. After all, he or she has lived without it for a very long time, so in the beginning he may simply not understand what he's being offered. Or he may not trust it, feeling certain that eventually you'll turn on him and be critical, as everyone else in his life has been. It may take a long time for Real Love to seep through his Protecting Behaviors, but what have you got to lose? Love is the only approach that will create a loving relationship, and even if your partner never reciprocates—which is unlikely—you will be happier yourself as you're loving instead of angry, afraid, and manipulative.

The only way to find genuine happiness in marriage is to submit completely to the principles of Real Love. On occasion, you must be willing to give up what you personally want, making instead a choice to be concerned about your spouse's happiness. That approach seems dangerous only if you're still looking for Imitation Love. When you give up manipulating and controlling, it's true that you'll often not get the Imitation Love you want, but if you consistently choose the path to Real Love, the reward is beyond description.

Giving up on your marriage before you learn how to feel Real Love and share it with your spouse is like giving up on learning to play the piano—or play baseball, or drive a car, or whatever—after you experience the initial frustrations of making the first few inevitable mistakes. Real Love has an unspeakable power to heal wounds and change hearts. Stay committed to your marriage and learn how to find that love. When I talk about the lifelong commitment of marriage, I am not saying there's never a reason to dissolve a marriage, but we'll talk more about leaving in Chapter Nine.

One-Sided Loving

After Katherine and her husband, Ray, had been unhappy with their marriage for years, she learned about Real Love, and she began to share with Ray what she was learning and how she was feeling. One day in a group meeting, she talked about her experiences.

"I've really been feeling loved in this group," she said, "and I've enjoyed that a lot. But when I go home and try to share this with Ray, he's not interested."

A woman in the group, Julia, spoke up: "Are you sharing your *love* with him, or are you just sharing *information* you've gotten in the meetings and hoping that somehow he'll change and become more loving toward you?"

"Well, now that you ask, I'm not sure."

"You seem a little irritated," Julia said, "that he's not responding to you in the way you want. So you must have some interest in changing him and getting him to meet your expectations. In that case, you're not offering him Real Love, and that's understandable."

"It's not fair that I have to work hard to change myself and learn to love him, when he doesn't do anything."

"What you mean is that you don't like it that he's not doing what you want. That's usually what we mean by 'fair,' isn't it? You've been coming to these meetings for several months, right?"

"Yes."

"And in all that time, would you say that you've *given* as much Real Love to the people here as you've *received*?"

"Well," Katherine stammered, "not really—not even close, actually."

"When you first start telling the truth about yourself, you need people to accept and love you unconditionally, and for quite a while you'll receive more than you give. That's just the way it has to be in the beginning. Nobody here thought it was *unfair* when they gave you more love than they received. They were more than happy to give you what you needed—without conditions—that's what Real Love is. Now, are you willing to do the same for Ray?"

Many people refuse to give love when they're not immediately rewarded with something in return. They abandon their marriages—or at least they abandon their efforts to improve their marriages—when the exchange of love becomes "unfair." Such people cannot create loving relationships. Before a relationship can break out of a pattern of self-protection and trading Imitation Love, one partner must be willing to tell the truth about himself, find unconditional love, and learn to be loving *without any promise of cooperation from the other partner*. He can then bring that love back to the relationship, which will unavoidably change as a result.

In any marriage, one partner will have more Real Love than the other. One will be more willing to tell the truth and change his or her life. That's just the way it is. If you're the partner with the greater ability to find and share Real Love, are you willing for a time to shoulder most of the burden for changing in your relationship? If you wait for your partner to take the first step, or even to cooperate and take each step after you, it's unlikely that any steps will be taken, and then you'll both lose. If you're looking for some kind of "fairness" with your partner, you will not be happy. Real Love does not keep score. *Somebody* has to be willing to take the initial steps to find Real Love and bring it back to the relationship.

The Power of Faith

We live in a society that *does* keep score. We're obsessed with winning—in sports, in business, and in relationships. That's understandable—when we're empty and afraid, every crumb of Imitation Love becomes very important, and we're willing to fight to get all we can. How can we break out of this paradigm and begin to love our spouses regardless of what they give us in return?

The answer is faith. In the beginning, when you're first learning how to feel loved and to share that with your spouse, no one can prove to you that telling the truth and choosing to be loving will make you happier. In fact, when you recall your consistently negative experiences from the past with being honest and trying to be loving, you may be certain that Real Love *won't* work.

Faith is a decision to take steps into the unknown, to take action when you can't entirely understand or control the consequences. Although there appears to be some risk in telling the truth about ourselves and pursuing Real Love, the risk becomes negligible when we consider that there simply isn't another way to be happy. If we *don't* tell the truth about ourselves—if we continue to use Getting and Protecting Behaviors—we can *never* feel unconditionally loved and genuinely happy. As we tell the truth about ourselves and choose to love our partners unconditionally, at least we create *some* chance that we'll find the Real Love we want. Actually, it turns out to be much more than a chance—Real Love is a certainty if we persist in taking the steps that lead to it.

If we want to find happiness and enrich our relationships, we simply have to make the *decision* to exercise faith—faith in the power of telling the truth, faith in the healing power of Real Love, and yes, faith in our partners. We must trust that when our partners are using their Getting and Protecting Behaviors, they're simply drowning. We must trust that they're doing their best, and that they behave in unloving ways only because they don't know *how* to be loving.

We can't afford to adopt the attitude proposed by so many, that trust is *earned*. That makes for a cute slogan, but it's really an insistence on proof rather than a reliance on faith. Relationships do not flourish under those conditions, as we see here in the case of Holly and her husband, Bruce.

Bruce often came home late from work—sometimes many hours late—and he never offered any explanation. He didn't seem to care that Holly had been waiting for him, or that dinner had been prepared. One day they were sitting in my office to talk about the conflict they'd been experiencing over this.

"I hate this," Bruce complained. "When I get home from a long day at work, she comes at me like a pit bull—barking and biting and demanding to know where I've been every minute."

Holly was not about to take this lying down. "Is it unreasonable," she demanded, "that I want to know where my own husband has been when he gets home five hours after work?"

"Certainly," I said, "it *would* be thoughtful of him to tell you where he is, but you don't have the right to demand that. Everyone has the right to make their own choices—the Law of Choice. You'll destroy your relationship if you insist that he meet your expectations. You've already proven that, haven't you? When you're demanding with him, how does that work? Does it make either of you happier?

"It sure isn't making *me* happy," Bruce agreed.

"I really do understand," I continued, "why you'd want him to tell you where he's been. I'm sure it's inconvenient, for one thing, to have him disappear for hours at a time. How do you plan dinner together, for example? His behavior also bothers you because he's telling you he doesn't care enough about you to share what he's doing. You feel like he's telling you he doesn't love you—and when he doesn't share what he's doing, that *is* what he's telling you. What bothers you most, though, is that you don't *trust* him. You don't trust that he's doing his best to love you."

"But he's not," Holly said.

"Do you ever behave in less than loving ways toward Bruce?" I asked her. "Like when you're snapping at him about getting home late?"

"I suppose so. Sometimes."

"So on the days when you're less than loving, do you ever begin the day by thinking, You know, I'm feeling pretty loving today. I *could* share that with my husband, but no, I think I'll withhold it instead. I'll make his life miserable and hurt our relationship."

"Of course not."

"Neither does Bruce, and your marriage won't change until you believe that. Bruce doesn't intentionally withhold Real Love from you. On many occasions, he simply doesn't have it to give. Then when you attack him about not loving you enough, he becomes even more empty and afraid, and everything just gets much worse."

"So what are you suggesting?" Holly asked. "That I just let him do what he wants?"

"Pretty much, yes. It sure isn't working when you try to control him, right? Don't you want a loving relationship?"

"Sure, but—"

"There is no *but*. If you want a genuinely loving relationship, you'll have to start with faith. You'll have to trust that he's doing the best he can with what he has, that he behaves as he does because he really doesn't feel unconditionally loved—he's drowning and uses Getting and Protecting Behaviors to keep his own head above water. That's selfish on his part, but when we're drowning, aren't we naturally selfish? Trust is not *earned*—it's given, like a gift. If you don't trust him to do his best to love you as he begins to feel loved himself, you'll find something wrong with everything he does. If you don't have faith in the power of telling the truth about yourself and finding love, and have faith that loving Bruce is the only happy way to live, your relationship will stay just like it is. Every time you demonstrate your lack of faith in him, he feels like you don't love him unconditionally—which you don't—and that's killing you both."

Holly made the conscious decision to accept that Bruce was just unable to love her. She chose to exercise faith in the truth and in the power of Real Love. She *demonstrated* her faith—faith is action—by saying nothing critical on the occasions when he got home late. Instead, when he walked in the door, she jumped up from whatever she was doing and gave him a hug.

Bruce felt Holly's concern for him, and he began to call home whenever he knew he was going to be late. In the absence of unloving demands from Holly—and in the presence of other evidences of her love for him—he no longer felt threatened by her and therefore had no need to lie to her, run from her, or be angry, all Protecting Behaviors. In fact, he began coming home right after work. It turns out that he'd only been creating things to do by himself after work—driving, shopping, eating out—because he didn't feel loved at home. We naturally go where we feel loved, and when he started feeling Real Love from Holly, he wanted to be with her. It all happened because Holly exercised faith. She told the truth about herself to Bruce—about her mistakes and Getting and Protecting Behaviors. She believed that being truthful and loving would be more effective than anger and controlling, and her faith paid off.

Mutually loving relationships develop only *after* many acts of faith. If you want such a relationship, you must be willing to tell the truth about yourself to your partner even on the many occasions when you're not sure he or she is being loving. In the beginning, you may be acting on pure faith, just hoping there's a chance your partner might accept you. Sometimes you'll find it easier to exercise faith and tell the truth about yourself to your spouse if you already feel sufficiently filled with the acceptance and love of wise men and women to whom you have told the truth about yourself on other occasions. With their love—with that twenty million dollars—you won't be afraid to tell the truth about yourself to your spouse, because you won't *need* his or her acceptance in that given moment. Under those conditions, telling the truth becomes easy. With that twenty million, you'll also find it easier to consciously choose to be loving toward your partner, even when he or she is not being loving in return.

Gratitude

In marriage, ingratitude is a natural condition. You have high expectations of your spouse, and if she has done something poorly a thousand times in a row, it's understandable that you would not be grateful when on one occasion she does that thing right. If, for example, she has been critical and angry for years, you may have a tendency to be less than impressed the first time she's accepting and loving. Rather than feeling grateful, you might think, "Well, it's about time." You might even regard it as an accident, not to be trusted. With ingratitude, however, you rob yourself of the enjoyment of positive experiences that do happen. Ingratitude will also negatively affect the motivation your wife feels to be loving the next time.

The Beauty of One

In every marriage the two partners are different—sometimes very different—and we often think of these differences as problems that have to be resolved. Not at all. The only thing that has to be "resolved" in a marriage is Getting and Protecting Behaviors. When those are eliminated with Real Love, what's left is two people with different qualities that can add to the relationship.

When you're insufficiently loved and loving, you're not complete. You're like half a person. When two half-people get together in a relationship, they don't make a healthy whole. In relationships, ½ + ½ does not equal 1. Two half-people can result only in misery, but when they find enough Real Love, they become whole individually, and then when they bring those qualities together, 1 + 1 equals far more than 2. Two whole people combine to create an effect many times greater than two people individually.

As you feel more loved and loving, and as your partner does the same, you'll feel your partner's roots and tendrils reaching out to you—and yours to him or her—not to smother or oppress either of you, but to bind you together in a mutually supporting and nourishing way. You'll become so mutually accepting and concerned about the other's happiness that on many occasions you'll forget you are two separate beings. You'll become *one,* and that is a miraculous feeling. Two unconditionally loving people combine to become something much greater than they would be separately. When you achieve oneness with your partner, you'll find your senses, your capabilities, and your joy magnified in ways you can scarcely imagine. This state is well worth whatever effort you'll make to reach it.

We're sometimes afraid of the idea of becoming one, anxious that somehow we might lose something, perhaps our identity. There is no fear of that when you're certain your partner loves you unconditionally. As you and your partner become one, you *add* to who you are, individually and together. As an individual you bring to your marriage a tapestry woven from the qualities and experiences of your life. Your spouse brings threads and colors of her own, and Real Love weaves all those threads together into a pattern far more beautiful than either of you could have created alone.

It's common to hear people say that we must be willing to meet our spouses halfway, but that approach will never create a great marriage. Picture you and your spouse standing on opposite edges of a deep canyon, one hundred feet apart. What would happen if you were willing to meet him or her only halfway, throwing out fifty feet of rope. Even if the ends of the rope happened to meet in the middle, you'd never reach each other. You must be willing to extend yourself all the way, without defense or manipulation, because only then can you come together. If you *both* extend yourselves all the way, the connection is even more secure.

To become one with your partner, you must be willing to extend yourself, and be thoughtful and considerate, in ways you may not be accustomed to, a lesson learned by Ellis one day as he talked to me about his wife, Deborah.

"She's always nagging at me about something," he said, "always complaining about something I've done—or haven't done."

"Give me an example," I said.

"If I get home late from work, she really gets mad. Wants to know where I was minute by minute. I don't have to tell her where I am every second of the day. She can't control everything I do."

"You're right. You don't *have* to tell her where you are, but what do you want in your marriage? Do you want to live with someone you're in conflict with all the time—constantly draining the energy out of both of you—or do you want to experience the miracle of being peaceful, loved, and loving? Are you willing to do what it takes to feel the power of becoming one with your wife?"

"That would probably be better than what we've got right now."

"A *lot* better, and in order to get that feeling, you have to think about how you'd behave with a genuine partner, someone you

want to really share your life with. Then make it your goal to behave that way with your wife. When that's your goal—to treat
your wife as a full partner—you won't feel *controlled* when you
share with her where you are and what you're doing. You'll share
all that with her because you *want* to, because you want to be her
partner in everything. When you share yourself with her freely,
she'll know that you care about her."

Exercise

Write several things about your marriage that you don't like: not
enough sex, too much sex, bickering about work, disagreements
about money, and so on. Ask yourself whether your conflict over
these issues could result in great part because you *want* something
you're not getting from your spouse. In other words, look at the
possibility that your unhappiness is due to your own selfishness,
that you're unhappy because you're thinking of *yourself* rather
than *your spouse's* happiness.

If you were to make a conscious commitment to learn how to
care about his or her happiness—the real purpose of marriage—
how would that change your behavior? Would you continue to
make demands? Or would you begin instead to focus on the loving acts you could share with your partner, some of which we
listed on pages 87–107? Make a written commitment to share
some of these loving acts every day for the next thirty days with
your partner. At the end of the thirty days, discuss with a friend
what difference it made in your marriage when you changed the
focus from what you wanted to what your partner might need.

6

ॐ

Making It Work

The Power of Requests and Agreements

When people first hear about the concept of Real Love, they often express concerns:

- "If I love my partner unconditionally, does that mean I have to do everything he wants? It sounds like I could really get used."
- "What if I'm not getting something *I* need? Am I supposed to put all that aside and only think about my partner? How do I get what *I* want?"

We never have the right to change or control our partners, nor do our partners have the right to control us. We are not obligated to give our spouses everything they want. We do have a right, however, to make *requests* of one another for whatever we need or want. Most of us, though, do not have an adequate understanding of how to make loving requests, and without that knowledge, we often feel helpless and frustrated—either we're afraid to make any requests at all, or we're constantly making demands of other people in ways that are irritating to them and frustrating to us. We'll now discuss the principles that will enable us to make requests that will contribute to our individual happiness and to the strength of our marriages:

- Realize that Real Love is always the most important thing.
- Ask, don't demand.
- Make requests clear and specific.
- Listen and accept.
- Modify your requests when necessary.

All these principles are helpful to both the person making the request and the person receiving it.

Realize That Real Love Is Always the Most Important Thing

Real Love isn't *one* of the most important elements in a happy marriage; it's *the* most important—by far. For that reason, whenever you're making a request, you must always ask yourself first, "Will this request—which includes the *way* I deliver it—interfere with the Real Love my partner needs to feel from me?" If it will interfere, do not make the request. No specific *thing* you want is worth any damage you might cause to the Real Love that's the lifeblood of your marriage. John learned about the importance of Real Love in requests as he talked to me about his wife, Laura.

"When we got married," John told me, "Laura had this little dog. At the time I didn't realize what it would be like to have a dog in the house—he wasn't big; how much trouble could he be, right?—but then I find out the dog isn't house-trained, and he pees on the carpet wherever he goes. He's cute, but I'd rather get rid of the dog than have him peeing all over the place. We got a little gate to keep him in the kitchen, so he could make his messes on a hard floor, but Laura is always letting him out and forgetting to put him back in before he pees on the carpet again. How can I make her take this seriously?"

"You can't *make* her do anything," I said, "but you can certainly *ask* her to take better care of the dog—house-train him, keep him in the kitchen, whatever works."

"I *have* asked her—a bunch of times—but it doesn't seem to make any difference."

"How does she respond when you ask her?" I asked.

"She still doesn't keep him in the kitchen, so I keep getting urine spots on the carpet."

"I understand that *after* you've made your request, she doesn't do what you want, but I mean, how does she respond right while you're asking her? Does she smile and say, Why sure, I'd be glad to?"

"No, she gets this huge scowl on her face, and then she starts defending herself. She says it wasn't *her* that left him out that time—that it was *me* who left the gate open—when I know that's not true. Or she brings up totally unrelated things *I've* done wrong. And if all that doesn't get me off her back, she stomps off in a huff."

"So when you ask her to take better care of the dog, she responds by lying, attacking you, acting like a victim, and running. We've talked about these behaviors before. What are they called?"

"They're Getting and Protecting Behaviors," John said.

"Right, and why do people use them—the only reason?"

"Because they're empty and afraid."

"Exactly," I said, "and they feel that way only because they don't feel loved. So what is Laura telling you when she does all those things in response to you asking her about the dog?"

"That she doesn't feel loved by me?"

"Right, and not just by you. She feels empty and afraid because she doesn't feel loved by *anybody*. And she's telling you that she needs to feel some Real Love from you. But what does she get instead? What do you do when she defends herself and attacks you?"

"I get mad," he said.

"And that's understandable, but when you respond to her with your own Getting and Protecting Behaviors, you're telling her quite clearly that you're primarily concerned about whom?"

"Myself."

"Yes. Right when she's telling you she needs Real Love, you're telling her you care more about yourself than her."

"No wonder it always goes so badly. I've tried a hundred times to tell her about that dog, but it never works."

"Because?"

"Because with the way I ask her about it, I'm also telling her I don't love her."

"Bingo. And as soon as she senses you don't care about her, she feels even more empty and afraid. In that condition, she can't hear a thing you say, except that you don't love her."

"So what can I do?" John asked.

"You can remember that what she needs most is to feel loved, not criticized. Also remember that what *you* need most is to be unconditionally loving and happy—that's far more important than keeping the dog from peeing on the carpet."

"So how do I ask her to take better care of him?"

"First, you need to learn more about Real Love. You can't leave that step out."

I then made some suggestions to John about how he might talk to Laura, and he called me two weeks later to talk about his experience with her.

"I really did some thinking about what you said," John told me, "and I could see that I haven't been loving toward Laura. Sure, she needs to take better care of the dog, but I've been causing more harm with my anger than she has by not keeping the dog in the kitchen. So I sat down with her and apologized for being selfish and unloving. I said I'd really appreciate her keeping the dog in the kitchen and off the carpet, but I was not going to nag her about it anymore. I said it was much more important to me that she feel loved and that we be happy together."

"What happened?"

"She couldn't believe what she was hearing. She put her arms around me and cried. She apologized for not taking better care of the dog and promised to do better. Since that time, she's only forgotten to keep him in the kitchen a couple of times. It's a lot better, and now we don't fight about it at all."

After John understood that Real Love is much more important

than anything else, he was able to make a *loving request,* demonstrating that Real Love is always the most important thing.

If you're empty and afraid, do not make requests of your spouse, because in that condition, you *will* use Getting and Protecting Behaviors, which will likely make your spouse feel more empty and afraid, too, and then the two of you will be mired in the mutual manipulation and protection that always make a loving interaction impossible. When you make requests, you need to diligently examine yourself for signs of emptiness and fear and of Getting and Protecting Behaviors such as these:

- Are you nervous about making this request? Are you afraid your spouse won't respond in a favorable way?
- Are you feeling insistent about getting what you're asking for?
- Are you irritated?
- Have you been putting off this request? You do that only when you're afraid.
- Would you feel annoyed or frustrated if the answer to your request were *no*?
- Are you inclined to exaggerate your needs in order to persuade your partner to agree to your request?
- Are you feeling hurt that your partner hasn't already done what you want?

If the answer to any of these questions is *yes,* it's very likely that you're feeling empty and afraid, and it's virtually certain that you'll make your request in a way that will not be loving. So don't do it. Talk to a friend first and explain your request and your fears. Talk until you feel more loved and loving, and then make the request of your spouse.

Above all, *never* make a request in anger—which means while you're feeling irritated, annoyed, frustrated, exasperated, and any of the other conditions we describe with words that disguise our anger. Anger always communicates to your spouse that you don't care about his or her happiness, only your own.

You also must remember the critical role of Real Love when you're *receiving* a request. Whenever your spouse asks you for something, always ask yourself, Will my response make a positive contribution to the Real Love my partner needs? If not, you might reconsider how you make your response, which does not mean that you always have to give your partner what he or she wants—more about that later in this chapter. Your partner may be asking you to take care of the dog, or clean out the garage, or accomplish some other specific task, but in addition, he or she is almost always evaluating your response—consciously or not—as an indication of your concern for her. And her interpretation is usually accurate. Most of the times our spouses ask us to do something, we *can* do what they've asked without great inconvenience and without compromising our integrity, so when we fail to do as they've requested, we *are* telling them we don't care enough about their happiness.

Even when you *agree* to do as your spouse asks, you need to remember that what she needs most is an assurance of your acceptance and concern for her welfare, not just the accomplishment of a task. The following couple, Larry and Patricia, illustrate this concept as they talk to me.

"Any time I ask you to do anything," Patricia says, "you resist me."

"Like when?" Larry protests.

"How about yesterday," she snaps back, "when I came in the house and asked you to help me carry in all those things from the car?"

"What do you mean? I *did* help you."

"Sure, after you sighed and rolled your eyes and walked as slowly as you could to the driveway. You looked like you were walking to your own execution."

"I was in the middle of doing something else."

"Larry," I suggest, "imagine that I'm directing you as an actor in a movie, and in this scene Patricia comes in and asks you to carry in some things from the car. I tell you to play the scene so that it will be obvious to everyone watching that you're madly in love with her and would do anything for her. Would you play the scene like you did yesterday? Did you respond to her in a way that left no doubt in her mind that you were excited to help her?"

Although they're rarely conscious of it, our spouses are constantly evaluating our behavior as evidence that either we love them or we don't, and with each decision we communicate our feelings and priorities more loudly than we know. When your spouse makes a request, remember that he or she needs to feel like the most important person in the world to you. Your primary goal is to communicate your concern for his happiness, and you will completely fail to achieve that goal if you pause, sigh, roll your eyes, and communicate other signs of hesitation and reluctance. It's not uncommon for my wife, Donna, to call from another room, "Greg, could you help me with this?" She knows she doesn't have to explain herself, or repeat herself, or wait for me to come straggling slowly into the next room with my shoulders hunched over in a loud tone of reluctance. Imagine how she feels when I bound out of my office, run to find her, and say, "What can I do for you?"

When you respond to your spouse's requests with genuine enthusiasm and without the slightest hesitation, he feels your concern for his happiness. It feels like a gift freely offered, *even though he made a request for it.* That's a great feeling to give your spouse.

If Getting and Protecting Behaviors do arise, on the part of the person making or receiving the request, review the principles for elimination of conflict in Chapter Four. Never allow a conflict to continue. It will only damage your relationship and your happiness.

Ask, Don't Demand

Megan and her friend Cynthia often got together for lunch. On one such occasion, Megan was obviously irritated as she said, "Tomorrow I'm helping my mother move from her house into an apartment—the house has just gotten too big for her. We won't get it all done in one day, but we do need to get started. I asked Ashton (Megan's husband) if he'd help us—he can load some of the heavy things, and he also has a pickup truck—but he said he was going to be fishing all day with a couple of his friends. It seems like any time I ask him to do anything, he has something else to do."

"You didn't *ask* him to help you," Cynthia suggested. "You *demanded* that he help you, and he could *feel* that. He didn't like it—most people don't."

"I didn't make a demand. I asked him pretty nicely, in fact."

"The difference between asking and demanding isn't the words you use, and often not even your tone of voice."

"So what *is* the difference?" asked Megan.

"Often you can't tell the difference until you *don't get* what you want. If you're truly *asking*, you won't feel disappointed or irritated when you don't get what you want. If you do feel disappointed or angry, though—as you were with Ashton after he refused you— you prove that you weren't really asking. We have those feelings only when we're making a *demand*, with expectations."

"But he can go fishing any time, and he knows I really need him tomorrow."

"Do you see what you're doing now? You're justifying your demand. You're showing why he *should* have done what you expected. And you might be right—if he were being thoughtful, he probably *would* help you. Maybe he's being unloving and selfish, but that's irrelevant, because you don't get to change him. What matters is what *you're* doing, and you're being demanding. He doesn't like that, and that's at least one of the reasons he doesn't like to do things with you or for you. Do you want to be right, or do you want to learn how to be loving and make a great marriage?"

We commonly make demands of our spouses, and we usually don't realize we're doing it. We make demands because we're afraid that if we simply *ask* for what we want, we won't get it. Demands and expectations are our way of *forcing* our partners to give us what we want. Sometimes with our demands we actually do get our partners to do some things, but the overall consequences of demands are always negative:

- Our spouses feel like we're trying to control them, which is exactly what we're doing when we heap expectations on them. We're telling them they're not quite acceptable as they are and have to behave in a certain way for us to like them. We're violating the Law of Choice and saying that they have to give up the right to make their own choices when it comes to making *our* lives convenient. Our spouses can feel our lack of acceptance, and that always injures our relationship.
- Although our spouses often don't know *how* to love us, they really do have a desire to be loving. If we're constantly making demands of them, however, they can't feel like they're offering us their love unconditionally. Our demands turn their potential gifts into payments we obligate them to make.
- Expectations make it impossible for *us* to feel loved. As we discussed in Chapter Two, you can't feel loved by me if you've forced me—with your expectations—to give you anything.

Don't Persuade or Convince

One way we attempt to force our partners—mostly unconsciously—to do what we want is to tell them the many reasons they *should* agree to our "requests." We try to persuade them that our requests are reasonable, necessary, and urgent, and therefore cannot be refused. When Megan "asked" for her husband's help, she told him she couldn't do it without him, which was intended to make him feel obligated. When he refused, she showed him how her requested activity was more important than what he had proposed to do, and she reminded him of the many times she had helped *him* with similar projects. When Cynthia pointed out how Megan was trying to make Ashton do what she wanted, she was frustrated.

Megan asked Cynthia, "So what am I supposed to do when I really need his help and he won't give it?"

Cynthia smiled and said, "Funny how we think that our needs justify our demands. Just because *you* need something doesn't obligate *him* to give it to you."

"So what can I do when he refuses?"

"You accept his refusal. He really does get to make his own choices, you know. Once you let go of your demands that Ashton *has* to be the one helping you, you'll see a lot of options. For example, without his help you could settle for moving just a few of your mother's things that day. Or you could put it off until another day when Ashton *can* help you—which he's more likely to do if you're not pushing him. Or you could hire a rental truck and get the help of some friends. Your frustration and your sense of being trapped are both a result of *your* expectations that *Ashton* must be the one to help you. It all becomes much easier when you quit making your demands."

We persuade people to do what we want more than we realize. We provide long lists of great reasons *why* they should do as we ask. Using that great logic, how could they refuse? Sometimes we persuade people to do what we want by offering something in exchange. Certainly we might get some things we want that way, but we won't feel loved when we buy or manipulate the attention we get.

Any time you make a request of your spouse, ask yourself, "Am I really willing to hear *no* for an answer?" Think about your demands, and talk to other people about them until you can make your requests without expectations. When you can do that, your spouse will feel the lack of expectations and feel more accepted by you. Then you'll be more likely to get his or her cooperation, and you'll feel more loved when you do get what you want.

Make Requests Clear and Specific

One afternoon, Emily called me to complain about her husband, David.

"I don't know why David even thinks we're married anymore,"

she began. "We never spend any time together. When I talk to him, he responds in grunts and single syllables. When he comes home, he either watches television or sits in front of the computer. Right now he's in there playing a video game on the computer, and he hasn't talked to me since he got home from work."

"What exactly would you like him to do?" I asked.

"Spend some time with *me*."

"Have you told him that?"

"Sure, lots of times."

"Have you asked him to spend some time with you *tonight*?"

"No, not exactly, but he should know that by now."

I chuckled and said, "It would be wonderful if David were more sensitive to you and understood better what you want, but he doesn't. And you can't expect him to read your mind. If there's something you want from him, you need to *ask* him."

We often fail to tell people what we want—sometimes *we* don't even know what we want—and then we're critical when they don't make us happy. That's not a great way to nourish a relationship. As we make our requests, we also need to be careful to make them clear and specific, and not to turn them into veiled attacks, which I explained to Emily as we continued our conversation. She agreed that she needed to ask David for what she wanted.

"Exactly what do you plan to say to him?" I asked.

"That I wish he'd spend more time with me."

"If you say that, I predict that you'll almost certainly have an argument on your hands."

"Why?"

"If you say, 'I wish you'd spend *more* time with me,' you're telling him that the time he's already chosen to give you is not enough. You're criticizing him, and he won't like that. Instead, just tell him what you want."

"Okay, how about if I just say I'd like to do something with him?"

"Much better, but it's not specific enough. Now he'll feel the burden of coming up with something to do that you'd like.

You're making him read your mind again, and that usually doesn't work out. What if he says, for example, that you can sit with him and watch him play the video game? You won't like that suggestion, but you will have created that situation by not specifically saying what you really want. If you want something, tell him specifically what it is. What do you want?"

Emily thought for a moment. "To talk to him, to feel close to him."

"That's clear, but it won't be specific enough for him. You're making him do the work of figuring out exactly what you want to do. Most of us don't have much practice at making specific requests without being accusing, so let me suggest some words, and you tell me if they'd work for you. You could say, 'David, I'd like to talk to you for a few minutes, but I don't want to interrupt your game. Do you know when you'll be at a place where you can stop and we can talk?' Also understand that many people—especially men—interpret 'I'd like to talk' to mean that they've done something wrong, so make it clear that you just want to talk about your day or some other non-threatening subject."

"He won't know when he'll get to a stopping place. He could play all night."

"Then keep being specific. If he doesn't give you a time, ask him if you can come back and check on him in fifteen minutes, or whenever. Then you keep that up until you arrive at a time when he'll be done—even if that's hours away."

"Then what?"

"When he's done playing, tell him you'd like to talk to him in the living room about what you've done that day. Or go for a walk with him. Hold his hand while you talk, ask him about his day, and discuss whatever else you'd like. You'll feel much closer to him than if you expect him to read your mind."

"What if he just doesn't want to talk to me at all?"

"He might not. Be careful that you don't have *expectations* that he'll do what you want, because then you're really delivering a demand, and he will *feel* that, which will make it far less likely that he'll want to spend time with you. If he does say *no*, you still have lots of choices. You can still do an infinite variety of things by yourself or with others. Then on another day you can make another request. If you keep talking to him without demands, eventually he will want to spend time with you."

When you make vague requests, it's unlikely that your partner will correctly guess what you want, and then you'll be frustrated, a condition you will have brought on yourself. It would be unthinkable in a business to write a memo to a supplier that said, "Please send us the things you know we need, and be quick about it," but that's just what we tend to do in our marriages when we pressure our partners to miraculously fill our needs. Following are some examples of the requests we make, and how we can make them more exact and productive:

Vague or General Request	Clear and Specific Request
I wish you'd pay more attention to me.	1. I'm not telling you what to do, but I'd feel a lot more like you were really listening to me if you'd put the newspaper down while I'm talking to you.
	2. I'd really like to go for a walk with you this evening. Would 7:00 be a good time for you?
I wish you were neater.	It would be helpful to me if you would consistently put your clothes in the laundry hamper. Would you be willing to do that?
The kids need you to spend more time with them.	Mike has a term paper that's due in two weeks. Can you choose two evenings this week to help him with that?

Vague or General Request	Clear and Specific Request
I hate it when you nag me.	I don't enjoy it when you say I *never* do something or when you tell me how many times you've asked me. I'd like it better if you'd just point out exactly what you want me to do.
The lawn needs to be mowed.	The grass is getting long. Could you have it mowed by Saturday?
I'd like to go out more with you.	1. How do you feel about going out to dinner this Saturday?
	2. How would you feel about setting up a time for you and me to go out together every Friday night for a couple of hours?

In many cases, being clear and specific about a request is aided by putting it in writing. My wife and I agreed long ago that there are too many things going on in our family to trust it all to our memories. If I want Donna to do something, I write exactly what I want done, *and* I date the note and indicate when the task needs to be finished. She does the same with me. Examples:

- March 14. Please pick up some additional copy paper next time you're out doing errands. I'll need that by March 17.
- May 7. The Book Page on the Web site needs to be updated in the next two days.

Being specific like this prevents the arguments couples commonly have about details. He says, "Three days ago, I asked you to get two gallons of antifreeze, and I said I needed it by yesterday." She says, "No, you didn't. You only asked for one, and you said there was no hurry." Such disputes can be difficult to resolve, and they are mostly avoided when your requests are written.

One reason we tend to make vague requests is that often we

don't know exactly what we want. It's lazy on our part to require our partner to figure it out for us, and then when they don't get it quite right, to criticize their attempt. We also tend to avoid specific requests because we don't want to be rejected. If our requests are vague, there's a greater likelihood that our partners will agree, because they can often imagine filling our request in a way that would require little effort on their part. Unfortunately, that rarely turns out to be exactly what we want.

᭟

Even when we're *receiving* a request, we need to remember the need for being specific, as Andre learned with his wife, Sheryl. As she went out the door one evening to a business meeting, she said, "Thanks for feeding the kids. When you get done with that, could you clean up the kitchen? That would be a big help."

Andre agreed and cleaned up the kitchen, but when Sheryl got home late that night, she was irritated. "I thought I asked you to clean up the kitchen," she said.

"I did," he responded, irritated that she hadn't appreciated the work he'd done. The unpleasant argument that followed was a result of their very different notions about what it meant to "clean up the kitchen." Andre thought it meant putting the dishes in the sink and scraping the leftover food into the garbage. He didn't know that she wanted the floor swept, the counters wiped off, and the dishes washed. To be sure, he didn't *want* to know what she meant by "clean up the kitchen," either, which is one reason he didn't ask.

The next time she made a similar request, he asked her to specify what she wanted done, and when he did as requested, she was quite pleased.

Make Lots of Requests

Often, when people tell me they're not getting what they want out of a relationship, I suggest that they're probably not asking for what they want. If you want a hug, for example, ask. If you want more time with your spouse, ask. Be clear and specific.

A Danger of General Requests

We discussed that one downside of making unclear, general requests is that you probably won't get what you want. But there are other, less obvious, dangers. Let's suppose you say to your partner, "I wish you'd spend more time with me." That general request can have negative consequences you might not think about, such as these:

- Because this generalized request has no definite time of completion, now it's always out there, like a constant pebble in your partner's shoe. Each time he or she thinks about this request, it feels to him like you're making it again, nagging him about it. And he has to wonder all the time whether his present level of attention toward you meets the standard for "more time." It won't be long before he'll resent the unrelenting feeling of pressure that can come from such an ever-present request.

- Each time he does something with you, now you have to wonder if he generated that effort on his own, or whether he acted out of a sense of obligation because of your ongoing request. The opportunity to feel his offer of an unconditional gift is greater when your requests are specific. Imagine, for example, that you ask him to do something specific with you this weekend. When *he* then asks you to do something with him the weekend after that, you know he generated that offer entirely on his own, and it will *feel* more like a gift to you.

Listen and Accept

In Chapters Three and Four we discussed many principles that contribute to effective listening, and we need to apply all those when we're listening to our partners make requests. Allow me to emphasize one of them, which was introduced on pages 119–120. The Third Rule of Seeing—the speaker describes *himself*. Frank and Allison illustrate this guideline in the following interaction.

"A couple of weeks ago," Frank said, "we talked about that bill we got from the hospital emergency room—remember that? Would you please call the insurance company today and work that out with them?"

Frank had a slight edge in his voice, and Allison felt it. She wisely understood that Frank was saying something about *himself*, and she lovingly *listened* to that part of his communication. "I'll be glad to do that. You seem to be uneasy—maybe even annoyed—about something, and if you want to talk about it, I'd really like to hear it."

Frank was immediately disarmed and even touched by what Allison had said. She could easily have felt attacked by him— since he really *was* attacking her, though unconsciously, with his anger—and responded by defending herself, which would have turned their conversation into a conflict. Or she simply could have done the requested task without addressing his irritation. But she didn't take either of those courses. She really *listened* to him instead, and as a result, he felt seen and accepted.

"I wasn't going to say anything," he said, "but since you've asked, I was annoyed that I got a second notice for that bill in the mail today. I was irritated that you didn't take care of it the first time we talked about it."

"You're right," she said. "I did ignore it. I shoved that bill in with some papers I meant to get to *someday*, so naturally it didn't get done. I should have done it right after we talked. Entirely my fault." She gave him a quick hug and said, "Thanks for loving me anyway."

While it's obvious that the person *receiving* the request must listen carefully as the speaker voices a request, so also must the person *making* the request listen carefully to the response to his or her request. On another occasion, Frank asked Allison to run a quick errand for him while she was doing some business at the post office. Allison agreed, but Frank noted the moment of hesitation she expressed.

"When you said *yes*," he said, "you paused. The errand doesn't *have* to be done right now, you know."

"Oh, thanks for saying that," she said. "I was just trying to be helpful, but I should have told you that if I do what you're asking, I'll be very rushed to get everything done on time. So can I put off your errand until later today or tomorrow?"

"Sure. It's a little thing. If it's done by tomorrow morning, that would be fine."

It's not difficult to imagine how seen and accepted Allison felt at that point. If Frank had not made his observation of Allison's nonverbal behavior, she would have felt pressured by the request, and then it's likely she would have resented it and in some way expressed her negative feelings later at Frank.

Modify Your Requests When Necessary

Notice that after Frank carefully listened to Allison, he modified his request. In the following interaction, Claudia and Jonathan demonstrate other ways to modify a request.

Claudia is tired when she gets home from work, and when she finds Jonathan collapsed on a couch in the living room, she says, "I know it's my turn to fix dinner, but I'm just too tired to do it. I'd love to go out and get something. Can we do that?"

"I don't think I can move off this couch."

Claudia has made a clear, specific, and nonthreatening request, but that doesn't obligate Jonathan to do anything, and he has declined her suggestion. Now what? She could give up and start fixing dinner, but she realizes that she can modify her request.

"I understand that feeling. So let's talk about what we *can* do. I really don't want to fix something to eat—too tired—so how about if I go out and bring something back? You don't look like you're eager to go anywhere."

"That would be great," says Jonathan.

"I don't want to eat out of a bag—I'd like to have a quiet, relaxing time with you at the dinner table—so would you be willing to put some plates and utensils out on the dining room table?"

Jonathan pauses for a moment and says, "Sure, I can do that. Thanks for going out to get something."

It's important to see the individual steps and principles involved in their brief conversation:

1. Claudia makes a clear, specific *request* without pressuring or persuading Jonathan.
2. Jonathan *refuses*.
3. She really *listens* to him and understands.
4. She makes an unconditional *offer* to do something for both of them.
5. She makes another request (set the table) that she believes will be more palatable to him. This request is not tied to her offer. (She did not say, "I'll get the food *if* you set the table.")
6. Jonathan agrees to the request.

It's critical to understand that Jonathan and Claudia were not engaged in a negotiation of demands here. If they had been, their conversation would have deteriorated the moment Jonathan refused Claudia's first request. Claudia simply modified her request after genuinely listening to her husband. Nor were they trading favors, which never leads to an increase in love in a relationship. Instead, because there were no demands, they both felt like the other was freely offering a gift.

That is the kind of interaction you want to have consistently with your spouse. No trading or feeling of compromise. You simply ask for what you want, you modify your requests where necessary, and you both freely *offer* what you *choose* to give. The Real Love in such a relationship grows rapidly.

An explanation is warranted here for the word *compromise*, since it characterizes the means by which so many agreements are reached in relationships. In most compromises each party gives up something—often grudgingly—in exchange for the other party giving up something of equal or similar value. There is usually a *feeling* or *spirit* of trading and score keeping, and these are not compatible with Real Love. In Real Love partners may certainly adjust what they offer or what they are willing to do—which on the surface could *look like* a compromise—but the *attitude* is not one of compromise, which suggests mutual, though often equitable, loss. In Real Love partners freely offer and receive.

As the person *receiving* a request, you, too, have a right to modify a request. Instead of just refusing her request above, Jonathan could have offered some alternatives or requests of his own. Instead of saying, "I don't think I can move off this couch," he could have said, "I don't want to go out, but I could throw a salad together, if that would help you fix something here. Or I could set the table while you go out and get something." It's helpful when we tell our spouses what we *are* willing to do, rather than just making a flat refusal of their request.

Keep Modifying Your Requests—Don't Pull Away

When you ask for something, and your partner says *no*, you might have a tendency to feel rejected, perhaps even to pull away. That will rarely help either of you, as Jonathan and Claudia learn in yet another interaction.

After coming home from another long day at work, Claudia finds Jonathan hunched over his desk, working on some papers. She stands behind him and puts her hands on his shoulders.

Jonathan senses that she would like to talk, but he is feeling far too stressed to offer anything to anyone, so he says nothing.

After a couple of minutes, Claudia says, "Could we sit on the couch and talk for a while?"

"I'm just too tired," he says.

This is a perfect opportunity for Claudia to feel offended and either attack Jonathan or run. Instead she decides to stay with him and modify her request. "Would it be all right, then," she asks, "if I sit here for a while and put my hand on your shoulder?"

"I guess so," he says, and Claudia sits next to him for several minutes, with her hand on his shoulder. In the process, she feels connected to him—which is what she wanted—and he feels supported while he's not feeling loving. Later in the evening, as Jonathan feels more accepted, he does sit and talk with her as she originally asked for.

If your partner doesn't have a response to your request, you might suggest that you'll be back in twenty minutes to talk about it again. Don't give up. Keep gently asking for what you need, while keeping your requests clear, specific, and realistic. Also understand that sometimes, no matter how specific and loving you make your requests, you'll still be refused.

Rating Your Desires

Sometimes, in the process of modifying your requests, it's helpful to ask questions to learn the relative intensity of your partner's desires.

On another occasion, Jonathan asks Claudia to go with him that evening to spend some time with his parents.

"I'd rather have my foot run over by a truck," she says.

"I can understand that," says Jonathan. "I know my mother can be difficult to get along with. I do need to spend some time with them, though. Tonight's just one possibility. Help me understand where you are with this so we can work it out. On a scale of one to five (five being the most), how much do you *not* want to go to my parents' house tonight? I am not trying to get you to change your mind here."

"Probably a four."

"I'd rate my *wanting* to go over there at about a two or three," he says, "so let's not go. *Not going* is more important to you than *going* is for me. Would you be willing to set up a time next week when we'll visit them?"

In this atmosphere of listening and acceptance, Claudia doesn't mind setting up a time for their visit, and Jonathan informs his family. When they ask why he and Claudia aren't coming over that night—as Jonathan previously suggested—he does not blame Claudia. He just says, "*We* decided next week would be a better time."

When you rate your desires, you could easily try to get your way by inflating your rating and exaggerating what you want or don't want. With that approach you might get what you want on occasion, but in the long run your selfishness will injure the trust and love in your marriage.

Refusal of Your Request

It's natural that you feel *some* disappointment when one of your requests is turned down—after all, you wouldn't have asked for something if you didn't have some interest in getting it—but in a loving relationship, your disappointment will be only brief, and you won't feel irritation. It's easier to accept a refusal of your request when you remember the following:

- The Law of Choice is always in play. Just because he married you and promised to love you forever does not mean he gave up the right to make his own choices. When you remember that—and when you care about *his* happiness as much as your own—you won't have expectations when you make your requests. You can easily accept *no* for an answer.
- You can always modify your request, as we discussed above, and suggest something your partner might agree to.
- Your greatest goal is to increase the Real Love in your relationship, not to get any particular *thing* you want.

When we make requests of our partners, we have a tendency to think—mostly unconsciously—*If you really love me, you will do this thing I'm asking,* and if our partners refuse, we often take that as evidence that they don't care about us. In effect, we're narrowly defining what love has to look like, and it is those expectations that cause our disappointment and anger. We need to expand our definition of love. We need to see that expressions of love are not limited just to those things we want, but also include whatever our partners are willing to give. That attitude will increase our gratitude and our sense of feeling loved.

Always be prepared for *no* as an answer, and prepare a back-up request. If you do that, you won't have that uncomfortable moment when your request is refused and you look disappointed. And your partner will be grateful when you gracefully accept his or her refusal.

෯

Also remember as the person *receiving* a request that you can do a lot to make your refusal graceful and loving. You can offer alternatives to the request. You can express understanding of the request, and genuine regret if you're not in a position to do as you've been asked. You can also explain *why* you're unable—or unwilling—to do as requested, but make your explanation brief. Long explanations often come across as defensive, and your spouse will often regard each point of your explanation only as another opportunity to argue. Do *not* keep responding to those challenges—it rarely helps. Simply restate your reason for refusal—once and without guilt—and offer to do something else, if possible.

Agreements and Expectations

Once your partner has agreed to your request, he or she has now made a *promise*, and that is an exception to the Law of Expectations (pages 46–49). The expectations associated with promises can actually be quite productive. Imagine, for example, that you've asked your wife to pick up something from the store on the way home from work. After she agrees, you have a right to expect that she'll do as she's promised. Without that expectation, you'd have to go to the store, too, which would result in needless duplication of effort and resources. In a marriage, promises and expectations can be a source of comfort. When agreements have been made, you can expect your partner to be faithful to you, for example, or to attend to certain tasks around the house, and from those healthy expectations, both of you can experience a comforting peace.

I can further illustrate healthy and unhealthy expectations as I introduce you to Terry and Jessica, who have been married for twelve years, have two children, and both work outside the home.

Because Terry works full-time and Jessica part-time, they've agreed that she will have a meal prepared—or brought in—each evening, and will also do the housekeeping. On many occasions, when Jessica fails to have the food prepared, or when the house is a mess, Terry says something unkind, and then she gets irritated about it.

Does Terry have a right to expect Jessica to fix meals and clean the house? Yes, because she agreed—promised—to perform those tasks. She made that agreement mostly in order to avoid Terry's disapproval, but she still agreed, and Terry therefore has a right to his expectations.

Terry, however, is making two mistakes here: First, he is disappointed and angry, which is always wrong, as we've discussed. Second, he expects her not only to do her work but also to make him *happy*. Every time we become disappointed or angry with people, we're declaring our expectation that they will add to our happiness in some way, or at least not detract from it. Even though we may reasonably have expectations that our partner accomplish certain tasks, we cannot expect him or her to make us happy. After childhood, no one has the right to that expectation.

You might object, Is Jessica stuck forever with doing all the work around the house? Is that fair? Jessica can certainly change her mind at any time. She's not a slave, nor has the Law of Choice been repealed here. But if Jessica is unhappy, she needs to talk to Terry about changing their agreement—instead of just reacting with irritation and resentment. Mind you, she does not need his *permission* to change the agreement. She just needs to tell him if she's unwilling to continue fulfilling her original promise.

In the case of a promise—other than for love or happiness—you *are* entitled to your expectations, but *having* an expectation and *demanding* that it be filled are quite different. Let me illustrate this concept with an activity most of us do every day: driving a car. Imagine that you pull up to a four-way stop at exactly the same moment that another driver pulls up to his sign on your left. In every state I'm aware of, you have the *right-of-way* because you're on the *right* side of the other driver. You therefore have the *right* to expect the other driver to remain stopped while you drive through the intersection. He's made a promise to that effect by accepting his driver's license, which requires compliance with all the driving rules of the state.

Just as you edge out into the intersection, however, the other driver also moves forward. You could insist on your right to proceed, but if you do that, you could be *dead right*. Being right about your expectations in relationships is similarly unproductive. You may be right, but if you insist on it, you won't like the results. If your spouse makes a promise, you're entitled to your expectations, but you'd be foolish to demand that they be filled. If she fails to perform as promised, you can simply make her aware of your expectation, but without insistence or irritation.

In a successful relationship, expectations always occur in an atmosphere of Real Love. If you unconditionally care about the happiness of your partner, you can still expect the promised performance of a task, but enforcing the letter of the law will never be more important to you than feeling and sharing love. And if you're focused on the happiness of others, they will actually tend to fill their promises with greater faithfulness, much better than if you make demands of them.

One major reason we need to avoid expectations is that they make gratitude and happiness impossible. Imagine that you expect me to bring you a dozen roses every morning at nine o'clock. On the first morning I bring you a dozen roses at nine thirty, but you're disappointed and angry, because you expected me to arrive at nine. You wonder why I don't care enough about you to do as you've asked. The next day I arrive at eight thirty, but that's no good, either, because I've interrupted your day by arriving too early. The day after that I arrive at exactly nine but with eleven flowers, so you have a fit that I haven't brought a dozen. Although I'm giving you a significant gift of time and resources each time, you can't be truly grateful for what you're getting because of your expectations, and then you can't feel loved or happy. Without gratitude, everything we have becomes meaningless and can't contribute to our happiness.

Notice that I didn't say anything about you being grateful *to me*. In order to be happy, you don't need to be grateful to me or anyone else in particular. Real joy comes from being grateful *for* what you receive, not from being grateful *to me*. In fact, if there's too much *me* in your gratitude, you'll feel only *obligated* to me, and that won't make you happy. I would insist on you being grateful to me only if I had some need for praise and power myself.

Making Agreements

One way to reach an agreement is to make a request of your partner, as we've already discussed. But you can also reach agreements mutually, without a request by one partner. If either of you perceives a need, you can sit down with your partner and reach an agreement about how that need will be filled, without an initial request. Geoffrey and Charlotte learned about the power of agreements as they argued one day in my office.

Charlotte began, "You never help with the kids."

"I do, too," Geoffrey countered. "How can you say that? I help all the time."

"Just last night Justin needed help with his homework, and you let him whine and whine about it, without doing a thing to help him."

"So why didn't *you* help him?" Geoffrey snapped.

Charlotte was becoming increasingly irritated and defensive. "You could see that I was busy putting Amber to bed."

I stepped in and said, "You could argue about this forever. Whose *job* was it to put Amber to bed, or to help Justin with his homework?"

They both looked at me as though I'd spoken in a foreign language. One of the most common sources of conflict in a marriage is that both partners assume that a given task will be done by the other person. When that expectation isn't filled, disappointment and irritation inevitably follow. But it turns out that these assumptions about who will do a particular thing are rarely warranted. There has been no clear agreement established about who is to do what in the marriage, so many things don't get done at all, or they're accomplished at the last minute, and it all happens in an atmosphere of confusion and tension. Making proactive agreements about responsibilities reduces confusion and the failure to accomplish necessary tasks. Agreements about responsibilities have the additional benefit of reducing the need for making requests for each individual task. Having to make a request for every single thing that needs to happen can become a real drag—you feel like you're always begging or nagging your spouse to do something.

I made some suggestions to Geoffrey and Charlotte—which I also recommend here to you—about how to make agreements:

- If possible, set aside a time when you will not be interrupted. Some issues are difficult to discuss when you're distracted by other concerns.
- Talk when you're both relaxed and not already upset about the issue you'll be discussing. Emptiness and fear do not make positive contributions to the establishment of agreements.
- Determine exactly what your needs are. What are the things that must be accomplished?
- Do *not* talk about past performance. Do not say, for example, "I've always been the one who . . ." Or, "You have never helped me with . . ."
- Determine who will be responsible for accomplishing each task.
- Set an exact timetable for completion of each task.
- Clarify how you will follow up on the assignments that are accepted.

Geoffrey and Charlotte really dug into their project. Let's examine just two of many agreements they made and see how they were guided by the principles above.

Agreement: The Kids' Homework

What: Their homework has to be completed each day before they watch television, talk on the phone, play with friends, or anything else. The parent responsible for homework must ensure that these guidelines are followed, and will talk to any child who fails to follow these rules. The parent will also talk to each child about the results of homework done the day before, test results, and so on.

When: As soon as the child gets home, the parent will ask what homework he/she has, and will follow up on its completion.

Who: Geoffrey to help the children Wednesday through Friday (he tends to get home late on Mondays and Tuesdays). Charlotte to help them on Monday and Tuesday.

Follow-up: Geoffrey and Charlotte will meet every Sunday at 2:00 p.m. to discuss the children's homework.

Agreement: Finances

What	When	Who
One person keeps checkbook	Every check entered same day, including those written by person not holding checkbook	Charlotte
Checkbook balanced	By fifteenth of month	Geoffrey
Pay bills	No later than one week before due date	Charlotte
Prepare personal taxes	By March 15	Geoffrey
No expenditures over $50 without mutual agreement	Always	Both

Follow-up: All the above to be discussed at regularly scheduled meetings, usually Sunday at 2:00 p.m.

In the beginning, it may be wise to put your agreements in writing—as this couple did—to eliminate confusion about what was actually said.

౿

There must be a division of labor within a marriage. It makes responsibilities clear, avoids duplication, and makes the best use of the individual abilities of the two spouses. One partner is often better suited for some tasks. Another partner might spend more time at work, in which case it would make sense that he or she would be given fewer assignments at home. When you both care about the other's happiness, and when you can avoid the consistently destructive effects of Getting and Protecting Behaviors, you *will* be able to work out an agreement for everything. If the agreement proves to be inequitable, you can always change it.

What If No Agreement Is Possible?

If you're having trouble working out a specific agreement—about the kids, finances, and so on—it is likely that one or both of you are feeling empty and afraid. Remember that there are people who love you. Tell the truth about yourself to your spouse and others, which will create additional opportunities for you to feel loved unconditionally. When you feel less empty and afraid, you can come back to that agreement and work it out. People have difficulty with agreements only because they're blinded by their own emptiness and fear. When Real Love eliminates those conditions, each partner can easily work with the other toward decisions that yield the greatest benefit to both.

Two people who are truthful and trying to be loving can work out anything. You are partners. Resist the temptation to take over and bully your partner into doing things your way.

Supporting the Agreement

Once you've made an agreement, remember that violating or neglecting it is an unloving act on your part. If you do fail to keep an agreement, freely admit your mistake to your partner, making no excuses. If your partner is in violation, simply inform him or her of your observation—when you're not feeling empty and afraid, and when you won't be accusing—and forgive the transgression. Hanging on to offenses is death to a marriage.

Sometimes your partner will need help keeping his or her part of the agreement. As Charlotte keeps the checkbook, for example, Geoffrey will have to inform her promptly when he writes one of the loose checks he carries around in his wallet. His failure to do that would make it difficult for Charlotte to keep her agreement about being responsible for the checkbook.

On some occasions, you'll notice that your spouse is having difficulty with fulfilling her part of the agreement. She may become burdened down by other responsibilities, for example, and be unable to help the kids with their homework on the night assigned to her. Don't just sit back and smugly point out what she should have done. Offer your help freely and communicate support for your partner.

One way to communicate support for agreements is to support the decisions of the person responsible for the job. When the living room needed new carpet, Geoffrey and Charlotte agreed that she would be in charge of the purchase. He had little interest in such things, and she had considerably more experience in interior decorating than he did. When Geoffrey came home and saw the installed carpet for the first time, he was dismayed—it was very different from what he would have picked out. In fact, he thought it looked hideous, but he remembered their agreement that she would be responsible for the carpet, and he instantly decided he could live with it. When she asked what he thought of it, he supported her decision completely.

Sometimes your partner will make decisions that work out poorly, and you might have a tendency to be critical or to say, "I told you so." You would *never* say that in a loving relationship. If she has the responsibility to make a decision, she also has the right to make her own mistakes and learn from them. Don't do the cheap thing by criticizing her best efforts.

Exercises

Exercise One

Make a list of several things you'd like your partner to do for you. Pick one of them and write exactly how you plan to make your request. Use the guidelines for making requests, found at the beginning of the chapter.

If possible, practice making this request first with a friend, asking your friend to tell you whether the request comes across as demanding, and whether it's clear and specific enough.

Now make the request of your partner. Later evaluate how you did, again using the five principles we've discussed.

Exercise Two

Write several things that are not being accomplished in your family as smoothly as you'd like—finances, the kids, household chores. Arrange a time to talk with your partner about how you can better address these tasks, using the principles above that guide us in the making of agreements.

Exercise Three

Identify something about your partner that provokes irritation in you. Now carefully consider the following:

- The Law of Choice. Everyone—including your partner—always has the right to do and say what he or she wishes.
- The most important goals in your marriage: to feel loved, loving, and happy. Is there any single thing about your partner that you're willing to change at the expense of losing some of the Real Love and genuine happiness you want most?
- The role of expectations in anger. If you're irritated, you *are* having an expectation that your partner will change in some way to suit your needs. In order to get something you want,

you're willing to violate the Law of Choice and destroy the possibility of a loving relationship.

In light of the above, make a plan to do one of the following:

- Completely accept and love your partner, without his or her changing the characteristic that now bothers you.
- Sit down with your partner and make a loving request—or work out an agreement—that addresses the behavior now interfering with your happiness.

7

Into the Lion's Mouth

Communicating Your Spouse's Mistakes

As I talked with Sharon one afternoon, she voiced the frustration she was feeling about her marriage.

"Months ago," she said, "I read your *Real Love* book and learned a lot. Since then I've been telling the truth about myself to some friends, and I've found several who can see me and accept me. I always hoped that Real Love existed, and now I know it does, because I've *felt* it."

I smiled. "It's a great feeling, isn't it?"

"The best. And it's helping me to accept and love my husband, Boyd. Naturally, I still make mistakes, but I'm loving him better than I ever thought I could. I have a problem, though. Even though I'm loving him a lot better, he doesn't seem to be any happier. He's still angry all the time. He yells at the kids and hardly ever speaks to me, even though I've quit criticizing him and arguing with him. He just seems miserable. I know a lot about the way he was raised, and I don't think he ever experienced a moment of Real Love in his entire childhood—still doesn't from his parents or his sister. And then he married me, and I didn't love him unconditionally, either. I'm learning to love him, but it doesn't seem to be helping. I don't know what to do next."

Why You Tell Your Spouse the Truth About Himself or Herself

Sharon's description of a spouse who is feeling unloved and unhappy is quite common, as is her desire to help her spouse. She simply wanted to share with her partner the joy she had thus far experienced with Real Love. So I attempted to describe to her a way she might be able to help her husband.

"Do you remember the first time we talked?" I asked.

"Sure."

"What do you remember about it?"

"Lots of things, but mostly that I felt accepted by you."

"Did I hug you and tell you I loved you? Did I tell you what a wonderful person you were?"

"No, you didn't."

"So how did you know I accepted you?"

"It was obvious. I could just feel it."

"What did we talk about?" I asked Sharon.

"Mostly we talked about how selfish and unloving I was—with Boyd and with other people, too. You showed me how I'd been lying, attacking people, and acting like a victim all my life [pause] I think I'm getting the point now. I felt accepted because you accepted me while I talked about my mistakes and flaws—my warts."

"Exactly. If you hadn't been willing to tell the truth about yourself, you wouldn't have felt accepted no matter what I'd done. It was your being honest that made it possible for you to feel loved, first with me and then with your friends."

"I understand."

"And your husband won't feel loved until *he* does what *you* did. He'll have to tell the truth about himself before he can feel the Real Love you're offering him. As long as he hides who he is—as long as he uses Getting and Protecting Behaviors all the time—he'll make it impossible to feel loved."

Although it is critical that we learn how to offer Real Love to our spouses, our partners will not benefit from the love we give unless they actually do what's necessary to *feel* it. On pages 55–56, I introduced the process Truth → Seen → Accepted → Loved. Our spouses cannot feel loved until they begin to tell the truth about themselves.

Most of our spouses have been hiding who they are for a lifetime—getting Imitation Love and protecting themselves from the people who have consistently failed to love them unconditionally—so in many cases, they will need some help from us before they can begin the process of being truthful. Sometimes, if we simply love them unconditionally and provide many examples of telling the truth about *ourselves*, that will be enough to create the safety and motivation they need to begin the process of truth-telling themselves. At other times, however, we may actually have to point out to them the Getting and Protecting Behaviors that are interfering with their happiness.

Just because your spouse *needs* to hear and speak the truth about his or her mistakes and Getting and Protecting Behaviors, however, does not always give *you* the right to assist in that process. Before you even think about offering your help with truth-telling, consider the two essential *reasons* for telling other people the truth about themselves:

- To create an opportunity for them to feel loved.
- To create the possibility for them to make different choices. As long as we blame other people for our problems, we're helpless to solve them. When we blame others, we place our happiness in their hands, and then we can't become happier until those people decide to change. When we concentrate on telling the truth about *our* mistakes and failings, however, we can begin to make wiser choices, especially if we also feel loved.

In short, you need to tell your spouse about his mistakes only to help *him*. Most of us have a lifelong habit of telling people about their mistakes for less than charitable reasons. We often point out the mistakes of others so we can feel powerful, or smart, or worthwhile, and sometimes we even describe the mistakes of others to hurt them. We can feel none of those motivations—to any degree—when we talk to our spouses about their mistakes and their Getting and Protecting Behaviors, or we'll cause only further injury to our marriages.

When to Tell Your Spouse the Truth About Himself or Herself

Our spouses hide who they are only because they're afraid that we'll see their flaws and then criticize or reject them. When people are empty and afraid, almost everything is threatening to them, and then they may not welcome your efforts to help them see the truth.

As we make attempts to tell the truth about our spouses, we must remember that they can listen to us clearly only if they're not distracted by emptiness and fear, and we can create the possibility of eliminating those conditions only if we are unconditionally accepting and loving toward them. Tell your spouse the truth about himself or herself only when

- you are feeling unconditionally loving, *and*
- your spouse is in a position to actually *hear* what you will say. If he or she is sufficiently empty and afraid, he won't be *able* to hear you, and then your speaking can only be unproductive.

You can't control your spouse's emptiness and fear, but you can be rigorously honest about your own ability to be loving in any given moment. As you anticipate talking to your spouse about his or her behavior, thoroughly examine yourself for signs of your own emptiness and fear, which include—but are not limited to—the following:

- You're nervous about talking to him.
- You have some expectation that she will actually listen to you

or change her behavior in some way as a result of what you're planning to say.

- You're afraid your comments will hurt his feelings. Partly you genuinely don't want to hurt *him*, but a great part of your fear is that he'll react to what you may see by not liking *you*.
- You're feeling irritated by the behavior you're planning to discuss.
- You're feeling hurt because of the behavior you'll be discussing.

These are all indications that you need your partner to listen to you and give you something you want, and in that condition it's quite unlikely that you'll communicate an unconditional concern for his or her happiness. Absolutely *never* talk to your partner about his or her mistakes, or Getting and Protecting Behaviors, when you are angry, which includes being annoyed, irritated, and frustrated. It's hard enough for your partner to face the truth about himself or herself without you introducing the pain and fear you provoke with your anger.

It should be noted that even when you *are* unconditionally loving, your spouse may still be empty and afraid and therefore unable to hear you—not everyone is capable of *feeling* the Real Love he or she is offered—but your Real Love is still the only way to create the *possibility* of his or her hearing you.

Taking a Risk

Sharon and I continued our conversation (from pages 220–221).

"So you're saying," she asked, "that Boyd won't ever feel loved and happy until he starts telling the truth about his anger and selfishness?"

"Yes."

"And you're saying that *I'll* probably have to be the one to talk to him about it?"

"If you don't, who will? With his anger, he makes everybody back away from him. Nobody dares tell him the truth about his anger, because they're afraid he'll bite their heads off."

"I'm pretty afraid of that myself. Any time I've talked to him in the past about his being mad, he's only gotten more angry. Why should it be different this time?"

"First," I said, "I'm guessing that when you've talked to Boyd in the past about his being angry, *you* were angry, too, and then he felt threatened and reacted to protect himself by becoming even more angry. Right?"

"I guess I always *have* been irritated when I've talked to him about his anger."

"You can change that. Now you understand that Boyd uses anger only as a Getting and Protecting Behavior when he's empty and afraid. You know he's just drowning and isn't doing anything with the primary intention of hurting *you*. So you can begin to give him the love he needs."

"I'm still afraid he's going to cut my head off when I try to talk to him."

"He might, but really, what have you got to lose? As things stand now, he's angry and unhappy most of the time, and if you don't say anything, he's likely to stay that way—or get worse. If you lovingly try to talk to him about his anger, though, at least you create a *chance* that he might hear you and begin the process of being truthful and feeling the love you're offering. The only way you can find out if that's possible is if you actually take the risk of talking to him."

"So what if I talk to him and he explodes at me? Or he won't listen? Then what?"

"First, you haven't lost anything, right? He was angry to start with, and if he's angry after you talk to him, nothing's really changed—so you haven't hurt anything. And then you can keep learning how to accept and love him, like you've been doing. The more you love him, the more you'll create a safe environment where he might finally be able to talk about his warts. And you can keep telling him the truth about your own mistakes and Getting and Protecting Behaviors, which will give him examples of what it looks like to tell the truth. Tell *other* people the truth about yourself, too, and you'll feel *their* acceptance and love. And remember that no matter how he responds, *you* will be much happier as a result of feeling loved and being loving."

How Hard Can You Push the Truth?

How hard can you push your spouse in the process of helping her see the truth about her behavior? How can you know whether it's better just to be accepting, or whether you should go beyond that and help her be truthful?

Usually, you learn the answers to these questions by making lots of mistakes. It's impossible to know what your spouse's reactions will be until you've actually taken the risk of helping her see the truth about herself. Accept the fact that you'll make mistakes, and learn from them.

If your spouse reacts with anger, lying, and acting like a victim as you attempt to help him see the truth about himself, back off. He's telling you he can't hear you. Try again later—when he's better prepared to listen, and perhaps when you're more loving.

Always examine your behavior as you're telling the truth about your spouse, and consider whether you could be more loving. Learn from your mistakes. Also keep in mind that just because your spouse won't hear you does not mean you didn't speak in a loving way. Sometimes when people are sufficiently empty and afraid, they can't hear the truth about themselves from anyone.

When *Not* to Tell Your Partner the Truth

Several days after our conversation above, Sharon called me and said, "I tried to help Boyd see that he's angry, but he didn't listen to a word I said. In fact, he just got madder."

"Tell me what happened," I said.

"He was making critical, snippy comments about something I hadn't done, and I said, 'Boyd, until you can admit that you're angry only because *you* are empty and afraid—not because of what *I* did or didn't do—you'll keep blaming me and you won't feel loved.'"

It's not difficult to understand why Boyd reacted badly to what Sharon said, and this couple illustrates two important principles to remember when talking to your spouse about his or her behavior:

- Don't try to tell your spouse the truth about his or her Getting and Protecting Behaviors right *while* he or she is using them. When people are getting Imitation Love and protecting themselves, they're telling you they're empty and afraid and are therefore unable to listen to you.
- Especially don't try to tell your spouse the truth about his or her anger while he or she is angry at *you*. Anything you say will then be perceived by your spouse as defending yourself.

Talk to your spouse about his or her Getting and Protecting Behaviors at a time when you're both relatively relaxed and not upset about the issues you'll be discussing. If possible, set aside a time when there will be no interruptions. It's difficult to discuss important issues while you're distracted by other concerns. In a few pages, we'll talk about exactly how you can talk to your spouse about these things.

Don't Tell Your Partner the Truth When It Doesn't Matter

Andrew and Lynn had been married for years, and one day I watched as Andrew listened to Lynn talking about her day. She said it had been really hot, setting a record for that date, but Andrew countered that the weather bureau had indicated that the day's high temperature had been only the third highest in the past fifty years. When she said she took the car in for an oil change, he said she'd done it too early—she could have driven two hundred miles more before the oil change was due. He corrected her several more times like that, and I saw that Lynn didn't like being interrupted and corrected all the time. Finally I said, "Andrew, are you aware that you keep correcting Lynn?"

"What do you mean?" he said.

"You've made some kind of correction or addition to almost everything she's said: temperatures, times, numbers. You may even be right about all of it, but does it matter, and is it worth it?"

He still didn't know what I was talking about, so I turned to Lynn and asked, "Do you like it when Andrew corrects you?"

"No, I really don't. It's been bugging me for years."

Eventually, as Andrew learned how to listen to Lynn—staying quiet when his corrections wouldn't really matter—Lynn felt much more accepted by him.

On many occasions, when your partner is wrong about something, you'll have an enormous temptation to say something about it. Before you speak, always ask yourself, "Does this really matter?" If her error won't result in emotional or physical harm to anyone, or the demise of the family finances, it's often wise to be quiet.

Don't Tell Your Partner the Truth When It Won't Help

On another occasion, Andrew said to me, "Lynn used to be really thin and attractive, but in the last several years she's gotten overweight and kind of dumpy-looking. What's the best way to talk to her about that?"

I chuckled as I imagined how that conversation would go. "Two things occur to me. First, does she already know she's overweight? Does she ever go on diets?"

"All the time," he said, "but she never stays on them."

"So she already believes she's overweight. If she already believes that, how could it possibly help for you to point it out? The second question is *why* you want to tell her. I'm sure a part of you is concerned about her health, but the first thing you said was that she used to be thin and *attractive,* but now she looks dumpy. It sounds like a big part of you is concerned about how she *looks.*"

"Well, sure. She's just not as attractive as she used to be."

"Attractive to *whom*? To *you.* It's quite understandable that you feel this way—I'm not criticizing you here—but when you talk about her weight, your primary concern is *yourself*, what *you* would get from her being thinner. If she lost weight, you'd be more sexually excited by her, and if you talk to her about this, she'll *know* you're thinking about yourself. It will only hurt her feelings and hurt your relationship."

It's not likely that you'll help your relationship if you tell your spouse something he or she already knows, or if you tell him or her the truth about something that will primarily benefit *you*. So when you want to tell your wife that she's overweight, close your mouth instead and think of something to say that's kind and loving. When you're dying to tell him that you don't like the shirt and tie he's wearing, put a lid on it and tell him how much you love him. Always ask yourself, *Is this important? Will this contribute to the happiness of my partner and strengthen our relationship?*

Sometimes the behavior we want to tell our spouses about *is* important, but often we should still be quiet, as Abby learned regarding her husband, Gene.

One day Abby called to tell me that Gene had just lost his temper and said some unkind things to her. She wisely chose not to confront him with his behavior *while* he was angry—that rarely helps—but after the situation had cooled down, she wanted to know the best way to talk to him about his anger.

"For some time now," I said, "you've been learning how to accept and love him, and you've been responding much better to him when he's angry, right?"

"Yes."

"For a moment forget about his little temper tantrum today. Think only about the pattern of his behavior over the past few months. Would you say he's less angry now than he was four months ago?"

"Sure. He blows up a lot less than he used to."

"Sometimes he even apologizes for his anger now, right?"

"Yes, he does."

"Then why do you need to talk to him about this particular

tantrum? He sees the truth about his anger, he apologizes for it, and he's angry less often than he used to be. He's learning and growing and becoming happier, so why not just be grateful for that and have faith that he'll learn from this event without your having to point it out to him?"

When you're thinking about pointing out a fault in your partner, ask yourself whether there's already a pattern of improvement. If so, maybe you don't have to say something about every mistake. What matters is that you and your partner are learning and growing. You do not need to speak just because something is less than perfect.

"So right while he's mad at me," said Abby, "I can see why it might not help to talk to him about it, but what *can* I say? Do I have to just sit there and say nothing?"

"Sure, sometimes that's exactly the thing to do," I said. "If you don't respond to his anger, eventually the fuel will burn out, and he'll quit being angry. On some occasions, though, you can help even more by telling the truth about *yourself.*"

"How do I tell the truth about myself when *he's* the one being mad over nothing?"

"Let's take a specific example. What got his tantrum started yesterday?"

"It was ridiculous," Abby said. "He came home late at night, when everybody was in bed but me, and there were a few lights on in some rooms here and there. He had a fit about how we *always* leave the lights on, and nobody cares how much it costs, and nobody appreciates how hard he has to work to pay for everything."

"Of course, we know that he was angry about a lot more than just a few lights that probably didn't cost a single dollar to run for the time they were on. To him the real issue was his belief that nobody listens to him or seems to care about him—and when you say his behavior is ridiculous, you're proving that you *don't* listen to him. Even though a few lights probably aren't all that important, what he's really trying to tell you is something about himself—the Third Rule of Seeing we've talked about—and you're not listening. You're telling him with your behavior that you don't care about what's important to him, and he can feel that."

"So what should I have said?"

"Has he asked you to turn off the lights before?"

"Yes, but—"

"There is no *but* here. He asked you to do something, and even though it isn't very important to *you*, it *is* important to *him*. It wouldn't take much effort to do this little thing, would it?"

"I guess not."

"So even though you weren't consciously aware of it, with your behavior you told him that he's not very important to you. Isn't that true?"

"I hadn't looked at it like that, but I see what you mean now."

"So tell him the truth about that. When he's mad about the lights being on, walk right up to him—real close—and touch him while you say, 'Boyd, you've asked me about those lights many times, and I keep ignoring you. I've been thoughtless about that, and I'm going to pay more attention to it in the future.' Then in a few days, ask him if he's noticed any change in the lights being turned off. He'll feel like you're really seeing him and caring about him. Eventually, as he feels more loved by you, it's very likely that he won't care much about the lights. It's really your love he wants."

How to Tell Your Spouse the Truth About Himself or Herself

On pages 220–221 and 224–227, we read about Sharon, who wanted to help her husband, Boyd, tell the truth about his anger. Her initial attempt was unproductive, but for several weeks, she practiced accepting and loving him, and eventually she tried to talk to him again. One Sunday morning, when there was no rush and no tension between them, Sharon asked Boyd if he would be willing to spend some time with her, either that morning or later in the afternoon. She had previously made arrangements for the children to be occupied so that she and Boyd wouldn't be interrupted as they talked.

When they were alone, she sat close to him on the couch, with her knee touching his. That seems like a small thing, but it's actually quite important, because when we're afraid of someone, or angry at them, we unconsciously move away from them physically, and they *feel* that, consciously or not.

"In the past several months," she said, "I've been learning a lot about relationships and unconditional love. You've probably noticed me talking to people on the phone about that."

"Sure," he said.

"I've learned that what everybody wants most is to feel unconditionally loved by the people around them—parents, spouses, friends, anybody—and I can see now that for many years I haven't given you much of that. Instead I get disappointed and irritated when you don't do what I want, and then you feel like I care more about myself than I do about you, which is true."

Boyd had no idea what to say in response.

"As a child," she said, "I never felt unconditionally loved. People always liked me only when I was doing what they wanted, so I tried hard to earn their affection, but that only made me feel empty and alone. Lately, I've learned that before people can accept me for who I really am, I have to tell them the truth about myself—about my mistakes, my selfishness, my inability to love people—and I've found some people who can really see me and accept me. I'm learning how happy I can be when I feel loved and loving instead of feeling hurt, or being angry, or manipulating people. Just being angry—that one thing—has cost me more happiness than I can describe. Look how much it's hurt our relationship every time I've been angry at you."

Disarmed by Sharon's honesty and sincerity, Boyd nodded his head.

"You haven't felt unconditionally loved all your life, either, certainly not by me, and that's a terrible feeling. To protect yourself from that feeling, and to get people to do some of the things you want, you get angry. But then you feel alone and unhappy. I am *not* saying you shouldn't be angry. I'm not criticizing you in any way. I'm just suggesting that being angry is making you unhappy, and there's a way to change that. If you could see how angry you are, and that I love you whether you're angry or not, you might begin to feel more loved and happy."

"I guess I've been angry all my life," Boyd said. "I can't remember when it hasn't been a big part of me. And I probably blame it on you more than I should."

As he told the truth about himself, he began to feel Sharon's love for him—just as the Wart King felt the love of the Wise Man when he finally told the truth about his warts. We can all learn to function as wise men and women for our spouses.

⚜

You may not get the kind of positive response from your spouse that Sharon got from Boyd, and you don't have to take an approach with your partner as direct as the one she chose, but any loving attempt to help your spouse begin to share the truth is often better than no attempt at all. We all have many opportunities to make such attempts, as illustrated here by Adam and his wife, Suzanne.

Adam walks in the door with a deep scowl on his face, an expression he's often used to get everyone in the house to back off and leave him alone. But Suzanne walks up close to him and asks, "How was your day?"

"Fine," he growls, and turns to walk away.

It would be so easy for Suzanne to allow Adam to walk off and be angry alone—who likes to be around people who act like that?—but she knows if he does that, he'll only feel more alone and miserable. So she reaches out and gently touches him on the arm. "You don't look fine, Adam," she says, "and you don't have to talk about it if you don't want, but I'd love to hear what happened today."

"Oh, it's just the same old stuff."

"When the same old stuff is bothering you day after day," she says, "it can really wear you down."

"I don't think the management at work is ever going to get the picture. They work us to death, and then they complain about how profits are down, and how we all need to do more."

As Suzanne listens and asks questions, Adam eventually tells her all about his frustration at work—about his anger and his fear that if things don't change, he could actually lose his job. Many other people have.

"That's a lot of stress," she says. "And I know you feel stress about some things here at home, too—the kids, money, me. What can I do to make things easier for you?"

Adam can't think of anything right away, so Suzanne suggests that they talk about it again the next day.

The results of this simple conversation are profound. Suzanne has demonstrated a genuine concern for Adam's happiness—the definition of Real Love—and Adam *feels* her love even more strongly after sharing his anger and fears. All the next day at work, he feels much less stress about his job, and although he doesn't realize it consciously, the change in his feelings is due to the love he feels from Suzanne. All day he looks forward to going home and talking to her about work and other things. It is the beginning of a gradual but powerful change in their relationship.

Eventually, when your spouse is certain that you love him or her, you can say almost anything, and he or she will be able to hear it, as Suzanne discovers one evening when she talks to Adam.

Adam has been putting the kids to bed, and when they don't move quickly enough, he begins to get angry and say unkind things to them. When one of them begins to cry, Adam sharply tells him to stay in bed and walks out of the room, slamming the door.

When he comes into the living room, Suzanne looks up at him with a grin on her face and says, "That sounded like a tender father–son moment."

Had she said this months before, Adam would have exploded, but for some time they had been sharing the truth about themselves and their acceptance of each other, so Adam knows she loves him. He smiles and says, "That wasn't very pretty, was it? Here my greatest goal with the kids is to love them, but because I was feeling stressed, I forgot all about that and yelled at Brandon just for being slow to get in bed. Embarrassing." Then he walks back to the bedroom to hug Brandon and apologize for his anger.

Notice that Suzanne talked to Adam about his anger *while* he was still irritated, in contradiction to the recommendation I made earlier that spouses not do that. But again, when you and your spouse are more certain of your love for each other, you can say almost anything at any time.

On other occasions, when Adam appears to be irritated, Suzanne crosses the room, takes him by the hand, and leads him to the couch, where she orders, "Sit down." Then she sits in his lap, smiles broadly, and says, "You look unhappy. Tell me about it." He simply can't resist talking to her under those conditions, and almost invariably his anger vanishes under the influence of her love for him.

As you and your spouse practice telling the truth and accepting each other, you'll become increasingly capable of making loving observations to each other about behaviors that are interfering with your feeling loved, loving, and happy. Our greatest goal is to find all the happiness we can, and a loving partner will point out to us the occasions when we're detracting from the happiness we could be experiencing.

Telling the Truth About Simple Mistakes

Sometimes you need to talk to your partner about simple mistakes—an assignment not carried out, an error made in the checkbook, and so on—rather than talking about Getting and Protecting Behaviors. A common blunder we make is to *accuse* our partners of a mistake, instead of just *informing* them of the mistake. It's not the words that distinguish these two approaches but how you *feel* when you speak. If you feel irritated because you were inconvenienced by your partner's error, you will be accusing—whether you mean to be or not—and should *not* talk about it then. If you wait until you feel accepting and loving, the results will be far better.

Adam and Suzanne shared the responsibility for getting the kids to soccer practice, school plays, and so on. Adam often waited until the last possible moment before leaving the house, and as a result, he often made the kids late for their events. In the past, Suzanne had approached a problem like this by saying, "You made the kids late again today. You're always doing that. When *I* take them, we're never late." This accusatory approach had always led to arguments.

But Suzanne had learned the value of Real Love in any discussion, so she said to Adam, "The last several times you've taken the kids to soccer practice, they've been late. When that happens, the team has to wait on them, and sometimes—to teach them a lesson—the coach cuts back the playing time for our kids. Is there anything I can do to help them get there on time?"

Suzanne's words were informative and helpful, rather than accusatory, and Adam could feel that she wasn't disappointed or angry. He felt her acceptance. Because she wasn't adding to his emptiness and fear, he felt safe and immediately admitted that he was the problem. He said he just didn't enjoy running those errands, so he put them off to the last minute. The problem improved considerably after that.

Even when you have an accepting attitude, avoid expressions like *you never*, *you always*, and *I don't know why you*. In the process of making a mistake, your spouse already feels inadequate. He or she needs your acceptance and support as you talk about what can be done to correct the mistake. Your conversations will never benefit from accusations.

Many of us allow our partners' mistakes to build up over a long period of time before we finally talk about them, and for much of that time we're not aware that our irritation is steadily building. It can be helpful if we take responsibility for our failure to bring up the troublesome issue sooner. For example, you could say, "Something has been bothering me, and I've let this go on far too long before talking to you about it. That's my fault. It's about the checkbook . . ." In this way, you can communicate that a problem has been going on for some time, but at the same time you can assume some of the responsibility for that yourself.

When Your Spouse Is Telling You the Truth About You

It's easy to make insightful observations about the mistakes and the Getting and Protecting Behaviors of your spouse. It's quite a different experience, however, to hear these observations about *yourself*.

Suzanne called me one day to say that she was angry about a conversation she'd just had with Adam.

"He can be so critical about things," she said, "and when he's like that, I don't know how to be loving."

"You may not be capable of being loving at those times," I agreed, "but you can certainly tell the truth about yourself. What was he criticizing you about this time?"

"We run a small business out of our home together. He says that every time I make a purchase that can be deducted as a business expense, I lose the receipts, and he's tired of it—but that's just not true."

"Okay, so he wasn't entirely accurate. That really has nothing to do with *you* telling the truth about yourself. You may not *always* lose the receipts, but *sometimes* you do, and that's inconvenient for Adam and causes you both to lose tax deductions, right?"

"I guess, but it doesn't help when he exaggerates it, and when he's irritated at me."

"Again, *his* mistakes are irrelevant. Just tell the truth. When he says you're always losing those receipts, *listen* to him—especially when he's angry. He's just telling you he wants you to hear him, but then you argue with him, which proves you're *not* hearing him. Instead you could say, "You're right. I do that a lot, and it's pretty inconsiderate. It's costing you time, and it's costing our business money. I need to pay more attention to that, and I will." If you do that, how much longer do you think he'll be angry?"

Which is more important to you, to be right, or to be loving and happy? When your spouse is pointing out your faults, he may not be motivated primarily by a desire for your happiness. So what? We all fail to be loving on many occasions. What your spouse needs is to be heard, and you can choose to do that. If he's angry, listen with acceptance. If his account of your mistakes and faults isn't exactly accurate, tell the truth about the part that is.

As you tell the truth and accept your partner, you'll create opportunities for both of you to feel accepted. You'll also remove the fuel for conflict. The tension you feel when your spouse is critical of you comes not from what you're hearing, but from your *resistance* to what you're hearing. When you're truthful, the conflict simply goes away. One of the primary reasons your partner is pushing you about your mistakes is that you haven't been listening. When you're truthful, he has no reason to keep being aggressive or irritated.

On rare occasions when you're really listening to your spouse, he might decide to take the opportunity to tell you about *all* your faults. Listen to him and tell the truth about yourself as much as possible. If it finally becomes too much to hear all at once, simply say, "You're right, all this is important for me to hear. Right now I'm feeling kind of tired (or uneasy, or anxious). Can we finish this in an hour or so?"

Exercise

Write down some of your partner's faults, the ones you've mentioned to him or her from time to time. Now, for each one, ask yourself these questions:

- Do I talk about this to my spouse in a way that actually *helps* her? Does she feel more loved? Does she use my suggestions to avoid her mistakes in the future?
- Do my spouse and I feel closer to each other as a result of my talking about this fault or mistake?

If the answer to these questions is *no,* consider taking one of the following two courses of action:

- Stop talking about that fault. If it's not contributing to the Real Love in your marriage, and it isn't helping your spouse avoid mistakes and be happier, then you're only hurting yourself and your spouse by continuing to talk about it.
- Learn to feel more loved and loving so you *can* eventually talk about the mistake or Getting and Protecting Behavior that's interfering with your spouse's happiness. Learn to talk about these issues in a way that uses the principles you've learned in this chapter, so you can lovingly offer her an opportunity to feel seen and accepted with this behavior.

8

The Agony and the Ecstasy

Sex in Marriage

We're surrounded by references to sex—in books, movies, magazines, calendars, and newspapers; on television, the radio, the Internet, and billboards; as well as in the jokes and stories we tell one another. The depiction of sexual desire and activity—sometimes subtle, but often quite graphic—has become so common that we accept it as normal. Sex is portrayed as a healthy appetite to be gratified as casually as eating a meal. We admire and envy sexually attractive men and women, and we're convinced that if we're sexually appealing ourselves, we'll feel worthwhile and happy. For that reason, we need to talk about the healthy and unhealthy roles sex can play in marriage.

Sex As a Form of Imitation Love

"Men want sex and women want romance. Men give romance to get sex, and women give sex to get romance." This statement is often used to explain the sexual conflicts between men and women, but it offers no solution, and it only widens farther the unproductive separation of men and women. It is much more useful and accurate to say that what both men and women need is Real Love, and when they can't have that, they use whatever form of Imitation

Love will make them feel good temporarily. Although both men and women use sex as a form of Imitation Love, they often differ in *how* they use sex—in other words, whether they mostly use sex in the form of praise, power, pleasure, or safety.

Praise

In the absence of Real Love, we desperately want to be valued for *something*, so we settle for earning the praise and admiration of other people. When people find us sexually attractive, for example, we feel acceptable, important, and even lovable. All our lives, we've seen the importance that people attach to physical appearance. Even when people gather around newborns, they invariably make comments like, "Oh, he's so cute," or, "She's such a pretty thing." If the child is ugly beyond redemption, making any comment about cuteness absurd, we still feel obligated to say something about the child's looks, if only to say, "He sure does look like his daddy." As a child grows, he or she continues to hear these comments about his or her physical appearance—positive and negative—and learns the importance we all place on that quality.

Eventually, when we begin to mature sexually, we learn that the term *physically* attractive is usually synonymous with *sexually* attractive. We learn that sexually attractive people are uniformly accepted, valued, and praised, so we work hard to be viewed as sexually appealing, and we envy those who possess that quality. Women especially spend a lot of time and effort—clothing, hair styling, exercise, dieting, plastic surgery—to be praised for their physical (sexual) beauty, and without that praise, they often feel worthless.

Power

When Monica was a little girl, she was praised when she behaved in the ways her parents liked, and she was the recipient of their disappointment and irritation when she was "bad," but mostly she was ignored. She felt small and powerless—as most children do—having little influence over the behavior of the people around her.

At age eleven, however, as Monica began to develop sexually, she noticed—as we all have—that sexually attractive women consistently receive more positive attention than women who don't possess that quality. Anytime we can influence the behavior of others—so they spend time with us, do things for us, let us get away with mistakes—we feel a sensation of power, and from the beginning of time women have used sexual attraction to get that feeling. Put a gorgeous model and an overweight, "unattractive" woman in any group of people and see if the two women are treated equally—by either the men or the women. Unthinkable.

As Monica noticed the effect her sexuality had on other people, she did whatever she could—modifying her physical appearance, clothing, and behavior—to enhance her sexual desirability and therefore her ability to influence the behavior of others. When she did that, she saw that boys would do almost anything she asked, boys and men of all ages looked at her when she passed, and even teachers were more accommodating with her—a welcome change from the powerlessness of her earlier years. Many women learn at an early age to offer sex and sexual desirability for the sense of power they receive.

Although I use the example of a woman above, I hasten to add that men also use their appearance for the purpose of getting a sense of power.

Pleasure

The physical pleasures of sex—sight, sound, touch, taste, and smell—are obvious and intense. Even the fantasies we have about sex are an enormous source of pleasure. When our lives are otherwise unfulfilling, sex provides an immediate thrill so powerful that we're often willing to risk serious social, emotional, health, and even criminal consequences to get it.

Safety

If you don't have enough Real Love in your life, during sex you can often achieve a few moments of safety from the pain of feeling alone and unloved. If your partner makes a commitment to be sexually faithful to you, that sense of safety increases considerably.

Trading Imitation Love in Sex

When we find a way to feel good—however brief it might be—we naturally tend to use that approach again, and that's just what Monica did when she met Anthony. She used all the tools available to her—clothing, makeup, hair, the way she spoke, the way she moved her body—to be physically appealing to him. Women often complain that men regard them only as sexual objects, but many women—perhaps even most women, to varying degrees—actually *work* at being sexual objects in order to get what they want. They trade sex—or at least the excitement they provide by being sexually appealing—for the praise, power, pleasure, and safety they want from the men in their lives.

We'll use Monica and Anthony's relationship to illustrate how men and women commonly use sex to trade Imitation Love, recognizing that the specifics vary from couple to couple. Throughout this chapter, I will generalize about how men and women get Imitation Love from sex. Although these generalizations are accurate most of the time, I recognize that there are marriages in which the stereotypes do not hold. If that is the case in your marriage, simply switch in your mind the gender being described and continue to learn the intended principle.

Neither Monica nor Anthony had experienced much Real Love before they met, so when they first became acquainted, they naturally tried to exchange as much Imitation Love with each other as possible. Sex was one currency of the trade they found useful. In Chapter One, I talked about *dollars* as an arbitrary unit of measure for Imitation Love, and I'll use that unit again here.

Early in their relationship, Monica felt about five dollars of praise from Anthony—in the form of acceptance and actual compliments—because of her sexual desirability. Anthony also felt complimented by Monica's willingness to have sex with him, although the sense of praise he received was less than Monica felt from him (two dollars for him, five dollars for her).

Anthony was quite accommodating about granting Monica's wishes—where they went together, what they did—in great part because he noticed that when he did what she wanted, she was more sexually receptive to him. Although she rarely manipulated him intentionally, Monica felt important and in control when he did what she wanted. From sex she got five dollars of power. When Anthony succeeded in getting sex from Monica, that also gave *him* a feeling of power—two dollars.

They both found sex physically pleasurable, although Anthony's enjoyment was greater than Monica's (seven dollars versus two). Their mutual promise of sexual fidelity gave them both a feeling of safety, although Monica felt less certain of Anthony's faithfulness than he did of hers (two dollars of safety for Monica, three for Anthony).

This sexual exchange of Imitation Love can be summarized in the following table:

Type of Imitation Love	Dollars Received in the Relationship by	
	Anthony	Monica
Praise	2	5
Power	2	5
Pleasure	7	2
Safety	3	2
Total Imitation Love	14	14

Although Monica and Anthony experienced the various forms of Imitation Love differently when they had sex, the overall exchange was sufficiently rewarding and fair that they both enjoyed it very much.

Like Monica, most women use sex to offer physical pleasure—along with some praise and power—in order to get a return of praise and power for themselves. This trading is rarely conscious, but it's nonetheless a serious affair, with meticulous accounting, and both parties are quite aware when there is an imbalance in the exchange.

The Imbalance of Trade

After years of marriage, Anthony and Monica became quite dissatisfied with the sexual part of their relationship, and they came to talk to me about it. He complained that they never had sex, and she complained that he was always pushing her to have sex, a scenario common in many marriages. I described to them why they had once enjoyed sex—because of the abundant and relatively equal exchange of Imitation Love detailed above—and suggested that the balance of trade had simply become unacceptable to Monica. The balance sheet now looked like this:

Type of Imitation Love	Dollars Received in the Relationship by	
	Anthony	Monica
Praise	1	1
Power	1	1
Pleasure	5	1
Safety	1	1
Total Imitation Love	8	4

Neither of them got much in the way of praise or power from sex any longer, for two reasons: First, the effect of Imitation Love had worn off, as it always does. The initial excitement that came from being praised for being sexually attractive, for example, had virtually disappeared. Second, as the effect of Imitation Love faded, both partners felt cheated by the other, and neither partner was then willing to give as much Imitation Love to the other, which further whittled away at the temporary satisfaction of the Imitation Love in their lives.

Although the overall enjoyment of sex had diminished for both of them, Anthony was getting twice the Imitation Love from sex that Monica was, mostly because sex still gave him considerable physical pleasure. Because sex was still rewarding for him, he was willing to push for it, while Monica didn't see it as something that gave her a sufficient return on her investment. Why should she be willing to participate in a trade that was obviously unfair?

All couples who are now experiencing less sexual enjoyment than they once did are feeling the fading effects of Imitation Love, as well as an imbalance of trade. Most men initially offer praise, power, and safety in exchange for the physical pleasure women give them, and when men no longer "pay" sufficiently, women withhold the physical pleasure of sex—often unconsciously. It should be emphasized, however, that for most men sex is much more than a physical experience. At work and at home they feel a constant competition and criticism. During sex they feel a warmth and connection that far transcends the physical pleasure, a closeness they may experience at no other time.

The Real Cause of Sexual Dissatisfaction

Many reasons are given for men and women not fully enjoying sex, but they almost always boil down to a single root cause: If you don't feel unconditionally cared for by your partner, sex cannot be an easy, fun, and fulfilling experience, as Carl learned when he talked to me about his wife, Sydney.

With considerable irritation, Carl said, "She's not even a wife anymore. We never have sex. She's always too tired or busy."

"And when you talk to her about it, are you as irritated with her as you are right now?"

There was a long pause. "Well, sometimes, sure. Who wouldn't be?"

"Do you like to be around people who are disappointed in you?" I asked. "Or mad at you?"

"Well, no, not really."

"Neither does Sydney. If she doesn't feel unconditionally accepted by you, she doesn't even want to be around you, much less share herself intimately with you. When you're mad about her not wanting to have sex with you, it's obvious to her that you're not accepting her unconditionally—you're primarily concerned about what *you* want."

When we don't feel unconditionally loved, we are so distracted by the pain of emptiness and fear that we can't fully enjoy any of life's experiences. The negative effect of an insufficient supply of Real Love on sex—where we intimately share ourselves with our partners—is especially noticeable. In the presence of Real Love, however, our enjoyment of every experience—especially sex—is multiplied.

The Big Difference

Although there are many factors that determine how men and women experience sex differently—hormones, social factors, spiritual considerations—one obvious physical difference can explain a great deal. It's a simple biological fact that men become sexually aroused—and achieve orgasm—more easily than women do. Even in the absence of acceptance or affection, most men can still have a physically pleasurable experience with sex, whereas that is not the case with most women. Women sometimes ask me, "How could he possibly want to have sex with me? He doesn't even talk to me all day, and then he wants to have sex? That doesn't make sense."

I answer that he wants to have sex because even without any exchange of praise, acceptance, power, or safety, he can still have a positive physical experience. Just because you're not getting anything out of sex doesn't keep him from enjoying it. He's not thinking much about your happiness.

Because sexual arousal and gratification are easier for men, they more often reach for sex to fill their emptiness. They use sex to *fill* their emptiness, whereas women often require their emptiness to be *filled* somewhat before they're willing to offer themselves in a sexual way to their partners. We'll talk more about the differences between men and women when we talk about sexual techniques later in the chapter.

Great Sex in Marriage

We often expect sex to create love in a relationship, but sex cannot create Real Love. Building Real Love in a marriage, on the other hand, guarantees the best sex imaginable. Sex can be a wonderful addition to marriage when it's an *expression* of Real Love, but it cannot long serve as a *substitute* for it.

It's Real Love we want more than anything else. When we have a sufficient supply, *everything* else in our relationships is enhanced: communication, decision-making, and sex. Imagine a marriage in which both partners are concerned about the happiness of the other. Under those conditions, everything they do together becomes enjoyable—how could sex *not* be a delightful experience?

In my conversation with Carl above, I explained that sex was not the problem in their marriage, only a symptom of a much more serious and long-standing deficiency, and he resolved to do whatever it took to address it. He learned to tell the truth about himself, and he found other men who unconditionally accepted him. Two months after we first met, he called me.

"I didn't really understand what you were saying at first," he said, "but I think I get it now. I've been pretty selfish. No wonder Sydney didn't want to have sex with me. Who likes to be used?"

"How's it going between you now?"

"I can't believe the difference. For years, I thought it would be amazing if we could have sex like we used to when we first got married, but what we have now is actually much better than that."

"So she's not avoiding you anymore?" I asked.

"Avoiding? I can't keep her off me. She wears me out. I have to beg for rest."

"Not exactly the problem you were having before, is it?"

Days later, I got a call from Sydney.

"What have you done with my husband?" she asked.

"In what way?"

"Over the past couple of months he's become a different person.

Most of the time now, he's thoughtful and kind. This is how I always hoped our marriage would be. For example, you probably knew that I used to avoid having sex with him."

"Yes."

"I just didn't enjoy it, but now I love having sex with him. In fact, it's even better than when we first got married. I've never had an easy time experiencing orgasm, for example. Hardly ever happened. I began to wonder what those women's magazines were talking about, but now it happens all the time. Now that I feel loved, sex isn't just more *emotionally* enjoyable—it's actually more *physically* exciting."

Can you imagine enjoying an ice cream cone while someone held a loaded gun to your head, or while a car was being driven over your foot? Our enjoyment of anything is seriously impaired while we're in pain—physical or emotional. Sex, for example, cannot be fully enjoyed while we're experiencing the pain of emptiness and fear. In the presence of Real Love, those distracting conditions are eliminated, and then we can more fully enjoy all our experiences, including sex. There is no aphrodisiac in the world like Real Love.

The Frequency and Enjoyment of Sex in Real Love

Months later, Carl called me again and said, "My relationship with Sydney is still amazing. It seems to get better and better all the time."

"I couldn't be happier for you," I responded.

"Remember when I told you that sex was better than I'd ever thought possible?" he asked.

"Sure."

"Well, for a while we had sex like rabbits. It was like we were sixteen again. But then I began to notice something that surprised me. Even though sex is still spectacular each time—like, amazing—I don't have this driving *need* to have sex as often as I used to. I'm in a place now where I can have sex with Sydney anytime, anywhere—that's no exaggeration, now that she loves it—but a lot of the time,

I'm perfectly satisfied with just sitting next to her or holding her. I never would have thought that could happen."

In the absence of Real Love, we desperately pursue anything that temporarily makes us feel less empty, and sex is one of the things we use. When you feel sufficient Real Love in your marriage, you'll enjoy sex even more, but as your emptiness disappears, you'll feel much less compulsion to fill it with sex. Sex becomes an expression of Real Love instead of a substitute for it.

The Physical Techniques of Great Sex

You may have noticed that in our discussion of great sex in marriage, I haven't yet mentioned a single physical technique to improve sexual pleasure. I haven't because Real Love isn't just number one on the list of factors that make the greatest contribution to fantastic sex—it also occupies positions two through ten on that list. If you find and share sufficient Real Love in your marriage, I promise you that everything else will become a relatively peripheral concern.

Dozens of books have been written—and uncounted videotapes and DVDs produced—that offer physical techniques for improving our sexual pleasure. In the short term, these can often seem quite effective, but not for the reasons we might suppose. Although sexual positions and other mechanical methods might produce some increased physical excitement, they have an even greater effect in other ways. To illustrate these other effects, picture a couple for whom sex has lost its exhilaration. They buy a sex manual and go through some of the exercises described. In the process of buying the book together, reading it, and practicing the techniques, the most important element is that he is spending more time with her—and is paying her more attention—than he has in quite some time. As a result, she feels accepted, important, even powerful—all independent of the physical pleasures generated by the sexual techniques themselves. These feelings of acceptance and worth have the greatest influence on the physical pleasure she feels and on her overall enjoyment of sex. As she feels accepted, and as she then demonstrates an increased interest in sex, he feels more accepted, too, and they draw closer together.

If there is insufficient Real Love in the marriage, however, all this excitement and fulfillment soon begin to decline, and they discover that happiness is not found in multiple sexual positions. There really is no pill, or book, or other magical method that will create genuine happiness in marriage. Having re-emphasized the importance of Real Love in sex, however, let's continue to discuss other factors that can add to our sexual enjoyment.

Timing, Foreplay, and Orgasm

Allow me to talk for a few moments to the men who are reading here. As we discussed earlier, it's critical to remember that your wife is almost always much slower to become sexually aroused and to reach orgasm than you are. This is not a physical disability, or an emotional handicap, or a problem intended to inconvenience you personally. It's just the biology she was born with. If you ignore that, you'll seriously impair the pleasure available to both of you.

Because you are easily aroused, and because orgasm is often just a few tantalizing moments away, it's understandable that you have a tendency to hurry things along. She, however, needs time—not just time for physical arousal, but time to soak in the acceptance and love that are so indispensable for her to have an enjoyable sexual experience. The slower you go, the more you communicate that you care about her, which is exactly what she needs to achieve orgasm.

Women actually require a background—a context—for great sex. Imagine that. To establish that context, you must remember that she simply needs to feel that you care about her. *That* is the most effective foreplay, and it takes real preparation on your part. You can't wait till the last minute to lay that groundwork.

For many years, the United States Marine Corps has used the CH-53 Sea Stallion helicopter to transport equipment, supplies, and personnel during the assault phase of an amphibious operation and subsequent operations ashore. For every hour this machine spends in the air, it receives *forty-four* hours of painstaking maintenance on its engines, hydraulic systems, electrical components, and so on. If this maintenance is neglected, system failures will occur in the air, with tragic results. There's a great deal more to flying one of these aircraft than hitting the gas and pulling off the ground.

Similarly, great sex requires considerable preparation that begins long before physical foreplay. If you have told your spouse that you love her—with your behavior, not just your words—a hundred times in the days and weeks before an actual sexual experience, that will be far more effective in generating a fulfilling sexual experience for both of you than any physical technique you could employ at the time you're having sex. The absence of that kind of preparation, in fact, will usually make "lift-off " impossible.

Truly effective foreplay consists of the loving acts described on pages 87–107: listening, looking, touching, talking, telling the truth about yourself, apologizing, saying "I love you," performing random acts of kindness, accepting, forgiving, and giving your time. When you begin to realize that washing a sink full of dishes makes a significant contribution to great sex, you'll have a much better understanding of how to make sex a loving and fulfilling experience. Offer to do an errand. *That* is what generates passion, because it indicates an interest in *her*. Touch her every chance you get. Whenever she walks by, reach out your hand and touch her gently. Stop what you're doing several times a day just to find her and give her a kiss. Doing that without any sexual overtones will do more to create a positive sexual experience than any kind of sexual touching you do in the absence of sufficient Real Love. Realize that often the most romantic three words you can say are not "I love you" but "I was wrong." Sit with her and say, "Remember yesterday when I was arguing with you about _____? I was being selfish and not really listening to you. I was wrong." In so doing, you're really listening to her and also creating an opportunity to be genuinely seen and accepted yourself. You're creating the kind of unconditionally loving and intimate environment that is indispensable to passionate and loving sex.

Anything you do or say that is *not* immediately followed by sex is usually more effective at communicating genuine affection than the things you do or say just before or during sex. If you are gentle and caring mostly just before sex, for example, there is often a lingering doubt in the mind of your partner about whether you are trying—however unconsciously—to get sex as a reward for the nice things you say or do.

If you want to communicate to your partner, for example, that she is physically beautiful and sexually attractive—which really adds to the sexual pleasure of any woman, since most are dissatisfied to some extent with how their bodies look—don't wait to flatter her until you're actually having sex. Most women are aware that during orgasm many men would find anyone—or anything—beautiful. Tell her she's beautiful on other occasions, and tell her often:

- When she's not aware that you're looking at her, put your head in your hands and stare at her until she notices. Then say, "You know, I could sit here and look at you all day."
- When you see her naked, or undressing, say, "Wow! Is this my birthday?" Then give her a peck on the cheek and go on about your business.
- As she walks past, look at her from behind and whistle. When she turns around—and she *will* turn around—say, "You are *so* fine."
- When she's showering, crack open the door and say, "I cannot get enough of this scenery."
- When she's getting dressed, say, "What a waste of cloth. It's a shame you ever have to cover up that body."

A word of warning about saying these things: Don't say them unless you mean them. What can you say, though, if your wife—or husband—is *not* physically attractive? Now what?

On pages 228–229 Andrew talked to me about his "dumpy" wife, Lynn. After months of telling the truth about himself and feeling Real Love from other people, he talked to me again.

"I can't tell you how much my marriage has changed," he said. "I'm learning to love Lynn in ways I never thought of."

I smiled. "Is she still dumpy?"

He chuckled in response and said, "Funny you should ask that. I've been embarrassed more than once as I've thought about that conversation with you. I really was being selfish."

"Has she lost any weight?"

"Probably not, but it just doesn't matter anymore. The more I learn to love her, the more beautiful she becomes—no kidding. Every once in a while, she'll make a negative comment about her weight. When she does, I hug her, squeeze her hips—which she thinks are too fat—and tell her I love every ounce of her. She was uncomfortable with that at first, but now she knows I really love how she looks."

When you learn to unconditionally love your spouse, you will find him or her more beautiful every day.

۞

Although orgasm is much more common when women feel unconditionally loved, even in the presence of Real Love women—and sometimes men—may not always be able to achieve orgasm. Instead of focusing on what you *can't* have, however, enjoy whatever physical and emotional intimacy you *can* have. Many people place far too much emphasis on orgasm, thereby creating a deep sense of disappointment when they can't achieve it. The greatest purpose of sex is to communicate affection. Everything after that is a bonus.

There is also a myth that simultaneous orgasms are somehow the ultimate goal. In many cases, the effort to achieve simultaneous orgasms is actually distracting. On the whole, women take longer to reach sexual climax than men, and climax is less predictable. For that reason, many couples have discovered that it's best when both partners focus on whatever activity will enable *her* to experience orgasm first. After that, they can focus on his pleasure, and if that leads to multiple orgasms for her, all the better. If, however, he allows himself to experience orgasm first, he seldom has any attention or energy remaining to see to her needs.

Variety

One evening Sydney sat beside Carl on the couch. With some hesitation, she said, "Are you satisfied with the sex we have?"

"Why do you ask?" he said.

"I don't quite know how to say this, because it could sound critical—but it's not. I'm just wondering. It seems like when we have sex, we pretty much do the same thing every time. The thing is, I *love* what we do. I love how I feel physically, and I love being close to you, but sometimes I wonder—you know, with the stuff in magazines and books about all the experimental things people do during sex—I wonder if you wish we were doing something different."

Carl smiled. "Here I've been worried," he said, "that I've been boring *you*. No, I love having sex with you. Sure, I used to think all those positions and techniques would be exciting, but now they just don't matter."

Many books on sex advise that variety is the spice that keeps the excitement alive in sex, but again, it's Real Love that matters more than anything else. If you and your partner are enjoying sex—if you feel a deep communication of affection and closeness as a result of sex—whatever you're doing is just fine. You don't need to wonder if you're lacking in some way. Shortly we'll discuss how to talk to your partner about his or her satisfaction regarding sex.

Anatomy

I've known many couples who have been married for decades but still don't have any vocabulary for the parts of their bodies involved in sex. It's difficult to talk to your partner about what you both enjoy sexually if you can't describe your own body, or your partner's. Many of us simply were never taught these words. Although we certainly talk about sex more than people did a hundred years ago, our conversations on that subject are not usually straightforward and open—instead, we joke about sex, whisper about it, and refer to it with words and tones that are lewd and suggestive.

There are many books available that describe sexual anatomy. Or you can type *male genital anatomy* or *female genital anatomy* into any Internet search engine (Google, for example) and obtain excellent drawings or photographs. This knowledge will be useful as you talk to your partner about your sexual experiences, a subject we'll address shortly.

Familiarity

Imagine that you've been invited to a party, and when you get there, you discover you don't know a soul. The next day you attend another party, but this time you know quite a bit about everyone, and you've had positive experiences with most of them. At which of the two functions did you feel most comfortable? Where did you enjoy yourself the most?

Familiarity is often quite helpful in eliminating the fear that interferes with the enjoyment of any experience, including sex. Regrettably, many people are quite unfamiliar with their own spouse's body. Having sex is then like going to a party with a stranger, and that can often detract from the intimacy and fun of the experience.

Sex can be more rewarding if you're both comfortable with each other's bodies. Take as many steps as possible to make that familiarity possible:

- When you're in the privacy of your bedroom, don't be in a rush to cover yourself up. Give your spouse opportunities to see you naked, and for you to feel accepted with all the flaws of your body.
- Shower together, not necessarily as a sexual experience, but just to be together naked.
- On some occasions during sex, just lie still and give your partner a chance to explore your body. In turn, explore his or hers. Say, "I love looking at you."
- Have sex with plenty of light—perhaps not all the time, but

often enough that you both overcome the embarrassment of seeing each other naked. You'll then enjoy better sex together.

Asking for Sex

Imagine that you've been lost in the desert for days. Without food or water, you've become quite hungry, thirsty, and weak. When you encounter a man having a picnic under a tree, you naturally ask him to share with you what he has. Consider, however, the *tone*—of voice and behavior—you would almost certainly use in making your request. Spurred by extreme hunger, your "request" would likely be accompanied by an air of desperation and insistence. You might beg for what you want, or you might even become aggressive if you meet resistance.

We often find ourselves in a similar position when asking our partners for sex. Without sufficient Real Love in our lives—a condition almost universal among us—every scrap of Imitation Love we can get becomes pretty important. Our requests for these scraps then easily turn into demands or manipulations or pleas. Or we're embarrassed about our pitiable state and ask for nothing at all. These attitudes are understandable, but they also make it quite difficult for us to feel or give Real Love. When we're desperate, we don't ask for sex—or anything else we want—in loving or effective ways.

In asking for sex, we can benefit greatly from remembering the principles that govern requests in general, as we discussed in Chapter Six:

- Realize that Real Love is always the most important thing.
- Ask, don't demand.
- Make requests clear and specific.
- Listen and accept.
- Modify your requests when necessary.

Realize That Real Love Is Always the Most Important Thing

When we make a request, we often forget that no single *thing* will ever be as important as the Real Love we feel and give in any situation. Real Love is *the* critical element that guarantees genuine happiness, while everything else—including sex—can only *add* to our happiness in the presence of Real Love. When we understand that, we become a great deal less insistent about getting any particular thing we want.

Although sex may seem to be your immediate need, if you push or manipulate your partner to get it in a way that interferes with Real Love, you'll discover that sex will actually detract from the happiness in your marriage.

It's also important to consider the importance of Real Love when you're *receiving* a request for sex, as Marie learns here with me in this discussion about her husband, Bryce.

"I feel like he's always leaning on me to have sex with him, and I don't like the pressure," she said.

"Why do you think he pushes you?" I asked.

"It's obvious, isn't it? He wants sex a lot more than I do."

"If he's *pressuring* you, what's obvious is that he's empty and desperate. But don't get distracted here. Even though he talks about *sex*, what he really wants is your *unconditional acceptance*, and judging from what you've said about many of your interactions with him, I'd say he's not getting that from you. Each time you're disappointed or irritated at him, he feels a lack of love from you. Each time you're too busy or tired to have sex, he also gets a confirmation that you don't care about his happiness."

"Are you saying I have to have sex with him whenever he wants it?"

"Not at all. I *am* suggesting that you look at ways to increase the Real Love in your marriage, and sex is *one* way you can communicate your affection to Bryce."

"But I don't enjoy it."

"I understand, but if you only give him what *you* like, and what's easy for you, he won't feel like you're making much of an effort to love *him*, will he?"

"I hadn't thought of it like that."

"The reason you don't enjoy sex with Bryce is simple. You

don't feel like he really cares about you. Sex is a selfish experience for him, and you don't like being used."

"That's exactly how I feel."

"Marie, he doesn't feel loved by *you*, either. If you want a happy marriage, *somebody* has to be willing to take the first steps and offer love without conditions, even when it's difficult or not enjoyable initially. You *could* wait for Bryce to take those first steps, but that might take a very long time, and it would be selfish on your part. Don't think of sex as something he's trying to *get* from you—even though he is. Think of it as a *gift* you can offer him as an expression of your affection."

Marie did begin to initiate sex with Bryce, and it had a powerful effect on both of them. He felt her concern for him, and as she made the conscious decision to be more loving, *she* also felt more loved and happy.

Ask, Don't Demand

You don't like it when people pile demands on you. You feel the pressure of all those expectations, and then, even if you do what is expected, you can't feel the pleasure of giving a gift freely. You can only feel that you were forced to give in to a demand. Your spouse doesn't like demands, either, and when you make demands about sex, you ruin any possibility of the genuine intimacy that should always be involved with sex.

How can you tell the difference between a genuine request and a demand? Often you can't until your request is refused. If you feel disappointment or irritation when you don't get what you want, you know that you were really making a demand. Sometimes you can sense a demand before making it. If you're feeling nervous or insistent about a request, you know you're empty and afraid, and you'll almost certainly make a demand.

Never make a request for sex if you're feeling irritated. If you're angry, tell the truth about your selfishness—at least to yourself but preferably to a wise man or woman capable of accepting you—and wait until you feel loved enough to make a genuine request. It will also be easier for you to avoid anger if you don't wait to ask for sex until you're desperate for it. Each time you think to ask—but don't—you're adding to an increasing pile of resentment. Then when you finally do ask, that entire pile has a negative effect on your "request."

Make Requests Clear and Specific

Don't require your partner to read your mind as evidence that he or she cares about you. It's lazy, and with that approach you'll not often get what you want. Although we often joke about sex, and comfortably watch other people talk about it in movies and on television, many of us have a difficult time making a clear request for sex. What we do instead is make vague hints—with our words and actions—about what we want: You might, for example, touch the back of her leg with your foot when you get in bed, as a sign that you want to be physically intimate. You might cast a longing look in his or her direction. In a marriage where Real Love is abundant, and where there is considerable experience with loving sex, such hints might be sufficiently clear and productive. In many marriages, however, the partner receiving the hints resents having to figure them out and respond to them.

Following are just a few samples of clear requests for sex:

- "In an hour all the kids will be out of the house. I'd love to take advantage of the time alone and have sex with you. Are you interested?"
- "You want to go upstairs and fool around?"
- "You wanna get naked?"
- "Today is going to be pretty filled with things we have to do. You want to set aside a time tomorrow when we can make love?"

I used four different terms here for "having sex." If you're not sure what words your partner prefers—make love, have sex, and so on—ask him or her.

Notice that in two of the examples, sex is suggested for a future time, in one hour in one case and the next day in the other. Some people believe it's not romantic to set a time for sex, but there are real advantages to it. When you approach your spouse with a request that will require her to stop what she's doing and pay attention to you, that can be distracting. Many spouses turn down offers for sex only because they feel distracted in that moment by the pressures of other things. Suggesting a future time allows your spouse to think ahead to a time when he or she might not be rushed. The anticipation of the wait can, in fact, add to the excitement of sex when the time comes.

Although it's common that one partner initiates sex more often than the other, don't let that pattern become a burdensome responsibility. If one partner always initiates sex, that person might eventually conclude that he or she is the only one in the marriage interested in sex, and that doesn't lead to intimate feelings.

Listen and Accept

You must be careful not to have expectations when you ask for sex. If you have them, your partner will almost certainly sense that you're manipulating or pushing her in some way. If you are honestly prepared to hear *no* for an answer, when that answer comes you won't communicate the disappointment or irritation that destroy Real Love in a marriage. With your acceptance of *no,* you'll be communicating a deep acceptance of her that will make it much more likely that your request will be accepted the next time. While you're accepting her, *you* will be happier, too.

Modify Your Requests Where Necessary

Suppose you've just asked your partner to have sex with you, and he's declined. Perhaps he's busy, or tired, or distracted by thoughts of other things. Now what? Is your only option to say, "Okay, not a problem?"

No, you can modify your request and try to find an activity and time that will please both of you. Be careful here. On some occasions, you might believe you're simply modifying a request, when you're really trying to pressure your spouse into giving you what you want. If you're feeling anxious or insistent when you make your request, your subsequent modification will almost certainly be a manipulation or demand. Ask yourself if you'd be significantly disappointed or irritated at having your request denied. If so, your request modification will be motivated by a desire to get what you want at your partner's expense.

When you offer a modification of your request, it's often helpful to clearly state that you're just making a suggestion. You might say, for example, "I am *not* trying to change your mind here. Let me make another suggestion, though, that you *might* like. If you don't like that one, either, don't hesitate to say so, or you can offer something you *would* like." Remember that if you are disappointed or irritated after your partner refuses this modification of your request, he will know that you're just trying to convince him to give you want you want, and that you were not truthful when you said you were not trying to change his mind. You can't fake the absence of disappointment and anger for long. Elimination of those conditions requires that you consistently tell the truth about yourself and get the Real Love you need from your spouse and others.

Following are some examples of "rejections" your partner might offer, and modifications you might make to your original request.

Your partner	You
"I'm too tired."	"If you'd like, you could relax while I take care of the kids for an hour. Would that make a difference in how you feel? If not, no problem. We'll talk about it when you feel more rested."
"I've got too many things to do before the end of the day."	"What can I do to help? *If* you want me to do some of those things, we could free up time for some fun. But you tell me what you want."

Your partner	You
"I just don't feel like it."	"Could we plan on going to bed an hour early tomorrow, so we can have some intimate time together then? In the meantime, if something's distracting you, I'd love to hear about it."

Again, you must communicate that you are not trying to change his mind here, just listening carefully to his objections and offering solutions. In some situations, there's no way you can modify a request without appearing to push for what you want. If he's obviously frazzled to the bone and distracted beyond repair, simply address what he needs. Ask what you can do to help without any mention of present or future sex. He'll feel accepted and will be much more likely to want sex with you when you bring it up later.

Following are some responses that are usually not wise to make after your partner indicates that he or she doesn't want to have sex with you:

- "You never want to have sex with me."
- "I just don't get it. Everything else is always more important than me."
- "Do you think there's any time in the near future when we *will* have sex? Any possibility that it will be this year?"
- "Is something wrong?"
- "Am I not attractive to you anymore?"
- "Why do you never want to have sex with me?"
- "What's the matter?"

The accusations and manipulations—direct and implied—in these responses will destroy any possibility of having loving sex, now or in the near future.

Modify Your Requests Where Necessary—As the Person *Receiving* the Request

When your partner asks you for sex, don't just say *no*. Requests for sex are very personal and often frightening for the person making them—your partner is really exposing himself to personal rejection when he asks you for sex. Don't make him do all the work of modifying his request, either. It can be quite difficult for him to guess what you *would* be willing to do. You can help a lot by offering suggestions. Instead of just saying *no,* there are many alternatives you could offer:

- "Right now I really do have a lot of things on my mind, so I just wouldn't be there for you if we had sex now. Can we talk about it again in a couple of hours? I'll know better then whether I'm going to get some of these things done on time."
- Throw your arms around him, look deeply into his eyes, and say, "I *love* having sex with you. I can't tonight, but what if we set a time for tomorrow?"
- "What I want to do is throw you down on the bed right now and make you beg for mercy, but I have four phone calls to make and several other things to do before I can go to bed. You do *not* have to help me with any of it, but if you do, I'll have some time to play with you."
- "I'd love to, but I don't have a lot of time. So you can choose: I'll be out of town tomorrow, so we can wait until the day after that. Or we could do something quick right now. I don't want you to feel rushed. I just don't have time for anything long, so if that means I don't get to have an orgasm this time, I don't care. We could do something just for you. I wouldn't mind a bit."
- "I'm embarrassed to admit it, but right now I'm feeling irritated about several things: you, the kids, my job. Do *not* worry about it—it's not your fault. If I were more loving, I wouldn't be irritated at all. I have to work this out in my mind—if I had sex with you now, I'd be a lousy partner. Let me do some thinking, and in a few hours I'll let you know how I'm doing."

With these responses you're clearly communicating that you're not willing to have sex at the time requested, but you're also expressing an interest in your partner and his or her desires.

Talking About Sex

How in the world can you enjoy the full potential of sex unless you *talk* to your partner about it? You need to talk about what you like, what you don't like, and what your partner likes and doesn't like. Many couples, however, never talk about sex, and for several reasons:

- They've never seen anyone speak openly—without guilt, shame, manipulation, or greed—about this subject, so they simply don't know how.
- Their past discussions about sex involved demands, expectations, and irritation, and they don't want any more of that.
- They're embarrassed to talk about it, a result of a lifetime of seeing sex portrayed as a dirty subject that decent people don't talk about.

There's no way to get over your discomfort about discussing sex other than simply to start. With practice, you'll become accustomed to such discussions and will find that they're actually fun.

Talking About What You Both Want

Let's suppose your partner cares about you and is willing—maybe even eager—to have sex with you. Why not maximize the experience by telling him what you like? Why not find out what *he* likes? We evaluate what works and doesn't work everywhere else in our lives—why should sex deserve any less evaluation and discussion?

One effective time to talk about what you like and don't like is *during* sex. Many couples don't speak during sex, so they're missing an element that could add a great deal to the fulfillment of their experience. There are many things you can say to your partner to indicate what you like, and to find out what he or she enjoys. For example:

- "You know where you were touching me just a few seconds ago? Could you touch me there again? A little more to your left. Yes, that's it. That's very nice." This is easier when you've mastered the vocabulary of some simple anatomy.
- "I know this is taking a while, but I'm really enjoying it. Thanks for being patient with me and caring about me."
- "Can you slow that down just a little? I'm loving this, and I'm not quite ready for it to end."
- "I really like this a lot, but I don't think I'll be able to have an orgasm. That has nothing to do with you—sometimes I just can't. You go ahead. It will still be fun for me."
- "Can you move your hand up just a little bit?"
- "This has been wonderful. What can I do right now that you'd like?"
- (pointing with your finger) "When you touch me right here, it's more exciting than when you touch me there."

When you make suggestions to your partner, he or she can easily take your comments as a personal criticism and be offended, especially if you say things like the following:

- "No, not like that."
- "Not there, that tickles."
- "Whoa, I'm not ready."

These are all variations on "You're doing it wrong," which is rarely a welcome sound to anyone, especially during sex. Instead, think about offering comments that give gentle direction, as I described above. You can also help avoid a sense of criticism during sex in the following ways:

- Make an agreement beforehand that you'll be talking and offering feedback to each other during sex.
- Be sensitive to your partner's nonverbal communication when you offer your feedback. If there is hesitation or resis-

tance of any kind, say, "It looks like you're bothered by what I just said. Do you want to talk about it now, or later?"

- After sex—several hours later, or even the next day—ask your partner if there was any part of your talking during sex that interfered with his or her enjoyment of the experience. If you made suggestions during sex about what he or she might do differently, ask if he had any objections to the *way* you made them. For example: "When I asked you to move your hand a little slower, is there a better way I could have said that?"

- Practice. The more you talk, the better you'll get at it. Eventually, you become so relaxed that you can talk during sex as casually as you would at any other time. Sex should be natural and fun, not an isolated, serious activity unlike every other.

It's also productive to talk about sex at times not associated with actual sexual activity. We often feel less threatened by feedback about something we're not actually doing at the time. Referring to the past is sometimes easier than criticizing the present.

Following are some examples of information you could exchange and questions you could ask your partner:

- "I love having sex with you. If it stayed like this forever, I'd be happy. If you're interested, though, I could tell you a few things that would make it even more fun for me. I can't expect you to read my mind. Are you interested in hearing them?"

- "Remember yesterday when you were touching my [body part] and kind of moving your fingers in a circle? That was fantastic."

- "What are some things I do during sex that are especially enjoyable for you?"

- "Is there something completely different that you'd like me to try during sex?"

- "Are there any things I do during sex that you enjoy less than others? I'd probably get defensive if you told me a dozen things, so let's start with one."

- "This morning, when you touched my [body part], it mostly tickled, instead of feeling good. Don't feel bad about it. You couldn't possibly have known how that would feel for me unless I told you, and I was nervous about telling you while you were doing it. The next time it tickles like that, can I just reach over and gently touch your hand to let you know that it doesn't feel very good?"
- "Remember yesterday when I _____? I was trying something different to see if you'd like it, but I didn't have the guts to ask you about it right then. Did you like that? Would you like me to do that again? Or is there something else you'd like better?"

When two people care about one another's happiness, these statements and questions are not threatening. Don't take any feedback as criticism of *you*—it's just an opportunity to increase the pleasure and the expression of caring in your marriage. You really do want to make your partner as happy as possible, and you want to talk about what your partner can do that would add to your own happiness. All that is possible only as you talk to each other.

You'll need to have many discussions with your partner about sex. It's impossible to think of everything you want in a single conversation, and as you learn more about loving each other, the feedback and questions will change.

Resolving Conflicts About Sex

It's virtually unavoidable that you and your spouse will sometimes see sex differently. When these differences are accompanied by Getting and Protecting Behaviors, you'll have conflicts. Let's see how Chuck and Rebecca handle their conflict over sex, and how I respond by using the principles for eliminating conflict, which are found in Chapter Four.

Realize That It's Always About Real Love
Tell the Truth About Yourself

Tell the Truth About Your Partner
Recognize What You Really Want

Like most couples, Chuck and Rebecca got married because they fell in love, but over the years, their dreams have been replaced with disappointment and unfilled expectations. Increasingly, they've been finding fault with each other—about many things—and now they're in the process of detailing the other's shortcomings to me. I ask Rebecca to focus on just one complaint, and she says, "Chuck wants to have sex all the time, and I don't."

"I'm not an animal," he says. "I don't want sex *all* the time. But you *never* do. It's like I have to beg you every time."

They begin to argue about the exact frequency of their sexual activity, but I interrupt: "These are just details. Let's talk about what you both really want from sex. It's pretty obvious that you [gesturing to Chuck] want to have sex much more often than you do [gesturing to Rebecca]. Agreed?" They nod their heads.

"So let's talk about *why* that is," I suggest. "Rebecca, do you have sex as much now as you did earlier in your marriage?

"No,"

"Why is that?" I ask.

Rebecca pauses and says, "I just don't enjoy it as much."

"When you do have sex, how do you feel toward Chuck?"

"Usually irritated. I only give in because he keeps pushing me."

Since anger is a response to the emptiness and fear that result from a lack of Real Love, the next question is easy. "Do you feel like Chuck cares about you when you have sex?" I ask.

A light goes on in Rebecca's head as she replies, "No. That's it—I feel like he's just interested in *himself*. He doesn't really care about *me*."

"Feeling unloved is painful," I say, "so it's natural that you'd protect yourself from that. When it comes to sex, then, your goal is to protect yourself from being used and feeling unloved. Do you see that?"

"I hadn't thought of it quite like that before," says Rebecca, "but yes."

"Now, Chuck, why do you want to have sex?" I ask.

Chuck looks at me like I'm stupid. He's thinking, *Have you never* had *sex?*

"Because it feels good, right?" I ask.

"Sure."

"So when it comes to sex, your goal is pleasure."

Chuck's silence and frown are a clear communication that he agrees but doesn't like how his motivation looks. I ask them both what they see as their greatest goal in life, and after a couple minutes of discussion, they both agree that they want to feel unconditionally loved by each other and be happy.

Rebecca and Chuck *say* they want to feel loved, loving, and happy, but with their *behavior* they demonstrate that they want safety and pleasure, respectively. *With their ideal goal in mind,* I ask them to tell the truth about themselves, their partner, and their relationship. This is a sobering moment for both of them, and after considerable discussion and reflection, I write in two columns what each of them has concluded:

Rebecca	Chuck
Chuck partly wants sex for pleasure, but he also sees it as evidence of my love for him.	Rebecca doesn't hate *sex*. She just hates it that I don't show her I love her in other ways, and then she feels used when I want sex.
I'm protecting myself instead of trying to make our relationship happier.	I'm manipulating Rebecca instead of thinking about what she wants.
I'm being selfish.	I'm being selfish.
What I'm doing isn't helping either of us to be really happy.	I'm not helping Rebecca to be happier, and it's not working for me, either.

As they tell the truth about themselves and each other, they experience several consequences almost immediately:

- They feel more accepted and loved by each other. When we tell the truth about ourselves, whatever acceptance we get afterward feels unconditional and genuine.
- Their anger vanishes. How long can you stay angry at me when I admit that I'm being selfish?
- They begin to see how they can change their behavior in ways that will contribute to what they really want. They can offer these changes as genuine gifts to each other—making contributions to their real and shared goal—instead of feeling like they're being forced to give what their partner wants.

Determine How *You and Your Partner Can Get What You Want*

Continuing our conversation, I say to Rebecca, "Now that you see what you really want—to have a loving and happy relationship, not to be right or defend yourself—tell Chuck exactly what you'd like from him regarding sex."

"I want to feel like you care about me all the time, not just when you want sex."

Chuck asks her to be specific about what she wants, and she talks about touching, talking, cuddling, and so on.

"So if I do all those things," Chuck says, "you'll want to have sex with me?"

Rebecca has a look of concern on her face as she says, "Well . . ."

I smile and say, "Chuck, if you do the things she wants just *so* she'll have sex with you, she'll still feel used instead of loved, and you won't have a loving relationship. And, Rebecca, if you *expect* Chuck to do the things you described, you won't appreciate them or feel loved when he does them."

As they keep in mind the goal of making one another genuinely happy, they begin to work out the details of what they're willing to do for each other. They write down their commitments—for their own individual benefit, not so their partner will have something in writing to nag them about. Chuck writes:

- I'll be less demanding, and I'll remember that it's much more important that both of us feel loved than it is for me to have sex right when I want it.
- I will be more affectionate—touching, talking—all the time, not just when I want sex.

Rebecca writes:

- When Chuck asks for sex, if my answer is *no,* I'll offer another time when we can have sex, or at least when I will bring up the subject again.
- When I don't want to have sex, I won't make those frowns and act irritated like I usually do.
- When Chuck wants sex and I don't, I won't physically avoid him, because that really makes him feel rejected.

Then they both agree that they'll talk in a week about how their agreements are being kept, and how it is affecting their relationship.

The Law of Choice

Several days later, Rebecca calls me in a state of agitation and says, "When we talked with you, Chuck said he understood that I needed more nonsexual attention from him, but he hasn't changed a bit. And he still expects me to have sex with him. He didn't learn a thing."

"Do you remember the Law of Choice?" I ask.

"Yes."

"Then you understand that he gets to make his own choices, after which you can always make *your* choices, preferably the ones that lead to your real goal. The next time you interact with Chuck about sex or the affection he gives you, remember the Law of Choice and let me know how it goes."

A week later Rebecca calls me again. "We got into one of our arguments about Chuck not being affectionate," she says, "and I was getting angry, as usual. But this time I remembered the Law of Choice. I *want* him to show me more nonsexual affection, but I don't have the right to *demand* it, and that's what I've been doing. He really gets to choose what he does, even if I don't like it, and when I remember that, my demands seem selfish and controlling."

"You're really learning something important."

"That's not all," she says. "You told me *I* always have my own choices to make. I can be loving and happy, or demanding and angry and miserable. So instead of insisting that he give me all the attention *I* want—which is always frustrating for both of us—I decided to do whatever I could to love *him*. I stopped pushing him to do what I want. I started *initiating* sex with him, too, and now it's a whole different experience for both of us. He's much happier, obviously, and I *like* being more loving toward him. Sex is a lot more fun for me *physically* now that I feel loved, too. He's more tender with me during sex, and he pays more attention to me at other times, too. Now I can see why he wasn't affectionate before—I was rejecting him and nagging him all the time. Why would he *want* to be with me when I'm like that?"

Understanding the Law of Choice helps us to eliminate the expectations that damage the Real Love in our marriages. Rebecca learned that and allowed Chuck to make his own choices, instead of pressuring him, which had never made either of them happy. She then made her own choice, to love him as well as she could without his changing in any way. Feeling her unconditional love, he responded with more love of his own.

Unfortunately, many conflicts are "resolved" only when both parties give up something they want. They make a compromise, a trade that fails to satisfy anyone entirely. Or they surrender out of the necessity of weakness, only to regret and resent their decision. It's compromise, trade, and surrender that characterize most human interactions: politics, business, and personal affairs. It doesn't have to be that way. Notice that Rebecca didn't trade affection with

Chuck. She didn't give him sex *in exchange* for what she wanted. There was no compromise in which they both gave up something, nor did she *give in* and surrender to his demands. Instead she freely offered him a gift, without the expectation of anything in return. As a result, the conflict instantly disappeared, and she enjoyed both the gifts she gave and the ones Chuck later offered. For more on the concept of compromise versus giving, see page 206.

Conflicts can be eliminated when you decide that you will simply offer your contribution freely to a relationship. If your offer is unconditional, you will not be disappointed or angry— key ingredients in any conflict—regardless of the response of your partner. But what if your partner isn't satisfied with your gift? What if he or she is still angry and demands more from you? Then you can make a *choice* to give more, not because you're being pressured but because you wish to be more helpful or loving. *Or* you can choose *not* to give more, knowing that you're still not responsible for the response of your partner. No matter how angry he or she becomes, *you* can still choose to be loving and happy. Although your partner is making a conflict *possible* with his or her anger, the conflict—which requires two or more participants—cannot happen without your cooperation.

In any interaction you can always choose to be loving and happy, regardless of the behavior of your partner. You can create a world in which you never lose. That pretty much eliminates your feeling like a victim, or being angry, or running.

Certainly, it would have been nice for Rebecca if Chuck had immediately begun to be affectionate after my first meeting with them, as he'd agreed. But he didn't. Before a relationship can change, *somebody* has to start making loving choices—and it might as well be *you*. That takes faith. And even if your partner doesn't respond in kind, your being loving always feels great. Rebecca, for example, began to enjoy sex more just because she was offering it unconditionally.

❦

Much of our discussion about sex in marriage can be distilled into a couple of general suggestions. If you are the spouse who is pushing for more sex, and if you express disappointment and irritation when you don't get what you want, you can probably make the greatest immediate contribution to the Real Love in your relationship by simply putting off your immediate sexual gratification and concentrating on learning how to love your spouse unconditionally. If you do that, great sex will eventually result. If you're the spouse resisting sex, you can make a great contribution to the Real Love in your marriage by *offering* sex, not to pacify your partner, and not because you're giving in to his or her demands, but as evidence of your love for your spouse.

Infidelity

Approximately 25–40 percent of wives and 45–60 percent of husbands have had extramarital affairs (study results vary widely). Because few things affect the health and survivability of a marriage more profoundly than infidelity, we need to talk about its causes and how to respond to it.

The Causes of Infidelity

Violation of the vows of fidelity in marriage has serious consequences: Marriages are destroyed, children are often torn from their parents, and extended families and other social relationships are affected. Considering all those weighty risks, why do people still have sex outside their marriages?

It's always about Real Love. Most couples get married with a woefully insufficient supply, and then they expect their partner to make them happy. In the beginning, with an abundant exchange of Imitation Love, they're both relatively satisfied. Both partners are getting more Imitation Love than they've ever gotten from anyone else, so they confuse that temporary satisfaction and excitement with genuine happiness. This mutual deception— almost always unconscious—is deadly. After a time—sometimes weeks, sometimes years—both partners notice that the effect of Imitation Love is wearing off. They feel empty, alone, and afraid again. They're in a desperate situation indeed: Not only do they not have Real Love, but the fountain of Imitation Love has dried up, too. Because they once made each other "happy," and now the happiness is gone, they naturally conclude that their partner is somehow failing to hold up his or her end of the agreement. They both feel abandoned and betrayed.

What can they do? Usually they demand more Imitation Love from their partner, using Getting and Protecting Behaviors more intensively. But that never works for long, so eventually they go elsewhere for their supply of praise, power, pleasure, and safety. Many people find these things at work, or in a hobby, or with their children, but sometimes they find what they're looking for with a sexual partner outside their marriage. We can see this in the following story of Diane and Christopher.

When they got married, Diane and Christopher were "happy," but they became increasingly disappointed and angry as the exchange of Imitation Love failed to meet their high expectations of each other. Over a period of many years, they used Getting and Protecting Behaviors more and more. Diane tended to attack Christopher for his lack of attention toward her, and he responded with anger and withdrawal.

They both felt alone. No longer getting the Imitation Love they wanted from each other, they began to look for it elsewhere. They both spent more time at work, enjoying the praise and power they received for achieving success in their careers. Diane began to pour herself even more into the lives of her children, from which she got a sense of importance and worth.

At work, Christopher met Alexandra, a single woman who liked him for the same qualities Diane had once found attractive—his intelligence, wit, ability to succeed at work, and sense of responsibility—and in return, she rewarded him with flattery, acceptance, and admiration. Christopher was excited to find someone who appreciated him and made him feel important, and before long he was sleeping with Alexandra.

When Diane learned of his affair, she talked to me about it.

"How could he do this to me?" she asked. And then she talked about her plans to divorce Christopher.

I explained Real Love to her, and how, in its absence, we behave badly in order to fill our emptiness. "Christopher was so empty that he was willing to get Imitation Love from anyone—in this case Alexandra—even though he knew the costs could be high. Although his behavior isn't excusable in any way, he didn't do this *to you*. Yes, I know it *affects* you, but he did this to dull his own pain, not primarily to hurt you. He really is drowning and trying to keep his head above water, not splashing you just to be hurtful. Now, the real question is, what are you going to do—leave him drowning, or help him out of the water?"

Responding to Infidelity

"Are you saying I shouldn't divorce him?" she asked.

"I'm not telling you to do anything," I responded. "I'm only suggesting that you see his behavior for what it is. Right now you see him doing this *to you*, and you're reacting to protect yourself by considering a divorce. But what if he's just drowning? Would you walk away from him, or would you help him?"

I can't tell you whether you should stay with a spouse who has been unfaithful—only you can make that decision. I *can* tell you, however, that infidelity does not have to be the end of a marriage. Most people who divorce an unfaithful spouse don't see the *cause* of the infidelity, nor do they see how they could respond in a healthy way that could strengthen their marriages.

Diane chose to take the steps to find Real Love, and as she felt more loved herself, she shared that love with her husband. It had a powerful effect on him and on their marriage. Several months after our initial conversation, Diane called me.

"I see now," she said, "that Christopher has never felt loved, not by his parents or anyone else, including me. He went out looking for somebody to make him feel better only because he wasn't getting the love he needed from me at home. In a way, I wasn't being faithful to him, either, because I wasn't loving him unconditionally."

I once received a letter from a man whose wife had been having an affair. When he learned about it, he talked to a friend, who recommended he read *Real Love*. He then wrote his wife a letter:

> I know what you did is a reflection of what you didn't get in our relationship. I know you've always been alone and empty, and I didn't give you the unconditional love you needed. It makes me sick now to see that I have only thought of my own needs and hurt you. When you didn't give me what I wanted, I would get angry, trying to get you to change. No wonder you didn't want to be around me. I really want you to be happy, even though I've done a terrible job of showing it. I want to learn how to love you better, and I think we can still have a loving relationship, but it's your decision whether you want to keep trying.

If your spouse has been unfaithful, you can be certain that he or she didn't feel loved by you. *That does not make you responsible* for his or her choice to have an affair, but you do need to consider the contribution you made to driving your spouse away from you. People like to feel unconditionally loved more than anything, and if your spouse feels Real Love from you, he or she will almost certainly stay with you. I also recognize that even if you love your spouse, he or she might not *feel* it because of his or her own choices to use Getting and Protecting Behaviors.

Varieties of Infidelity

Most of us agree that in marriage we make an agreement not to have sex with people other than our spouses. Without having sex, however, you can still be unfaithful to your spouse in many ways. When you were married, you made a promise not only to love your spouse, but to love him or her in a special, exclusive way—more intimately and with greater intensity than with anyone else. When you do anything that detracts from that unique loyalty and level of commitment, you're being unfaithful. In the following discussion, Jerry learns about infidelity as I talk to him and his wife, Andrea.

"Everywhere he goes," Andrea begins, "he looks at other women—at the mall, while we're driving, at the grocery store, wherever—and it really bothers me. And when we're in groups of people, he goes right to the pretty babes and spends his time with them. And he's always touching them. I don't like it."

Jerry protests vigorously. "I can't believe you're making such a big deal of this. Sure, I look sometimes, but so what? And I touch people all the time when I talk. I'm just being friendly."

I turned to Jerry and said, "Think for a moment about *how* you touch pretty women. And what you are thinking about—how you feel—when you're touching them and looking at them. Would you touch your *sister* that way, or think those thoughts? Would you touch *me* that way?"

"Well . . ." It was obvious that Jerry was somewhat sobered by this new perspective.

"Clearly you wouldn't. When you married Andrea, you promised to be faithful to her sexually—completely, not just most of the time or in most ways. You look at other women, and you touch them, because you find them *sexually* attractive. You're sharing your sexual attention with women other than Andrea, and that is violating the commitment you made to her."

You can have an affair without having sex and without even touching another person. If you flirt with other men or women, you're being unfaithful. If you look at pornography on the Internet, you are sharing your sexual attention in a way that violates your exclusive commitment with your spouse. Even in the absence of obvious sexual overtones, we're often being unfaithful in the conversations we have. Infidelity is any emotional or sexual intimacy that violates your primary loyalty to your spouse.

We can't live with the pain of feeling empty and alone, and we will do whatever it takes to eliminate those conditions. It's only natural that we would reach out to other people for a sense of connection when we don't have it with our spouses. Many of these connections can be healthy. I have repeatedly suggested, for example, that we have frequent contact with wise men and women—including people other than our spouses—in the process of finding Real Love. But when do these conversations become emotional affairs?

In any relationship with someone other than your spouse, consider the following questions:

- Do you share with your spouse the conversations you have with this friend? You don't need to share with your spouse every word you say to other people, but generally, do you share with your spouse what you do and say with others? Or at least would you be *willing* to share if asked?
- Do you say negative things about your spouse to this person? That does not mean you can't *mention* some of the negative behaviors of your spouse in the process of telling the truth about your own Getting and Protecting Behaviors—a common event when talking to a wise man or woman.
- Would you feel comfortable if your partner were watching and listening to a videotape of your conversation?
- Do you touch each other differently when you're alone than when you're with other people?
- Do you ever wonder what it would be like to have sex with this person?

Certainly we do need to have associations with many people in our lives, but when we don't feel sufficient Real Love, it's very easy for us to look for a kind of intimacy in those relationships that interferes with the loyalty we have promised to our spouses.

Preventing Infidelity

Although it's important to understand the causes and varieties of infidelity, it's more important to understand how we can keep it from ever happening. If you follow these steps, you'll prevent the violation of your marriage vows and will make great contributions to the strength of your marriage:

- Tell your spouse about your other friends—when you meet with them and what you say. That doesn't mean you have to share every word, but you do need to sketch out generally what relationships you have, and at least be *willing* to fill in all the details.
- Tell your spouse the truth about yourself—your mistakes and Getting and Protecting Behaviors—which will create the opportunities for you to feel genuinely accepted by him or her.
- Tell the truth about yourself to other people, and as you fill up with Real Love, you'll lose any need to find the artificial excitement of sexual intimacy outside your marriage.
- Avoid placing yourself in situations where you'll be physically alone with people toward whom you feel sexual attraction.

Exercises

Exercise One

Following are strong pieces of evidence that you are using sex as a form of Imitation Love. Answer these questions honestly and consider how you use sex as a form of Imitation Love in your life:

- Do you feel more worthwhile when people see you as sexually attractive?
- Exactly what efforts do you make to increase your sexual desirability?
- Do you ever withhold sex from your spouse when he or she has behaved in a way you don't like? If so, you're trading sex as a form of Imitation Love for something you want (praise, power).
- Do you sometimes seek the physical pleasure of sex for yourself without thinking about what your partner might be getting from the experience?
- Do you ever manipulate or push your partner for sex?
- Do you find yourself obsessing about sex?
- Do you use pornography?

🜨

Exercise Two

Consciously make a decision to do three or more loving acts—as described on pages 87–107—for your spouse each day for the next week. Assess what difference it makes both in your spouse's being sexually receptive to you and in your own enjoyment of sex.

Remember that you're not doing these things for your spouse for the purpose of *getting* more or better sex—you only want to *see* the role Real Love plays in creating great sex.

🜨

Exercise Three

At a time when you're *not* about to have sex, talk to your spouse about what he or she would like during sex. Ask the following:

- "What are some things I do during sex that are especially enjoyable for you?"
- "I really want to make sex more fun for you. Is there something completely different that you'd like me to do during sex?"
- "Can you tell me one or two things I do during sex that are less than enjoyable to you?"
- "Remember yesterday when I _____? I was trying something different to see if you'd like it, but I was afraid to hear your reaction right then. Did you like what I did—would you like me to do that again?—or is there something else you like better?"

Also make an agreement with your partner that he or she will talk to you *during* sex and tell you something that would increase his or her pleasure. If there are particular ways you'd like that communicated to you—hand signals, pointing, verbal directions, nonverbal noises—work that out with your partner.

9

When It's Over

Divorce

Fifty to Sixty percent of marriages end in divorce. Lest we suppose that the remaining 40–50 percent live in a state of marital bliss, one study found that 45 percent of married women wish they could replace their present husbands. One half of people marrying in the 1990s had been married before. A quarter of Americans today, ages eighteen to forty-four, are children of divorced parents.

These statistics strongly suggest that there is something pervasively wrong with our understanding of marriage, or our commitment to marriage, or our preparation for marriage, or a combination of all three. This entire book to this point has been dedicated to promoting the success of marriage—and therefore to the prevention of divorce. Because it is not possible to save all marriages, however—and because divorce is so common—we must discuss the nature of divorce, how to make the decision to divorce, how to navigate through the process of divorce with as little destruction as possible, and how to feel loved and love others after a divorce is completed. This will be a discussion of general principles, with some specific examples. An entire book would be required—many such have been written—to deal with all the individual elements of divorce: custody, property settlement, visitation, the effect of divorce on extended families, and so on.

Understanding Divorce

Divorce is a terribly traumatic experience. When two people get married, they have dreams of great success and delicious happiness, and divorce is a violent destruction of those dreams. I've seen people agonize for years after a divorce, repeatedly asking themselves and others, Why, why, why did this happen? We hate unexplained mysteries. They make us feel helpless—if we don't understand the cause of a mistake or failure, we're afraid it will happen to us again.

There's often another reason we vigorously seek the cause of a disaster. We want to certify to ourselves and to everyone else that it wasn't *our* fault. We want to pin the blame on someone else and avoid the intolerable position of being responsible for something that's gone badly. We've learned that if we're at fault, people might think less of us, and we just can't have that. During and after a divorce, therefore, it's only natural that we're quite eager to blame everything on our partners. To support our positions, of course, we present great piles of evidence that prove the villainy of our partners. In so doing, however, we only further isolate ourselves, alienate our partners, and make ourselves more blind to the real cause of our unhappiness.

Accompanying all that blaming is a profusion of excuse-making, which is both destructive and based on lies. We must understand that although we certainly try very hard to make our marriages work, when they fail it's almost always because of mistakes *we* make. No matter how badly our partners behaved, *we* invariably have made major contributions to the divorce. To be sure, we often lack the *ability* to avoid those mistakes—primarily because we don't have sufficient experience with Real Love—but the mistakes are still ours. We must tell the truth about them, and stop making excuses or denials, before we can begin to correct them and create the possibility of a great marriage—either with our present partner or the next one. Let's observe one couple who learned about the futility of blaming and making excuses.

Elliott and Michelle had been divorced for more than a year when they came to see me because of their continuing conflicts over their children and finances. They were both even more miserable than when they were married, and their behavior was severely affecting their children. They began our conversation with a long list of grievances against each other, both of them absolutely certain they were right and their partner was wrong. Had I said nothing, I'm sure they could have continued to blame each other for the entire evening.

"Michelle," I finally said, "when you were married, did you feel like Elliott loved you unconditionally? Did he care about your happiness without wanting anything from you in return?"

"No," she said emphatically.

"Elliott, did Michelle love you unconditionally?"

"Not at all," he said.

"*That,*" I said, "was the central problem in your relationship. It wasn't the conflicts about money, or the kids, or sex, or nagging. Those were all just symptoms of the real problem, which was that neither of you felt loved by the other—or by anyone, for that matter. You both got married hoping that the other person would love you and make you happy, but *neither* of you had ever felt enough Real Love, so you couldn't possibly have given that to your partner. Your marriage was virtually doomed from the beginning."

When Elliott and Michelle got married, they didn't *try* to fail—divorce wasn't a goal. They sincerely hoped they'd be happy, and they really did pour their best efforts into creating a successful relationship. But neither of them had the one ingredient—Real Love—essential to make a marriage work, so they were drowning. To keep their heads above water, they naturally used the Getting and Protecting Behaviors that temporarily gave them Imitation Love and diminished their fears. As they used these behaviors, however—thrashing about in the water with their anger, withdrawal, deception (conscious and not), blaming, acting hurt, clinging, and so on—they made it even more difficult for their partner to keep his or her head above water. Both of them had their hands around the throat of the other, trying to push themselves up and screaming to their partner, "Save me!" There can be no positive outcome in a scenario like that.

Elliott and Michelle really thought all their reasons for divorce made sense. After all, how could they continue to live with someone who was irresponsible, thoughtless, withdrawn, nagging, oversexed, sexless, or left his or her socks on the floor? If we believe these are the real reasons for divorce, however, we'll ruminate over them endlessly, and we'll use them to justify ourselves and to make our partners look bad, which will never give us real satisfaction.

After my initial conversation with Elliott and Michelle, they both began to take the steps necessary to find and share Real Love. A year later, Elliott talked with a friend he hadn't seen in quite some time. "I heard you got divorced," the friend said. "What happened?"

A year before, Elliott would have supplied his friend with the hundred reasons he couldn't possibly have lived with "that woman," but now he understood the real reasons. "In order for a marriage to be happy," he said, "there has to be enough unconditional love in it. I had never felt loved unconditionally—not as a child or as an adult—so when I married Michelle I didn't have any Real Love to give her. I only accepted her when she was doing what I wanted, and that really hurt our relationship. I didn't really learn how to be loving until we were divorced."

His friend was obviously surprised. "Never in my life," he said, "have I heard somebody say a divorce was *their* fault. But what about Michelle? She must have been part of this. Living with her must have been hard, or you wouldn't have left."

Elliott smiled, realizing with profound relief how much he had lost his need to blame anyone for his own unhappiness. "Sure, she had her flaws," he said, "but who doesn't? Talking about other people's mistakes has never helped me be happy. The real problem was that *I* didn't know how to love her unconditionally, and I really regret that."

With an understanding of Real Love, you can see that virtually without exception your divorce and the unhappiness in your marriage prior to the divorce were caused by a lack of Real Love—the love you didn't receive from others long before you were married, the love you didn't give your spouse, and the love your spouse didn't receive from others before you were married. We don't need to administer any beatings to your parents and others who failed to love you unconditionally, nor do you need to be whipped for not sharing the love you didn't have. People don't intentionally withhold unconditional love—they just don't have sufficient experience with it. With an understanding of Real Love, you can eliminate the anger and guilt that cause almost all the misery following a divorce.

࿐

Divorce is much less painful when you understand the behavior of your spouse or ex-spouse. It's natural that you would see all the inconsiderate and unloving things he or she has done as being directed at you. After all, those behaviors *have* involved you, but you'll experience an enormous freedom when you understand that people who behave badly are simply not feeling loved, and that they are reacting to their unbearable emptiness and pain by protecting themselves from others and filling themselves with Imitation Love. When you see this, you will be released from the dual anguish of both anger and guilt. As we discussed in Chapter Two, when you saw that the man splashing you from the pool was drowning, you lost your irritation in an instant, feeling instead an unconditional desire to help him out of the water. How can you remain angry at an ex-spouse who was—or is—drowning, even though his or her behavior has splashed you on many occasions?

Understanding human behavior in this way can help you avoid the deadly pitfall of staying angry at an ex-spouse, and, perhaps more important, it can also help you avoid a divorce in your present marriage. This understanding can also help you avoid the useless burden and pain of excess guilt. How long can you continue to flog yourself with guilt when you understand that your own unproductive behaviors in marriage have been a result of *your* drowning?

When you tell people you've been divorced, many of them will believe that you're defective in some way: You must not have had a real commitment to your marriage, you must have done something terribly wrong, you were selfish, and so on. Married people who have not been divorced often regard themselves as morally superior to those whose marriages have dissolved, and you can feel their condemnation and condescension. To avoid the criticism of others, and to win sympathy for yourself, you may have a tendency to describe the divorce in a way that blames everything on your ex-spouse and exonerates you. But guilt and blaming both destroy happiness. We must change the way we perceive the behavior of our ex-spouses, and the way we see our own behavior, so we can eliminate those two destructive feelings.

We tend to see divorce as a sign of weakness, a moral crime, evidence of a defect in character, and proof of irresponsibility. We must begin to realize that people get divorced because they don't feel enough Real Love, and because they simply cannot stand the pain of living any longer in a relationship where that need isn't being filled. They're protecting themselves from the constant reminder that they don't feel loved, and they're leaving the marriage because they feel betrayed by the failure of their partners to deliver the "happiness" they once supplied with Imitation Love.

The Destructive Power of Anger

In the entire process of divorce—making the decision and every subsequent stage of living with it—anger is a common feeling. That's understandable—after all, look at the justifications we can provide for our irritation:

- You promised to love me, but you *lied.*
- Now I'll be alone, and it's *your* fault.
- My finances will now be limited—because of you.
- Now I have to go through the awful process of dating again.
- You've made me look like a fool.
- I've lost some of my friends because they've sided with you.
- The kids look at me and wonder why I've done this to them.

We get a real payoff from being angry: We feel less helpless, we can get people to do some of the things we want, we appear to be in a morally superior position, and we're distracted from the emptiness and fear that are always the real problems. The short-term rewards of anger are many, but it never produces genuine happiness. Never. Your blaming and anger will only hurt you, your ex-spouse, and your children. Anger is the biggest obstacle to making wise choices and being happy. It will poison you and everyone around you.

As you go through a divorce, and in all the years after, you'll be much happier if you strictly adhere to two rules: Never make a decision while you're angry, and never speak to your spouse or ex-spouse in anger. Ever. As we discussed in Chapters One and Four, anger is always wrong. I am not suggesting that you *shouldn't* be angry, nor that you hide it. I'm only saying that you should never make decisions in that condition, and you should never express anger to your spouse or ex-spouse *while* you're angry. If you make decisions while you're angry, for example, you will succeed only in protecting yourself and filling yourself with Imitation Love; you will not make choices that contribute to your highest goal of finding and sharing the Real Love that will make you genuinely happy. If you speak to your ex-spouse in anger, he or she will almost certainly receive your words as an attack, and she will respond with Getting and Protecting Behaviors, which will make you feel even more empty and afraid.

So what *should* you do when you're angry? Take the steps described on pages 124–129: Be quiet, be wrong, feel loved, get loved, and be loving. Certainly you can talk about your anger—you need to do that in order to feel loved unconditionally—but not to the person you're angry at *while* you're angry. Instead of blowing up at your ex-wife, talk to a friend about your anger, and describe the real cause—the lack of Real Love in your life, your expectations, your fears, and your selfishness—which will create an opportunity for you to feel accepted and loved. It's Real Love you want, and you can feel the healing power of that love when you get it from any source. It's natural to want your ex-spouse to finally give you the love you always expected—and to make up for all the years you didn't get it—but that approach can only end in misery. When you feel sufficiently loved by friends, you'll be able to make more productive decisions and will have much better conversations with your ex-spouse.

Preventing Divorce

Studies have been done to assess the level of stress people feel during a number of difficult circumstances. Divorce is in that tiny group of disasters that causes more emotional pain than anything else—right up there with the death of a loved one or blindness. Anything we can do to prevent divorce from happening is well worth our attention, while recognizing that on rare occasions divorce is unavoidable and perhaps even desirable.

Getting the Love You Need

Cole and Amy had a miserable marriage, filled with unfulfilled expectations, disappointment, anger, and mutual accusations. Cole read *Real Love* and decided to begin the process of telling the truth about himself. Amy was delighted that he was being more accepting and less angry, but on the occasions when he didn't give her exactly what she wanted, she became angry and blaming. He often reacted with anger and accusations of his own, and one day he talked with me on the phone about his desire to change the pattern of their interactions.

"I don't know what to do," he said. "I tell her the truth about myself, and that doesn't help. I try to accept her, but she never notices that. She still criticizes me all the time, and then sometimes I blow up. I'm frustrated. This just isn't working."

"You're only frustrated," I said, "because she's not filling your expectations. You still expect her to love you unconditionally, and she's not ready for that yet. Keep telling her the truth about yourself, as much as you're able, and as much as she's prepared to hear it, but do not expect her to love you. For now, you'll have to get that elsewhere. Tell the truth about yourself to the wise men in your group, and get Real Love from people who have it."

"What can I do when she attacks me? I don't handle that very well."

"Again, tell the truth about yourself—about *your* mistakes. If she keeps it up, tell her you love her and that you're trying to learn to love her better. If she still keeps it up, tell her you need to continue the conversation later."

Cole did find the Real Love he needed from his friends, and as Amy gradually began to feel what he was sharing with her, she felt safe enough to tell the truth about herself.

If you diligently follow the principles we've already discussed about finding enough Real Love in your own life, learning to share the Real Love you have, and eliminating conflict, it's unlikely that you'll become an addition to the divorce statistics. People who feel unconditionally loved, and who are committed to loving their partners, rarely have a need to leave a marriage. Sure, there are exceptions—where one spouse feels loved, for example, and is doing her best to be loving toward her husband, but is regularly threatened with potentially life-threatening physical abuse—but those exceptions are rare.

Cohabitation

Many people live together for months, even years, getting to know each other before they make the commitment of marriage. Does that approach work? Does it help to test drive the car before you buy it?

In 2002, the Centers for Disease Control and Prevention released the results of a study of eleven thousand women ages fifteen to forty-four.* They found that 75 percent of women had been married by age thirty, and about half of those had lived with their partner outside marriage. Those couples who lived together before marrying were *more* likely to be divorced after ten years of marriage than those who had not cohabited before marriage. There was no suggestion that living together before marriage was the cause of those divorces, but it certainly didn't decrease the divorce rate.

There is no way to simulate the sense of complete commitment that comes with a public and legal declaration of marriage. Without it, backing out of a relationship is always easier.

Making the Decision to Divorce

Few decisions are more difficult—to make and to execute—than the one about whether you should divorce your spouse. It affects not only you but your children, friends, and extended families. First, we'll discuss *your* decision to divorce, and later in the chapter we'll talk about what to do if *your spouse* announces that he or she wants a divorce.

Certainly, many marriages continue because both partners love each other, but many other marriages "survive" only because both partners are motivated by fear to stay together. We often stay together out of a fear of

- letting go of our dreams. We'd hoped our marriages would signal a new beginning, a promise of the genuine happiness

---

*"Cohabitation, Marriage, Divorce, and Remarriage in the United States" by Matthew D. Bramlett, Ph.D., and William D. Mosher, Ph.D., *Vital and Health Statistics*; Series 23, No. 22 (July 2002)

we've always sought. It's an awful feeling when we have to abandon those dreams.

- being alone. Sure, we may fight with our spouses, but some companionship—even when it's often difficult and manipulative—can seem better than none at all.

- admitting we're wrong. When a marriage fails, *somebody* has to be at fault, and we don't want to create an opportunity— which divorce does—for other people to blame us for anything.

- not being able to find something better. Our spouses may have lots of faults, but what if we can't find anyone better? After all, we married the person we thought would be a great partner, and that didn't turn out so well. And how many great marriages have we seen?

- the unknown. Marriage is often difficult, but what if divorce is even worse?

- inconvenience. We naturally like to do whatever is easiest, and divorce is not convenient: legal maneuvers, changes in finances, child visitation horrors, and so on.

- hurting the kids. We've all heard the terrible stories about what divorce does to children, and we don't want that to happen to our own children.

- the condemnation of other people. Nothing spurs gossip like a juicy divorce, and we don't want to be the subject of everyone else's advice, criticism, and condescension.

- not keeping a commitment. When we were married, we made a commitment to stay with our spouses, and divorce is a painfully obvious failure to do what we said.

- the condemnation of God. For many of us, there are serious religious and moral implications in getting divorced.

You'll have to decide whether any of these reasons—or combination of them—is enough to preserve a marriage, but none of them will create the genuinely loving relationship you want. Only a desire to find and share Real Love will do that.

Making Decisions About Divorce in the Absence of Children

Divorce is complicated enough without thinking about the consequences to children. First we'll talk about divorces that affect only couples, and then we'll address how children factor into things.

Don't Be in a Hurry

There are few things in life more painful than an unhappy marriage, and if you're in one, it's understandable that you would be eager to find relief from your pain. Although divorce is often a tempting solution, never make that decision while you're still empty and afraid. In that condition, you will be capable only of making decisions that protect you and fill your emptiness with Imitation Love. Such decisions never lead to lasting happiness.

Before you consider divorce, first learn to tell the truth about yourself and find the Real Love that will fill the emptiness that haunts you. With enough Real Love, you'll lose your need to use the Getting and Protecting Behaviors that cause so much confusion and harm in any marriage. As you share that love with your spouse, miracles become possible. In some cases, your partner might be slow to accept your love, but keep trying. It may take months, sometimes longer, of unconditional loving before your partner begins to feel it. You'll make lots of mistakes, and so will your partner, but don't give up easily. Don't be in a hurry. It's tragic that so many marriages are abandoned when an effort on the part of either partner to find Real Love would have produced a loving and rewarding relationship.

Simply Make the Decision to Stay in the Marriage

In rare cases, your partner will simply be too afraid to ever trust your love. He'll justify his fear by pointing out—to himself or to you—the mistakes you make in loving him, which he'll use as proof that you really *don't* love him. Keep at it. Keep learning to love him. Keep practicing. Even if your partner never accepts your love—which is unlikely—*you* will be much happier as a result of becoming a loving human being, as we see in the following case of Marlene.

When Marlene learned about Real Love, she couldn't wait to share it with her husband, George. But he had been empty and afraid all his life and was thoroughly entrenched in his pattern of Getting and Protecting Behaviors. He believed he was doing "all right," and had no interest in changing his life, despite Marlene's assertions that there was a much happier way to live. After it became clear that George didn't want anything to do with Real Love, Marlene began to share with friends the truth about herself, and gradually she found the happiness she'd always wanted. George certainly enjoyed her increased acceptance and love, but he was never willing to discuss his own faults, so instead of feeling Real Love, he just believed Marlene was finally giving him the attention and cooperation he'd always demanded and deserved. As a result, he was angry less often, but only because he was getting more of what he wanted, not because he felt more loved unconditionally. He was certainly not unconditionally loving toward Marlene, although he was unkind to her less often, because she was being nicer to him.

Marlene, however, understood the meaning of unconditional love. She continued to love her husband without conditions, without his returning the love she was giving. After several years of this, a friend asked her why she stayed with George.

"When we got married," Marlene said, "I said I'd stay with him and love him, even when things got difficult. I'm keeping that commitment. He doesn't beat me. It's true that he's not very loving, but I believe he's as loving as he knows how to be. It's easy to love somebody who returns your love. I'm learning a lot about how to be loving as I love George even when he doesn't seem to be giving much back. As I love him, I'm always much happier, regardless of what he does."

If we were perfectly loved and loving, we could probably experience some degree of genuine happiness while married to anyone. I realize that may seem like a fantastic claim, but I have known real joy as I've learned to love people who are selfish, dishonest, angry, manipulative, and outright destructive. Many others have had similar experiences. Loving under those conditions stretches and transforms the soul. You will grow as you learn to accept and love people of all descriptions. As you are unconditionally loving, you will become happy under all conditions, instead of feeling good only when other people treat you well. The latter condition isn't true happiness at all.

It's Never Too Late

Dean called my office one afternoon from a pay phone and said that his wife, Sallye, was at that moment filling a trailer with her belongings from their house. She had previously filed for divorce and had even gone to a pawn shop in a fit of anger to sell everything he'd ever given her. Dean wanted to know what he could do.

After explaining the effects of Real Love—and its absence—in marriage, I said, "Go to the house and tell her you finally realize that all she ever wanted from you was your love—your unconditional love—and now you see that you didn't give it to her. Then give her several specific examples where you've been selfish and haven't accepted and loved her as she's needed. Tell her that you're making a commitment to learn how to love her. You're not trying to change her mind, just explaining that you've begun to learn some things that can make a big difference in your marriage. Then it's up to her whether she wants to have faith that such a change is possible."

"Wow, that's a lot to say," he said. "But what about all the things *she's* done wrong?"

"If you keep doing the same things you've been doing all these years—pointing out her faults and getting angry—your marriage is over," I said. "It's your choice: You can keep doing it the old way, which has never worked, or you can try something quite different—an approach that has been consistently effective for a lot of other people."

Dean drove over to his house and found Sallye. Taking her gently by the shoulders, he said all the things I had talked to him about. She dissolved in tears and stopped packing the trailer. Over the following months, they learned how to have a loving relationship.

Never assume that your marriage is beyond hope. Instead begin to tell the truth about your mistakes and flaws—to your spouse and also to others. Find the Real Love that will enrich your own life and has the capacity to change your marriage. Even if your changing doesn't resurrect your marriage, *you* will be much happier, and you'll also be much better able to have a loving marriage in the future.

When Divorce May Be the Only Way

Even though we can learn a great deal from loving a spouse unconditionally and unilaterally, there are still some cases where divorce may be the best decision the participants can make at the time. If a woman is being physically abused, for example, she *may* need to withdraw from that environment—either with a temporary separation or a divorce—before she can find the love and happiness she needs. In cases of physical abuse, the decision to leave a spouse may be relatively obvious, but there are other kinds of abuse we need to consider that are just as damaging as a physical beating. Take the case of Anna, who talked to me about her husband, Blake.

Anna had grown up empty and afraid, and she married Blake in the hope that he would make her happy. But neither of them came to the marriage with sufficient Real Love, and when the effects of trading Imitation Love wore off—which they always do—they were both quite disappointed. Blake began to criticize everything Anna did—and didn't do—to the point that Anna began to feel emotionally beaten all the time. She lost weight, her hair began to fall out, her blood pressure rose, and she was unhappy all the time.

I recommended that Anna learn to tell the truth about herself, first with her husband. As she talked about her mistakes and flaws, however, Blake used whatever she said as yet another weapon to beat her with. But she didn't give up easily. Without blaming him, she repeatedly told Blake the truth about herself and took responsibility for the unhappiness she was feeling in their marriage.

Eventually, because she wasn't getting the Real Love she needed from Blake, she told the truth about herself with some friends, and she began to feel the Real Love that several of them offered. She'd been drowning all her life, and they helped her to the side of the pool where she could breathe. Each time she began to feel a sense of hope, however, her husband attacked her with his criticism and anger, figuratively kicking her right back into the pool. She was finding Real Love, but when Blake attacked her, the effect of her friends' love simply vanished, and she remained miserable.

Anna finally divorced her husband, and although it was a painful experience, in the absence of her ex-husband's attacks she was finally able to feel Real Love from her friends with enough consistency that she began to climb out of the pool, where she could breathe and grow. I am not blaming Blake for Anna's unhappiness, only explaining that leaving him *may* have been the only way she ever could have overcome her emptiness and fear. Her emotional and spiritual wounds were every bit as serious as the physical injuries of someone who is slapped with a hand or punched with a fist.

Marriage is such an important commitment and opportunity to learn about loving that divorce is the last step we should ever take in approaching the problems in a marriage. I cannot know whether divorce is the right thing to do in any individual marriage, but I do know that it is sometimes the only way some people can make progress toward feeling loved, loving, and happy.

Questions to Ask Before Divorce

As you're considering a divorce, you might find it beneficial to answer the following questions:

- Have I learned enough about Real Love to even make a sensible decision about divorce?

- Do I have enough Real Love in my own life—and have I brought enough into my marriage—to have any idea whether my marriage could succeed? Because Real Love is essential to the success of any marriage, until one or both partners has enough of it to contribute to the marriage, divorce can often be a sadly premature decision.
- If I were to get a great deal more Real Love in my own life— and if I were to share it with my partner—is it possible that I could find the happiness I've always wanted in my marriage? Many couples have done just that.
- If I leave this marriage before learning how to be unconditionally loving, what will prevent me from experiencing the same misery in the next relationship?
- My spouse may not be unconditionally loving now, but if I were to learn how to be loving toward him or her, is it possible that he or she could learn how to be loving, too?
- Do I want to quit before I've tried the one thing that really makes a marriage work?

I am not saying that all marriages can or should succeed. I am saying, however, that in most cases, proceeding with a divorce before implementing the principles of Real Love is like permanently abandoning your stalled car on the side of the road before you put any fuel in your empty gas tank.

Responding to Divorce Initiated by Your Spouse

We've discussed how *you* can make a decision about divorce, but what should you do when your spouse presents you with *his* or *her* decision to divorce you? A woman once wrote to me with a variation on this question, and my answer to her applies to many others in similar situations.

> I've been married for eight years. Two weeks ago my husband came to me and said he wanted a divorce. I think there's another

woman involved, but he denies it. He says he's just tired of our marriage and wants to move on with his life. After spending my whole life on him and giving him three children, the coward actually said, "I need my space." I can't believe he could say that! What can I do to stop this from happening? Does he not understand what this will do to me and the children?

Following is my response:

A relationship is the natural result of people making independent choices. You're allowed to make only your own choices, not his—even when his are inconsiderate, irresponsible, and destructive. That means that you don't get to "stop this from happening."

Allowing him to make his own decision in this matter, however, doesn't mean you have to stand by and do nothing. You need to talk to him about his decision, but not in an angry or accusing way. You already know he doesn't feel unconditionally loved by you—that's one reason he's leaving—and if you're angry when you talk to him, you'll only drive him farther away. Talking to him in a loving way will be easier for you if you've read *Real Love* or *Real Love in Marriage*, and if you've told the truth about yourself to enough people that you've begun to feel some of the early effects of Real Love in your life.

Feeling loved, you can sit down with him and say, "Lately I've been learning some things about unconditional love, and I can see now that I haven't loved you unconditionally. I didn't know how, and I'm terribly sorry that I've hurt you. Now I'm learning how to love you in the way you need, and I believe that if you stick around while I learn this, our marriage will be great. But it's still your choice whether you want to have faith that things can be different."

When your husband sees that you're finally really listening to him, it might affect his decision to leave—as it has in many marriages. But he still might decide to leave you, and if that happens, you have your own choices to make:

- You could be bitter and angry at him for the rest of your life, which will guarantee only that you'll be miserable until you're dead. It will also have a terrible effect on your children. Nonetheless, after a divorce many people do make the bitter and angry choice.
- You could completely accept his decision and move on with making the rest of your life happy.

We spend so much time grieving our losses in the past and worrying about what bad things might happen in the future—all a waste of time. How much more productive it is to have faith that if we just do the next right thing now, we'll be happy. And the right thing is so simple. If you keep telling the truth about yourself, you will create opportunities for people to accept and love you, and you *will* feel loved. Then you'll learn to love others, which results in the greatest happiness imaginable. Don't waste your time doing anything else.

If your husband finally decides to leave, let him go—freely. Then fill your life with the unconditional love that will always make you happy. When you have an abundance of Real Love and genuine happiness, you won't miss your ex-husband. I've seen that happen in the lives of many others.

Talking About Your Divorce

You will have so many opportunities to talk about your divorce. It's a big event in your life, and people will ask you about it everywhere you go. You will often experience an extraordinary temptation to speak ill of your partner, because then you'll feel right and justified and powerful. If you give in to that temptation, however, you will feel only more unloving, irresponsible, bitter, and alone.

If instead you take complete responsibility for your own mistakes and avoid the compulsion to point out the faults of your partner, you will experience an enormous freedom, as Elliott did on pages 285–287. Some of the people who ask you about your divorce will just be casual acquaintances, to whom you probably wouldn't offer a long explanation as Elliott did with his friend. There are many honest things you can say that will answer the question without going into great detail. You could say, "It was my fault. I just didn't know enough about how to be a good husband." No matter what our ex-spouses did, it's always true that we could have been more loving. We're afraid that if we openly take responsibility for our mistakes like that, people might think less of us, but if you do this with a real friend who accepts you, you'll feel accepted and loved for who you really are. If you're honest with someone, on the other hand, and he or she is critical of you, have you really lost anything? That person wasn't capable of unconditionally accepting you, and you simply learned the truth of it.

What About the Children?

Many couples stay together "for the sake of the children." They suffer through horrible marriages for years, even decades, and, in many cases, as soon as their children are out of the house, they separate. Did they actually do their children a favor by staying together, or would it have been better had they divorced years earlier? What is the effect of divorce on children?

For many years it was accepted as common knowledge that divorce is harmful to children, and some studies have demonstrated that children from divorced families experience more unhappiness, mental illness, drug use, divorce, and economic disadvantage. Other respected studies, however, suggest that children from divorced families may not have significantly more problems than other children.

None of these studies, however, really help us make individual decisions about our own marriages. Suppose, for example, that we do a study of ten thousand families, and we learn that, indeed, children from divorced families are 20 percent more likely to use drugs, have trouble in school, and spend time in jail. Would that prove that divorce itself caused any of those problems? No, it would not, because we still wouldn't know whether *divorce* was the cause of the problems in those children, or whether there were other factors that caused both the divorce *and* the subsequent problems with the children. Such a study would not help you make a decision about your individual marriage.

What children need more than anything else is Real Love. Without it, they're in terrible pain, and they respond with the anger, rebellion, disobedience, withdrawal, drug use, indiscriminate sex, and other behaviors we find problematic. The unhappiness and unacceptable behaviors of children are all indications of—and responses to—a lack of Real Love in their lives. Children from divorced homes have problems not because of divorce itself, but because they don't feel loved—because their parents have been unable to give the children sufficient Real Love before, during, and after the divorce. It's the lack of Real Love in the parents that causes *both* the divorce and the unhappiness of the children.

When two people are divorcing, they're *proving* they don't have enough Real Love—for each other *or* for their children. On average, divorcing parents have less Real Love to give than couples who stay married, and *that* is why we see more unhappiness in children of divorced families. Children suffer from a lack of Real Love in their lives long before the divorce. It's true that events related to the divorce *add* somewhat to their injuries, but the vast majority of their pain is caused not by the divorce itself but by the Getting and Protecting Behaviors their parents have been using all along. What we can't know for certain—but seems very likely—is that two warring parents may cause just as much damage to their children by staying together as they would by getting divorced. We'll talk more about that in a moment.

Children need all the Real Love they can get. If you're *already divorced,* don't waste time worrying about the effects of divorce. Just learn to tell the truth about yourself and find the Real Love you can then give to your children. If you're *considering* a divorce, the question is not whether you should stay together for the children. The real question is what you could do to increase the Real Love in your own life, so you can give that life-saving element both to your spouse and to your children.

You also need to think about what the divorce will do to the Real Love that will be available to your children—from both you and your spouse. If divorcing your spouse will significantly lessen the anger and frustration in your life, which will allow you to feel more loved and share that with your children, your children might actually benefit from divorce. Many couples are so occupied with hurting each other—consciously or not—that they create an intolerably toxic environment for their children. When they divorce, they're better able to begin the process of telling the truth about themselves, feeling loved, and learning to love others. After divorce, some parents become more capable of loving their children than when they were in constant conflict with their spouses.

This is not to say that we should use the welfare of our kids as an *excuse* for divorce: "Let's get divorced because our conflicts are hurting the kids." Divorce is still the last resort. In almost every case—perhaps being married to a serial killer who is known to have murdered his last wife and children would be an exception—the ideal approach to difficulties in marriage is for one or both spouses to tell the truth about their mistakes, find the Real Love they need for themselves, and save the marriage.

Making Decisions About the Children in Divorce

When we get divorced, our buckets are obviously not filled to the brim with Real Love. Reacting to our emptiness, we have strong and selfish impulses to use Getting and Protecting Behaviors with our ex-spouses, and those behaviors always get in the way of making decisions that would be best for our children.

When you're making decisions about custody, visitation, property, child support payments, family rules, and shared family events (birthdays, graduations, and so on), your primary guide must always be this question: *What will make the greatest contribution to the Real Love and happiness of our children?* In the sections that follow, we'll examine the effect of this question—as well as the effect of implementing the guidelines in Chapter Four for eliminating conflict. Keep in mind that my first counsel to couples is always to do everything possible to increase the Real Love in their marriage, thereby *avoiding* divorce. Any advice I give in later sections about children in divorce is meant only for people who have already determined that there is no possibility of saving their marriage, and for people who are already divorced.

The Actual Divorce

A woman once said to me, "It was hellish enough living with my husband and going through all the mess that led up to the divorce. But I wasn't satisfied. No, I chose to be angry and bitter through every step of the divorce, making it hell all over again. I wish I'd done that differently."

Many of us use divorce as an opportunity to take revenge on our spouses for all the wounds they inflicted on us during marriage. That is a tempting course of action, but it can create only misery for ourselves. You can avoid this pitfall if you accept the fact that your spouse is only empty and afraid, and was doing the best he or she could in your marriage with the skills he had. He didn't intentionally try to hurt you, although it may have seemed like it at times. He really was drowning, and as he thrashed about in the water, he splashed you—perhaps nearly drowning you.

Do not use the divorce as a time to teach him a lesson, or punish him, or prove a point of some kind. Divorce is difficult enough without these additional agendas. Do not behave in a way that will continue to cause misery for both of you for years to come. If you punish your partner, your anger and bitterness will poison you in far worse ways than you will hurt him.

In addition to being the termination of a *relationship*, divorce is also a *legal* agreement. Regrettably, our legal system is adversarial in nature. Characteristically, the two parties in a legal dispute are not battling to determine what is true or right but are struggling to use the law to get the most for themselves. This adversarial approach is especially harmful in a divorce. It leads to demands, blaming, manipulation, intimidation, and bitterness. You've already had countless painful experiences in the process of arriving at your divorce. Do you really want to multiply the blood and gore by adding the powerful weapons of the legal system? If you choose that course, you may get a brief sense of vindication or revenge, but you—and your ex-spouse and children—will pay for that choice for many years.

As you work out a divorce, never forget the central purpose of your life—to feel loved, to be loving, and to be happy. As you make any decision, therefore, ask yourself whether it will lead to more love and healing, or whether it will cause more pain. That perspective will help you determine the healthy role of attorneys in your divorce. With genuine happiness as your goal, you'll see your attorney as a source of *information* and *advice*, instead of as a gladiator who will mercilessly beat your spouse and force from him or her everything you want. Certainly you want to know your legal rights as you *discuss* decisions with your soon-to-be-ex—an excellent role for an attorney—but *make* these decisions with your spouse. Do not allow the lawyers to scratch and claw out the agreement. The latter course is very expensive and much more traumatic.

It's tempting to use divorce as a way to hurt a partner who has hurt you, but the consequences to *you* will be severe, as Evan learned during his divorce with Ellen. Evan hired a powerful lawyer to represent him, while Ellen settled on a friend who was primarily a tax attorney but agreed to represent her at no charge. Evan took advantage of her choice. He had orchestrated a divorce that would gut Ellen emotionally and financially, but just before it was finalized, he talked to me.

"It sounds like you're getting everything you want," I said.

"Yeah, pretty much," he responded.

"Except what you really want."

"What do you mean?"

"What do you really want in life? A few more dollars? The

knowledge that you took Ellen to the cleaners and hurt her? Will that make you happy? Or do you want to learn to be loving?"

There was a long pause before Evan said, "I've really gotten caught up in this, haven't I? I guess I am being pretty selfish, and maybe I need to re-examine what I'm doing."

This change of heart on Evan's part could appear sudden, but he and I had been discussing the principles of Real Love for some time. In the heat of the divorce, he was just having a hard time re-membering them.

The next day Evan sat down with Ellen to talk about what would be more fair and beneficial to her. The divorce became a much more loving experience than it would otherwise have been.

You may need help as you reach a divorce agreement with your spouse. You may need the advice of a lawyer. You'll need good friends to accept and love you at the times when you're being self-ish and angry. You may choose to enlist the assistance of a profes-sional mediator, thereby avoiding much of the conflict generated by two antagonistic lawyers. After all that help, you can then use lawyers to simply draw up the agreement you've both made.

The Division of Property and Spousal Support

We often view the division of property in a divorce as a wonder-ful opportunity to balance the scales of justice in our lives. We say the following to ourselves and others:

- "I've worked harder than she has all these years. I went to work every single day, while she sat home doing nothing. Why should she get half of anything?"
- "I've put up with his behavior our whole marriage, and now he's going to pay."
- "When my mother gave us that couch, she meant it for *me*."
- "She's been spending money like water all these years. It's about time she learned how to tighten her belt, like the rest of us."
- "But this is *mine*. I'm the one who bought it, and I should be able to keep it."

As you negotiate the division of property and income, you must recognize that one of you might require financial support from the other. If your spouse worked while you went through school, and she took care of the children while you were building a career, she gave up critical years when she could have increased her own earning power. It would be inappropriate for you to say at the time of divorce, "Well, just get a job," because it's not likely she'll be able to earn a sufficient income to maintain her present lifestyle.

Even if you both maintained careers from the beginning of your marriage, one of you may require financial assistance from the other to make it possible for both of you to live in *relatively equal* lifestyles, which may not mean the same lifestyle you enjoyed before the divorce. After a divorce, expenses increase—there are two households, changes in car and health insurance, and so on—while the combined income often remains the same. It may not be reasonable, therefore, for the spouse with the lesser income to expect the other spouse to support him or her in exactly the same lifestyle as before the divorce. It's much more beneficial to have as a goal that you'll both have a relatively equivalent lifestyle.

You may be able to think of a hundred reasons why your spouse should suffer, but don't act on that fantasy. Also don't go to battle over exactly who ran up the telephone and other specific bills. As much as possible, divide the assets and income and debts in a way that will benefit and encumber both partners equally. In some cases, a spouse who previously had not been required to work outside the home may have to get a job to supplement the combined income of both spouses.

Custody

Gabe and Caroline were bitterly contesting everything in their divorce, including the children. The divorce was precipitated by Gabe's affair, and Caroline maintained that he didn't deserve to be with the kids after what he'd done. She was demanding sole custody of their two daughters.

"There's no doubt that Gabe made a terrible mistake," I said, "and I'm sure he's made many more I don't know about. It's understandable that you're angry, and it's tempting to punish him by withholding your kids from him, isn't it?"

Caroline stammered a bit as she experienced the discomfort of seeing her motivation out in the open like that. "I'm not punishing him," she said, intent on justifying herself. "I just think they'd be better off with me."

"Do the girls love their daddy?" I asked.

Shrugging her shoulders, she admitted, "Yes, they do."

"You and Gabe have already proven that you know how to hurt each other, and how to insist that you're right, wouldn't you say? You're both so good at it that you're about to get divorced because of it. You can keep up this fight, but not only will it make both of you more unhappy; it will seriously injure your daughters. The important question here is what will make *them* feel more loved and happy. Caroline, I'm not justifying a single wrong thing Gabe has ever done. I *am* suggesting that your *children* will be happier if they have as much contact with their father as possible. With your divorce removing much of the conflict you two often generated when you lived in the same house, they might even feel more loved by each of you than before."

Caroline agreed to joint custody for the benefit of her daughters.

In most cases, joint custody is the arrangement that will be most loving and effective for children. Sole custody communicates to children that one parent's love is being cut off, and that is not constructive. In most cases, you *can* work out a joint custody arrangement. When parents are motivated to help their children, they can become quite creative. Some parents have the children shuttle back and forth during the week: four days in one home and three in another. Others alternate weeks, or months, or even years in rare cases. Some families have even arranged for the children to stay in one house while the *parents* alternate the weeks or months they live in that house with the children. Although it's not always possible, when you're both interested in the welfare of the children, you will find ways to stay in the same town, even though that may require personal and career sacrifices.

☙

Although Caroline became accommodating about establishing joint custody when she understood the needs of her children, some spouses are not as understanding, as we see with Matt and Cheryl.

For years, as she saw their marriage crumbling, Cheryl talked to everyone she knew about what a horrible husband and father Matt was. Some of what she said was true, but it was mostly exaggerated and even fabricated for the purpose of allowing Cheryl to feel like a victim. When Matt lost his job, and their financial situation became difficult, Cheryl could see no reason to stay in the marriage. One day, while Matt was out of the house, she bolted—taking the children with her—to live in the hometown of both their parents, several hundred miles away. She filed for divorce and lined up allies by the dozen—including his parents—to support her suit demanding sole custody of their two sons. In court, she planned to assassinate his reputation in every way she could. She would talk about his two years of prescription drug abuse, which had ended years before, and she found people who would testify to minor events that would cast ugly doubts on his fitness as a father.

Matt called me and asked what he should do. He knew he could find people who would say negative things about Cheryl—and he'd already begun the search—but he wondered if that was the right thing to do. I suggested that he abandon all efforts to smear the character of his wife, and instead simply tell the truth about himself in court. When the custody hearing arrived, Cheryl brought out all her guns and viciously attacked Matt in front of the judge. In response, Matt calmly admitted to all the mistakes he'd made—his past drug use, his failure to sufficiently love Cheryl, some financial irresponsibility on his part, and so on—and added that he had always tried hard to be a good father. After the hearing, and before he heard the judge's ruling, he called me to say, "I'm so glad I didn't fight her. I would have been bitter and angry, and I would have said and done things that would have caused unhappiness for myself and my family for a long time."

The judge was impressed with Matt's honesty, and his refusal to attack Cheryl, and he awarded Matt joint custody of the children. The lesson here is not that being loving will win you what you want in court, but that it *will* enable you to avoid the anger and bitterness that will destroy you.

Another benefit to joint custody—in addition to increasing the availability of love to children—is the positive effect it has on compliance with spousal and child support. Studies have proven that spouses who are cut off from their former families by the restrictions of sole custody are much less likely to meet the financial responsibilities they have to their children and former wives.

Child Support Payments

With many couples, there is a significant difference between the incomes of the two spouses, such that after divorce one partner will require financial assistance to care for the children. As the spouse who is paying child support, you may feel that the payments are too high. As the spouse receiving these payments, you may be certain you're not getting enough. Again, if parents are concerned about the welfare of the children, fair and effective child support can be arranged.

Earlier, when we discussed spousal support, I mentioned that with the increased expenses that occur when one household becomes two, adjustments in the lifestyles of both spouses may be necessary. For the same reason, after divorce children may have to do without some of the things they once enjoyed. They may have to give up the private schools, the golf lessons, and the expensive vacations. Children should not be pampered at the expense of putting an overly stressful financial burden on either parent.

Child support payments are for the benefit of the *children*. The receiving parent should not use them to elevate his or her own lifestyle. The paying parent, however, should not assume the responsibility of judging how these payments should be spent. Some paying spouses are eager to tell the receiving spouse exactly what should be done with the money, and if the receiving spouse doesn't comply, the paying spouse withholds the support payments. That is not a great way to communicate love to children. If the paying spouse does withhold payments, or is late in making them, the receiving spouse should not use this as a weapon to turn the hearts of the children away from the paying spouse. Children are severely affected when one parent says to them, "Your father is late on his support payments again."

Visitation

If you or your spouse has sole custody of the children, visitation of the children by the noncustodial parent must be arranged. If you're the parent with custody, there was often a compelling reason that led to the sole custody—a neglectful or abusive spouse, an affair, and so on—so you probably feel justified in limiting visitation of your spouse. Many times I've heard one parent say something like, "He doesn't deserve to see the kids any more often than every other weekend. He didn't spend time with them before, and I'm certainly not going to help him do it now." Such feelings are understandable, but the motivation is vengeance, not the welfare of the children. Arrange visitation that will maximize the opportunities for your children to be loved by both parents.

After the Divorce

Many people obsess over a divorce for the rest of their lives. They blame their ex-spouses for their misery, or they heap guilt upon themselves, or they do a combination of both activities. They ask, "How could he do this to me?" or, "If only I had been more _____," referring to their mistakes as a marriage partner. After a divorce, it's a waste of time and happiness to keep reliving the agony of the past.

Think about your divorce only in terms of what you can *learn.* How were *you* selfish? What Getting and Protecting Behaviors did you use with your spouse? What can you do to increase the Real Love in your life, which will enable you to avoid making the same kinds of mistakes again? How can you be a more loving and effective parent? Remember that your spouse's mistakes are not your concern. He or she was drowning and using the Getting and Protecting Behaviors that briefly kept her head above water. You have no right—nor the ability—to judge what he or she should have done differently. Let it go.

Friends

During and after your divorce, you'll experience a natural tendency to blame your partner for the failure of your marriage. If you indulge that inclination, and share your feelings with friends, you'll probably be quite successful in convincing most of them that you are right and your partner is wrong. You'll be able to line those friends up in support of your position, and they will take your side in opposition to your spouse. In the process, you'll make your spouse feel even more alone, which might give you a certain perverse satisfaction.

In most divorces, one spouse communicates his or her dissatisfaction far more verbally than the other, and the more communicative spouse will convert many friends to his or her "side." If you criticize your ex-spouse, not only does that injure him or her, but it also hurts *you*, since what you're winning from your friends is not Real Love but Imitation Love in the form of sympathy and power.

If you have friends who are getting divorced, be aware that *both* partners need your love and support. It is not productive for you to take sides and treat one partner like a victim—which would mean of course that you would treat the other as a perpetrator. Simply accept and love them both. If possible, you can even help them tell the truth about their own mistakes, which will help them far more than giving them sympathy or criticism.

After the Divorce—Without Children

When children are involved, contact between the ex-spouses is virtually unavoidable—mutually raising small children, attending school events and weddings with older children, and so on. When no children are involved, however, you can choose to completely sever your relationship, and in some cases that may be the best thing to do. If you feel sufficiently unloved, and if association with your ex-spouse makes you feel even more unloved and unhappy, withdrawing completely from the relationship may be the most healthy decision. In such cases, you should not feel obligated to interact with your ex-spouse just because he or she demands it. It is your choice entirely how much contact you have with that person. Healthy withdrawal is quite different from the Protecting Behavior of running, which is associated with blaming, attacking, and acting like a victim. You cannot be happy if you feel like a victim, or if you feel angry at your ex-spouse.

After divorce, learn to tell the truth about yourself, and fill up with the Real Love essential to your happiness. When you feel sufficiently loved by other people, you will eventually lose the guilt and anger associated with your divorce. As you feel more loved and loving, you may decide that you're capable of spending time with your ex-spouse and remaining happy.

Whether or not you spend time with your ex-spouse, your healing will not be complete until you can completely forgive him or her, and until you ask for his or her forgiveness. Yes, I know you can think of a hundred reasons to justify your claim that your spouse was more at fault in your marriage and divorce, but those reasons will help you only to keep the fires of anger and resentment alive. You need to tell your ex-spouse the truth about *your* mistakes and ask for his or her forgiveness. Ask her if there are any issues from the past still bothering her, and if so, tell the truth about the mistakes *you* made. When you can do that, you'll feel a great burden lifted from your shoulders, whether or not your ex actually forgives you.

After the Divorce—With Children

If you can remember that your children's primary need is Real Love, you won't make the mistakes that most divorced parents do. You can fill that overarching need much better if you follow these guidelines:

- Never express anger about your ex-spouse to your children. Children need to feel your love, and if you're critical and angry toward your ex, the feeling they sense from you will not be loving. Unconsciously they'll also be wondering when *they* will become the objects of your anger.
- Don't involve your children in disagreements with your ex-spouse. Do not say, "I'd like to get you guys a computer, but your father says he can't spare the money to get it." Do not say, "I'm sick and tired of your mother being late to pick you kids up." When you criticize your spouse, you're tarnishing the image of someone very important in your kids' lives.
- Don't pick at the little mistakes. If your ex is late only occasionally with the support payments, or fails to fill his or her responsibilities for taking care of the children only here and there, let it go. If you say, "But in the divorce agreement it says . . . ," your spouse will usually take that as criticism. Don't make a big deal of it and cause unnecessary conflict. Sometimes you do need to point out your ex-spouse's behavior, and we'll discuss an example of that shortly.

Sometimes your children will attempt to draw you into a conflict with your ex-spouse. Your son might say, for example, "Mom won't let us watch television. She never lets us do anything." He's hoping you'll side with him, and you'll be sorely tempted to agree with him—you might even want to add a couple of brilliant, sharp-edged observations of your own about her—because there's an immediate payoff. You'll be getting revenge for some of the terrible things she's said about you, and you'll win the approval of your child, but the consequences of that approach are awful—you'll feel more selfish, unloving, and unhappy yourself, and you'll further alienate your child from his mother's love.

So what can you say when your child complains about his mother's behavior? You could say, "That's something you can discuss with your mother. She and I just do things differently, and when you're with her, you need to listen to her."

Custody and Visitation

Even after custody is established, there will still be conflicts about specific details. Your husband has agreed, for example, to deliver the kids to your house every Sunday night by six o'clock. But he's often late. If he's late by only a few minutes, and it's not causing a true inconvenience—as opposed to simply offending you—leave it alone. If you make a big issue out of every mistake, your anger *will* spill over and affect the love your children feel—both from you and from him—and you do not want that consequence. Thank him for bringing the kids back.

If he consistently brings them back quite late, however—adversely affecting the schedule of the children—you may need to say something. Barking at him while he's in the process of delivering the children—while he's in the middle of making the mistake, and while you're irritated—will rarely be productive. Arrange a time when you can meet to discuss how the children are doing. Meet at a neutral place and be clear that you don't want to take up a lot of his time. After Gabe and Caroline (pages 308–309) finally settled on joint custody, they illustrated how to approach a conflict like this one.

Gabe had consistently been late when delivering his daughters back to Caroline's house, and it was becoming a problem. Caroline called him at home the day after he'd returned the children to her for the week and asked to meet him in a local restaurant for lunch. At the meeting, after several minutes of small talk, Caroline said, "Gabe, I'm pleased at how this is working out for the kids. They really do enjoy the time they spend with you."

"And I love the time I spend with them," he said.

"I just wanted to meet with you from time to time to talk about how it's going for everybody. Is there anything I'm doing that's creating problems for you?"

"No," Gabe said, "everything's fine. How about for you?"

"I do have one thing I need help with. When they get to my house at six on Sunday night, they have time to get ready for bed, finish a little homework if necessary, and get to bed by eight thirty. For quite a while now they've been getting home at seven, seven thirty, eight. I want them to have all the time with you they can get, but when they get home late, they can't get ready for bed on time. Then they feel rushed, and they don't get as much sleep. I just don't want us to do anything that interferes with their happiness."

"That's my fault," he said. "I just haven't been paying attention to the time like I should. I'm glad you brought it up. I'll do better."

Caroline nicely illustrates how to bring up a problem in a way that focuses on the needs of the children rather than talking about how her spouse had personally inconvenienced *her*. She didn't say, "You're supposed to _____," or, "You *said* you would _____," or, "You *promised* that _____," More important, she didn't *feel* angry as she spoke. When you're angry at your partner as you speak about an issue, he or she will feel even more empty and afraid, and then that person will respond to your *anger*, totally unable to respond to the actual content of your message.

You'll find it much easier to talk about problems with your ex-spouse if you establish beforehand an agreement that you will regularly speak with each other about how the children are doing. Such discussions can then become routine, instead of being treated like a crisis each time.

Family Rules

You and your ex-spouse each have the right to establish your own rules for the children when they're in your home. You do not have to do things exactly like your ex-spouse. In some cases, however, consistency can be beneficial to the children. If you require the kids to do their schoolwork before they play, and give them household chores, and limit their television watching, while your spouse requires no schoolwork and no chores, and allows unlimited television, the kids can become confused about what is the responsible way to live. You also might come across as a strict, uncaring parent. You don't have the right to tell your spouse how to behave in his or her home, but you might get together to talk about what's best for the children. Your spouse might then be willing to adjust the rules in his or her house so the kids will experience some consistency from one household to the other.

Shared Family Events

Imagine that this year your daughter's birthday falls on a day when she'll be living with you. Your ex-husband wants to be there for the celebration, but you don't want him in your house—you're just not feeling loving enough yet to have him in your private space that much. When it comes to your children, you must be willing to make some personal sacrifices. Ask your daughter what *she* would prefer. Would she like to celebrate her birthday twice, first at your house and then again on another day with her father? Would she like to have both of you there at one party? If you can't stand the idea of having your ex-husband back in your house, perhaps you could arrange to meet at a neutral location—a pizza restaurant, a skating rink—for the celebration. Offer her multiple options, and be flexible.

Again, your children need all the love and support they can get—from both parents—and you need to work with your ex-spouse to make that possible.

Exercises
☙

Exercise One

Write down all the behaviors of your ex-spouse that drove you crazy while you were married. Identify how each one was a Getting and Protecting Behavior that resulted from a lifetime of not feeling loved. Then repeat to yourself, "He [she] was drowning. He was empty and afraid and only doing whatever he could to keep his head above water. He was doing the best he could, and he hurt me only because he didn't have the knowledge or ability to behave any differently." Say this until you believe it in your bones, and then notice how your anger disappears.

🍂

Exercise Two

Write down some of the unkind things you have said about your ex-spouse to your friends. Talk to at least two of those friends and tell the truth about the mistakes *you* made in your marriage, and apologize for blaming your ex-spouse in the past.

🍂

Exercise Three

Write down the mistakes you made in your marriage—for example:

- I was not unconditionally loving
- I was pretty selfish a lot of the time.
- With anger, I manipulated her to do what I wanted.
- I withdrew from him at the very times he most needed my unconditional love.

Then ask your ex-spouse for an opportunity to meet, and describe to him or her those mistakes. Apologize for them and acknowledge that you caused a lot of pain in your ex-spouse's life.

🍂

Exercise Four

Write down several of the issues where you and your ex-spouse disagree about raising your children: bedtime, schoolwork, television, religion, diet. Then write down how you could change your position on each of these issues in ways that would benefit your children. Meet with your ex-spouse and share your observations.

Exercise Five

If you're considering divorce, make a solemn promise to yourself that you will not get divorced until you have learned a great deal more about telling the truth about yourself and finding Real Love. Commit to learning how to love your spouse unconditionally before you blame him or her for your unhappiness and abandon the marriage.

Conclusion

A s you apply the principles in this book, it's likely that you'll begin to notice significant changes in your marriage. As your partner feels the Real Love you're sharing, he or she cannot help but be affected. Conflicts will diminish and, ideally, eventually disappear. You'll begin to express a more regular concern for one another's happiness, and you'll want to be together more.

In some marriages, however, one partner is too afraid to participate in the process of Real Love. You might have such a partner, but that is no reason for you to jump back into the pattern of Getting and Protecting Behaviors yourself. Even if your partner doesn't change as you become more loving, *you* will become much happier in the process of feeling loved and learning to unconditionally love others.

Finding and sharing Real Love isn't yet another thing for you to do in an already busy life. It *is* life. Real Love produces the happiness that is our entire reason to be alive. Don't look at the principles of Real Love as another burden or list of things to do. They are, rather, the way to realize the ultimate goals of life. Use them.

Imagine that I have found a great treasure: an entire fleet of Spanish galleons sunk in a sixteenth-century storm while carrying Aztec treasure back to Spain. It's worth billions of dollars, and I will sell it to you in exchange for all the money you have—whatever sum that is, small or great. Would you be willing? Who wouldn't exchange what they have for something worth much more?

Now imagine that I give you another choice. Instead of buying the treasure, you could also buy from me a bag of household garbage—newspapers, old food, empty cartons, and the like. The price for the garbage is the same as the price of the treasure—all the money you have. Which choice would you make? Would you buy the treasure, or the garbage?

The answer seems obvious, but in our lives we choose to buy the garbage almost every day. With each decision we make, we choose the unspeakable treasure of Real Love and happiness, or we choose a life of emptiness, fear, and Getting and Protecting Behaviors. With everything we have—our time, effort, resources, our very lives—we buy freedom or bondage, life or death, joy or pain. Which choice will you make?

Make a commitment that you will not settle for less than a profound joy in your life and in your marriage. Never give up. Only in Real Love will you find the genuine happiness you've always wanted. Persist in being truthful about yourself, which will create opportunities for other people—your spouse, friends, family members—to love you. Remember that the annoying behaviors of other people are only a response to their drowning, and never waste your time and happiness being irritated at them.

Sometimes the process of finding Real Love, changing your own life, and contributing to the happiness of your marriage can take years. In most cases, however, if you are fully committed to being truthful and loving, you will see remarkable changes much more quickly than that. Be patient. You will make many mistakes. You'll think you understand Getting and Protecting Behaviors, and you'll think you've learned to be accepting and loving toward your partner, and then something will happen that exceeds your ability to be loving. You'll become empty and afraid, and will jump back into the pattern of using behaviors that can only make you and your partner unhappy.

Again, don't give up. Review the principles you've learned, and make a decision to do the next right thing. You don't have to do the next hundred right things, just the next *one*. Tell the truth about your mistake. Take responsibility for your anger. Perform a loving act. A richly rewarding life and marriage are the result only of continuing to do the next single right thing.

You get to make mistakes. You're allowed to stumble and fall. But don't get discouraged. Don't constantly compare yourself to perfection, or to any other person. Just keep trying to avoid the mistakes you made yesterday. Stop periodically and compare how you're doing with how you did a month ago. Appreciate your own progress.

As you apply the principles of Real Love, you can lose only if you quit. When you experience failures, there is a natural tendency to say the principles don't work, but changing the direction of a lifetime requires effort, persistence, and time. You reach the top of a mountain by taking thousands of small, persistent steps, not by taking a giant leap.

If you will persist, the reward will be more than you can even imagine at this point. Recently, a woman called me on the phone and said, "I was doubtful in the beginning that this Real Love stuff would work. In fact, at first it didn't seem to make any difference, but I had nothing to lose, so I kept going. Now I'm happier than I've ever been, and my marriage is better than it's ever been. Actually, I'm happier than I ever even imagined it was possible to be." We can all find that kind of happiness, in our individual lives and in our marriages. Achieving that kind of joy is well worth any effort we make to get there. I know that from personal experience and from observing the marriages of thousands of others.

Additional Resources

In *Real Love in Marriage* you have learned how to tell the truth about yourself, how to find Real Love from your spouse and others, and how to share that love in your marriage and in other relationships. The process of learning how to find and share Real Love, however, continues for a lifetime, and Dr. Baer has provided a number of resources to assist with an ongoing education in Real Love.

- The book *Real Love: The Truth About Finding Unconditional Love and Fulfilling Relationships.* This is the foundation of any Real Love education, teaching the real meaning of love and giving us the power to consistently choose peace and confidence instead of anger and confusion in our individual lives and in our relationships. Available at retail and online bookstores.

The following are available *at* www.RealLove.com:

- The *Real Love Audiobook*, an audio recording, on six CDs, of the book *Real Love.*
- The book *Real Love in Dating.* How to eliminate the confusion and frustration of dating and instead create the lasting and loving relationships you've always wanted.

- The book *Real Love in Parenting.* How to apply the principles of Real Love in the process of raising happy and responsible children.
- *The Essentials of Real Love* on six DVDs. A video recording of a presentation of the basic principles of Real Love by Dr. Baer before a live audience.
- *The Essentials of Real Love* on six CDs. An audio recording of a presentation of the basic principles of Real Love by Dr. Baer before a live audience.
- *The Essentials of Real Love Workbook,* a companion to *The Essentials of Real Love* on CDs or DVDs that will make the principles of Real Love come alive in your life.
- *The Essentials of Real Love Bible Workbook,* focusing on how the principles of Real Love are taught in the Bible.
- The book *Real Love for Wise Men and Women.* This is a continuation of the *Real Love* book, focusing on how you can *share* love with the people around you.
- The book *The Real Love Companion,* a workbook that accompanies the *Real Love* book.
- The *Real Love in Dating Audiobook,* an audio recording, on six CDs, of the book *Real Love in Dating.*
- The *Real Love in Marriage Audiobook,* an audio recording, on nine CDs, of the book *Real Love in Marriage.*
- The *Real Love in Parenting Audiobook,* an audio recording, on thirteen CDs, of the book *Real Love in Parenting.*
- *The Truth About Love and Lies,* a three-CD audio recording of Dr. Baer describing the basic principles of Real Love.
- Membership on RealLove.com, which includes:

  1. *The Essentials of Real Love* seminar online: a video recording
  2. Video Coaching with Dr. Baer: video presentations three to five times a week, in which Dr. Baer answers questions and discusses the principles of Real Love

3. The Real Love Radio Network: weekly online radio talk show, hosted by Dr. Baer
4. Real Love Chat Rooms: Available 24/7, monitored during limited hours by Real Love Professionals
5. Telephone coaching by Real Love Professionals

Acknowledgments

As I present this powerful approach to creating and maintaining a fulfilling and exciting marriage, I feel an enormous gratitude to those without whom this work would not have been possible. I'm grateful to

- the thousands of people who courageously shared with me the details of their relationships. I learned a great deal from them.
- those who loved me. I can repay them only by sharing what I've learned with others.
- those who allowed me to practice these principles on them while I was still learning the principles myself. All the material in this book was field-tested on thousands of brave souls who were willing to try what I suggested.
- my wife, Donna. It is she who has demonstrated for me the power of Real Love in marriage.

I'm also grateful to those who were so helpful in the development and production of the book itself:

- to my literary agent, Wendy Sherman, who has expressed an

energetic faith in me and held my hand through the publication process of two books.

- to Bill Shinker, Lauren Marino, and Hilary Terrell, at Gotham Books, for all their assistance in the process of publication.

Index